The Mys

Varieties of Mystic Experience *is a documented inventory of mystic experience from the third to the seventeenth century. Elmer O'Brien, the noted Jesuit scholar, has carefully selected those writings that best show how men and women of religious genius have experienced direct confrontation with God. His introductions to each mystic and to each mystical school combine mastery of his subject with a style at once witty and lucid.*

"This book fills a most important gap in mystical literature. For a long time I have felt the need for a comprehensive and inclusive anthology that would include with the selections a hand-core analysis of the essence of the particular insight and the pertinent written testimony of the mystic quoted. I find in what Father O'Brien has done an answer to this need."
—Howard Thurman, Boston University

"We find erudition, urbanity, and wisdom in O'Brien's thought and style; but it is the beauty of what he and his mystics have to say that pervades the whole and gives to mystic experience a unity that the title refuses to impose."
—*Commonweal*

Other MENTOR BOOKS of
Related Interest

Varieties of
MYSTIC
EXPERIENCE

An Anthology and Interpretation

by ELMER O'BRIEN, S.J.

A MENTOR-OMEGA BOOK

Published by The New American Library, New York and Toronto
The New English Library Limited, London

COPYRIGHT © 1964 BY ELMER O'BRIEN

FIRST PRINTING, NOVEMBER, 1965

Imprimi Potest: Angus J. Macdougall, S. J.
                    Provincial of the
                    Upper Canada Province

Nihil Obstat: Rt. Rev. Msgr. James T. Clarke, S.T.L.
                    Censor Librorum

Imprimatur: ✠   Most Reverend Jerome D. Hannan, D.D.
                    Bishop of the Diocese of Scranton,
                    Pennsylvania
                    September 2, 1964

The *Nihil Obstat* and *Imprimatur* are official declarations that a
book or pamphlet is free of doctrinal or moral error. No implication is contained there in that those who have granted the
Nihil Obstat and *Imprimatur* agree with the contents, opinions,
or statements expressed.

MENTOR-OMEGA BOOKS are published *in the United States*
by The New American Library of World Literature, Inc.,
1301 Avenue of the Americas, New York, New York 10019,
in Canada by The New American Library of Canada Limited,
295 King Street East, Toronto 2, Ontario,
in the United Kingdom by The New English Library Limited,
Barnard's Inn, Holborn, London, E.C. 1, England

PRINTED IN THE UNITED STATES OF AMERICA

Acknowledgments

THE AUTHOR wishes to thank the following for their kind permission to use selections from the works cited below.

Aquin Press, London: *Signposts to Perfection. A Selection from the Sermons of Johann Tauler,* edited and translated by Elizabeth Strakosch (Blackfriars Publications, 1958).

Burns & Oates Limited, London: *The Cloud of Unknowing, and Other Treatises,* edited and translated by Dom Justin McCann, 5th edition (1947); *The Dialogue of St. Catherine of Siena,* translated by Algar Thorold, new and abridged edition (1925); *The Complete Works of Saint John of the Cross,* translated and edited by E. Allison Peers, Volumes I-III, new edition, revised (1953).

Philip Caraman, S.J.: For his kind permission to revise and include material from my article, "St. Ignatius Loyola," *The Month,* XXVI (1961), 325-333.

Faber and Faber Limited, London: "Classics of the Contemplative Life": Blessed Jan van Ruysbroek, *The Spiritual Espousals,* edited and translated by Eric Colledge (1952); Henry Suso, *Little Book of Eternal Wisdom* and *Little Book of Truth,* edited and translated by James M. Clark (1953); *Richard of Saint-Victor, Selected Writings on Contemplation,* edited and translated by Clare Kirchberger (1957). (These works are published in the United States by Harper & Row, New York.)

Victor Gollancz, Limited, London: *Theologia Germanica,* Winkworth-Bernhart-Trask (1950).

Harper & Row, Publishers, Incorporated, New York: *The Book of the Poor in Spirit* by a Friend of God, edited and translated by C. F. Kelley (1955).

B. Herder Book Co., St. Louis: *Signposts to Perfection. A Selection from the Sermons of Johann Tauler,* edited and translated by Elizabeth Strakosch (1958).

Iona Community, Scotland: *The Revelations of Mechtild of Magdeburg,* translated by Lucy Menzies (New York-London: Longmans, Green & Co., 1953).

David Knowles: *The English-Mystical Tradition* by David Knowles (New York: Harper & Row, 1961; London: Burns & Oates Limited, 1961).

Longmans, Green & Co. Limited, London: *The Book of the Poor in Spirit* by a Friend of God, edited and translated by C. F. Kelley (1955); *St. Maximus the Confessor, The Ascetic Life* [and] *The Four Centuries on Charity*, translated by Polycarp Sherwood, O.S.B., "Ancient Christian Writers," Volume XXI (1955).

John Murray (Publishers) Ltd., London: *From Glory to Glory*, edited by Jean Daniélou, S.J., and translated by Herbert Musurillo, S.J. (1963); *The Mediaeval Mystics of England*, edited and translated by Eric Colledge (1962).

The New American Library of World Literature, Inc., New York: Lao Tzu, *The Way of Life. Tao Tê Ching*, translated by R. B. Blakney (1955).

The Newman Press, Westminster: *The Cloud of Unknowing, and Other Treatises*, edited and translated by Dom Justin McCann, 5th edition (1947); *The Dialogue of St. Catherine of Siena*, translated by Algar Thorold, new and abridged edition (1943); *The Complete Works of Saint John of the Cross*, translated and edited by E. Allison Peers, Volumes I-III, new edition, revised (1953); *St. Maximus the Confessor, The Ascetic Life* [and] *The Four Centuries on Charity*, translated by Polycarp Sherwood, O.S.B., "Ancient Christian Writers," Volume XXI (1955).

Pantheon Books, Inc., New York: *Theologia Germanica*, Winkworth-Bernhart-Trask. Copyright 1949 by Pantheon Books, Inc. Reprinted by permission of Pantheon Books, a Division of Random House, Inc.

Marcel Rodd Incorporated: The original publisher of *The Song of God: Bhagavad-Gita*, translated by Swami Prabhavananda and Christopher Isherwood. Copyright by The Vedanta Society of Southern California, Hollywood, California.

Charles Scribner's Sons, New York: Extracts from *The Mediaeval Mystics of England*, pp. 126, 127, 131, 137-39, 151-52, edited and translated by Eric Colledge are used by permission of Charles Scribner's Sons. Copyright © 1961 Charles Scribner's Sons. Extracts from *From Glory to Glory*, pp. 34, 40-41, 42-43, 44, 45, 118, 127-28, 241, 242, 245-47, edited by Jean Daniélou, translated by Herbert Musurillo, are used by permission of Charles Scribner's Sons. Copyright © 1961 Charles Scribner's Sons.

Sheed & Ward, Inc., New York: From *The Complete Works of St. Teresa*, Volume II, translated and edited by E. Allison Peers from the critical edition of P. Silverio de Santa Teresa, C.D. (1946); *The Confessions of St. Augustine*, translated by F. J. Sheed (1943); *Saint Catherine of Genoa, The Treatise on Purgatory and The Dialogue*, translated by Charlotte Balfour and Helen Douglas-Irvine (1946).

The Vedanta Society of Southern California, Hollywood: *The Song of God: Bhagavad-Gita,* translated by Swami Prabhavananda and Christopher Isherwood. Copyright by The Vedanta Society of Southern California, Hollywood, California (New York: New American Library, 1954).

James Walsh, S.J.: *The Revelations of Divine Love of Julian of Norwich,* translated by James Walsh, S.J. (London: Burns & Oates Limited, 1961; New York: Harper & Row, 1962).

Preface

I HAVE NOT had the leisure, even in such instances where I might have had the competence, to translate anew many of the selections herein. Hence it is with an uncommon gratitude that the conventional acknowledgments have been made.

Particularly gratifying, however, is it to salute in especial here the following owners of copyright material for co-operation, much beyond the customary, in the making of this book: Aquin Press, Burns & Oates, Philip Caraman, Harper & Row, Herder of St. Louis, the Iona Community, David Knowles, Newman Press, and James Walsh.

E. O'B.

Loyola College
Montreal
July 1, 1963

Contents

Introduction

WHAT IS A MYSTIC?

MYSTICS are as like as peas in a pod. Mystic experience—
perhaps a good thing, perhaps a bad thing—is everywhere
the same thing: a singular pietistic twitch of the human psyche
that has proved to be not altogether devoid of interest to the
occasional scholar.

Assertions of this sort continue to be made today and,
doubtless, will continue to be made tomorrow. That they
should, seems something of a pity, for in the whole wide range
of that eminently challenging science, the history of ideas,
there is no subject more enduringly provocative than mysticism. To accord mystics and mystic experience such short
shrift, as do the majority of our laconically assertive contemporaries, is—to say the least of it—to miss rather more than
half the fun.

It is also to miss the point.

If he would not miss out here as elsewhere, the historian of
ideas must move upon, not one, but two levels of understanding—one after the other. The first level (upon which he is
forever tempted to dally unduly) is that of the generic intuition of categories. For example, it is perceived and it is
affirmed that there has existed through the course of centuries
an approach to reality which may be termed "the philosophic"
as distinguished from "the poetic." Such perception-affirma-
tion, however necessary, is elementary. In any scientific enterprise it is merely preparative to one's entry upon the second
level of understanding, that of particularity. It is there, upon
the second level, that the historian of ideas is most properly
engaged, because it is there alone that the intuition of individual manifestations within the generic is achieved, and the individual, not the generic, is the historian's business.

The first level is that on which the layman moves, the man

for whom Aristotle, Hegel, and Kierkegaard are "philosophers" and thus distinguishable from Fielding, Dostoevski, and Kafka who are "novelists." For the historian to disport himself exclusively on that level must inevitably result in the fantastic or the simply foolish, as in the assertion (if one can imagine it) that Aristotle, Hegel, and Kierkegaard are as like as peas in a pod. Or that all mystics are.

The past three decades have witnessed the appearance of a small noble band of historians, more venturesome than most, little given to the fantastic or the foolish, who move with ease upon both levels of understanding. Their assertions about individual mystics make it possible now for one to say, with assurance, what in general a mystic is and to conjecture, with a fair degree of reliability, about the nature of particular differences.

The Generic in Mystic Experience

1. *The object confronted in mystic experience is thought by the mystic to be somehow ultimate.*

The avowal is constant that the object is the absolute limit to which, at least here on earth, human awareness can be extended. With a man like Richard Rolle, the object is the fire of divine consolation. With St. Bernard, it is comparable to the awareness accorded by the Beatific Vision in Heaven. With Jan van Ruysbroek, it is precisely that awareness—although briefly and obscurely given.

In some instances it is asserted that the object is the ultimate possible to human awareness because it is the ultimate reality —the Deity. Thus with St. Catherine of Siena the "Sea Pacific" in which she felt herself immersed is quite simply God. Thus with Origen the word spoken at the deepest interior of his being is the Word, the Second Person of the Trinity, newly and experientially come to birth. Thus, too, with St. Gregory of Nyssa and St. John of the Cross the object is God, although within that experience of the ultimate there is a continual progression.

That the object is conceived of as a *religious* ultimate is only to be expected. Yet, even here, there are interesting and instructive variations. In some instances the confrontation with the ultimate is esteemed to be itself the terminal ethical enterprise, all other ethical endeavor being mediating and preparatory to it. So it is with Evagrius of Pontus: one exercises oneself in virtue in order to achieve contemplation. Or it is held that, although other ethical efforts have their own final value and continue to preserve them, this—in another and more exalted form—by implication fulfills them all. So it is with a Maximus the Confessor or a William of St. Thierry. Or, again, it can be that all else is reputed to be only deception and snare, so that this confrontation is the sole ethical act and an essential escape from the human condition that attaches to everything else and renders it invalid. So it is with Plotinus and, speaking quite generally, in Buddhism.

Yet, always religious and always with ethical overtones, the experience need not always imply a moral transformation of the mystic, either as necessary prerequisite or as necessary consequence. The mystics of Islam are, more than most, insistent on this point.

2. *The manner of confrontation is immediate, direct.*

It can be intuitive, a one-to-one cognitive relation between subject and object—as in St. Augustine.

Or it may be insight, the unmediated perception of a higher coherence within the materials of one's more or less usual knowledge. So it is with St. Ignatius Loyola and St. Teresa of Avila.

Or it may work entirely the other way around. It may be a "received knowledge" in which the subject is wholly passive— an experienced invasion of the ultimate, as in St. Bernard or St. John of the Cross.

3. *The confrontation is always different from the familiar exercise of either sense perception or of reasoning.*

The diverse philosophic backgrounds of individual mystics, or the total lack of any such background, will result in that difference being variously expressed and explained. But, in the last analysis, it would seem to come down to this: the self, itself, becomes awareness. For there is none of the externality that characterizes sense perception nor any of the progressive linking together of partial insights that characterizes intellection. Yet, so thorny is the path of the interpreter, he must remain on his guard even when advanced this far because precisely those mystics who use the notion of spiritual senses (as Origen, Gregory of Nyssa, William of St. Thierry) do so to convey the idea, not of exteriority, but of intimacy; and precisely those who use intellectual knowledge as their helpful analogue are the most insistent (as Meister Eckhart, as St. Teresa) that one cannot properly express what occurs because it defies understanding.

A Question of Method

The analysis of the writings of mystics, reputed or real, is no easy matter. That, by now, should be clear. The very rehearsal above of recent findings on the common general characteristics of mystic experience involved, inevitably, advertence to particular differences. Apparently all one can do is attempt, explicitly, one thing at a time while aware—and on one's guard—concerning possible implications.

One possible implication, everywhere present, is that the "mystic" is no mystic at all but is simply making it up out of whole cloth. Yet the historian cannot exclude anyone from his area of investigation who has been conventionally, whether rightly or wrongly, referred to as a mystic. Only as his investigation proceeds, particularly when he moves onto the second level of understanding, does it become allowable to notice that some seem to be merely aping or echoing what seems to have been personally experienced by others. The distinction, most tentative, may then suggest itself: pseudo-mystics and authentic mystics. Authentic mystics will be solely those who have had, once or often, briefly or habitually, an experiential awareness of the presence of God. It is an admirable distinction, surely, but how apply it? Three rules, upon reflection, suggest themselves:

1. *The reputed experience does not follow as a doctrinal conclusion from the person's basic philosophic or theological position, but is counter to it.* For example, in the writings of the Pseudo-Dionysius or of Meister Eckhart the experience that is so highly extolled is the logical last step in a rigid speculative process. Either of them may have been authentic mystics, but one cannot come to that conclusion from their writings. Each of them had, from his speculative suppositions, necessarily to draw the conclusions he did. When the experience (as that of St. Augustine) does not fit in at all with the person's speculative suppositions, the chances are that it was a genuine experience.

2. *The reputed experience is not an instance of wish fulfillment, but is counter to one's wishes.* The writings of the early St. Augustine reveal the wish being father to the thought. Those of St. Paul of the Cross or of St. Mechtilde show the opposite.

3. *The reputed experience alone gives consistency to the speculation.* This rule is the least easy to apply. In some instances, as that of St. Catherine of Siena, it is not too difficult,

so chaotic otherwise does her thinking become. But, in people like St. Gregory of Nyssa or St. John of the Cross, only advertence throughout to the chronology of the writings and to the doctrinal influences of the time makes possible its sure application. Thus, in Gregory, the experience will be seen to be the luminous center in the light of which Bible and philosophy and current theological controversies are understood. Similarly, in John of the Cross, everything takes its coloring from the experience: his interpretation of the Pseudo-Dionysius and of St. Thomas Aquinas, his modification of the poetic themes current in his day. As a rule for using this rule, one would do worse than to begin with the consideration of the seeming doctrinal inconsistencies and then proceed to seeing how the author resolves them: the resolution will not be doctrinal but experiential.

So much for rules.

The rules applied, one directs one's chief attention to the authentic mystics. But the pseudo-mystics are anything but irrelevant to this more limited purpose; they can serve as excellent foils for setting the authentic more clearly in relief.

"Schools of Mystics"

Few readers will have wandered far in the history of mysticism before encountering a phenomenon which it is difficult not to greet with a large and ample skepticism. What, indeed, is one to think of "Schools of Mystics"? Although academic overtones are not wholly absent from this conventional designation for such groups as appeared in ninth-century Persia, the fourteenth-century Rhineland, and sixteenth-century Spain, what is mainly meant is the sort of crowding a person has in mind in speaking of "schools of fish." And that is quite bad enough. The suspicion intrudes that at such times in such places it was, for whatever reason, very much *à la mode* to be a mystic. So there were mystics. By the score. So skepticism is the order of the day in reading the "mystics" of these times and places.

Yet, as healthily full of skepticism as ever he may be, the historian is soon brought up short at the number of undeniably authentic mystics he comes upon. In the century preceding, there were few or none. In the following, there were few or none. But in this particular century they swarmed like haddock in the springtime. What is the explanation?

The explanation is not that a time and place favorable to mysticism brings mystics into existence. Rather would it seem to be that a time and place favorable to mysticism bring into existence the recording of their experiences by which, alone, we have knowledge that the mystics existed. Other times, other places likely have had mystics in much the same quantity; there is no reason for thinking they did not. Mysticism, however, was not in favor. So a literary silence cloaks them wholly.

Literary Forms

The historian's task would be easier if all mystics recorded their experiences in the same fashion. The same vocabulary, the same form, especially the same directness as in the writings of Marie of the Incarnation or of St. Paul of the Cross would, in a way, be most welcome.

But, in another way, one would not want it. One would not wish to be deprived of the pleasure that comes (cheek by jowl with problems) from reading such varied literature as this: general exhortations, pastoral homilies, theological treatises, personal advice, poems, confessions, spiritual accounts.

The laws of interpretation for each type differ slightly. The informative content increases by degrees from "general exhortations" (a minimum) to "spiritual accounts" (the maximum). A few words about each of the seven types may prove of help to the reader.

General Exhortations: Here are meant urgings on to the mystic way addressed pretty much to the world at large. The writings of Jacob Boehme fall into this class. So also, despite their epistolary form, do the mystical works of the Pseudo-Dionysius: he pretended they were letters, apparently in order to accord them an added authority from the dignity of the (fictive) recipient. So also the aphorisms (usually called "Centuries" because they were put together in lots of one hundred) of Evagrius and Maximus the Confessor. The information they provide is minimal precisely because they are so general and sweeping. They seem intellectual exercises rather than statements based upon experience.

Pastoral Homilies: One does not, these days, expect to hear in sermons the expression of the preacher's most intimate communings with the Godhead. Nor, perhaps, did one expect to in Origen's or Augustine's or Bernard's or Eckhart's. In any day it would be, at best, a mildly embarrassing experience for the congregation. For one who reads now the transcripts of such sermons, the experience can be positively unnerving: how much is one to believe?

If applied with caution, the rules outlined above should

serve to determine the measure of one's belief quite as well as when applied to other types of mystical writing. Caution, however, is especially to be exercised in disengaging the personal from what is simply mandatory in the content because of the Biblical passage that is being, professedly, explained. The difficulty is rather less with one, such as St. Bernard, who indulges in personal asides. The difficulty is least with one, such as Meister Eckhart or John Tauler, who manifestly is using the Bible merely as a prop to the highly personal. But, whatever effort the interpreter may have to expend, it is well worthwhile; much of the most beautiful mystical writing we have is in the form of homilies.

Theological Treaties: Being deliberately directed to the analysis of the experience, these are rather more informative. But the personal element in such works can be isolated only if they are read against the background of the doctrinal sources upon which they draw. With Ruysbroek and Suso and Denis the Carthusian, the three chief practitioners of this type, one can do this with relative ease because the doctrinal sources of each of them are known. Then Denis promptly appears to have been no mystic at all; and Ruysbroek and Suso, mystics very different from one another.

Personal Advice: In this category fall such anonymous works as *The Book of the Poor in Spirit* and the *Theologia Germanica* and *The Cloud of Unknowing* and works as easily identifiable as those of Walter Hilton, St. Teresa, and St. John of the Cross. They all have this one thing in common: they were written to meet the need for instruction in the mystical way of some definite person or persons. The advice, accordingly, is personal in two ways at once: author-mystic, in the light of personal experience, counsels reader-mystic according to personal need. The information imparted, similarly, is limited in two ways at once: only that amount of the experience—limited—of the author which is relevant to the need—limited—of the one advised is described. It is one of the less pleasant curiosities of religious history that the writings of such authors should have come to be esteemed as complete Baedekers of the mystical life.

Poems: So long as compensation is made for the stylized patterns in which they inevitably must appear, poems can be exceptionally informative mystical documents. One reason for this is that the poet expresses experience by experience. Rābi'a, the Moslem mystic, used this literary type most informatively, with St. Mechtilde of Magdeburg a rather close second. St. John of the Cross was perhaps a better poet than either of them, but his poems are informative only when complemented by his book-length explanations of them. Even the aphoristic verses of Angelus Silesius manage, quite of themselves, to say more.

Confessions: I find myself forced to use the word "Confessions" simply for the lack of a better. I intend it in the specialized meaning that it has in the writings of the most famous practitioner of this particular type of thing, St. Augustine: self-profession before God. Few have ever had difficulty in properly assessing William of St. Thierry's use of the form in his *On Contemplating God*. With others, it is none too easy. The dramatic form—complete with *dramatis personae*—adopted by such as St. Catherine of Genoa presents special problems: one's sole recourse is to read her *Dialogue* as one would read a play by Shaw, aware that whatever the name a character may bear it is always the author who speaks and it is always of himself that he speaks.

Spiritual Accounts: These, after what have preceded, are child's play. They are direct and to the point. Their purpose is single: to tell what happened. That they are so uniformly uninspired in their mode of expression awakens the unworthy suspicion that, however it is with the rest of mankind, mystics write well only when there seems the prospect of their being read by more than one or two people. The suspicion, still unworthy, is reinforced when one recalls that three who used this type had more lofty experience to describe than any other mystics known to history: St. Ignatius Loyola, Marie of the Incarnation, and St. Paul of the Cross. The reader may know what to make of this. I do not.

SELECTED BIBLIOGRAPHY

All shades of the spectrum are, without apology, represented here. For easy reference the listing is alphabetical, since the chronology of such speculative studies is, unfortunately, irrelevant.

C. M. Addison, *What Is Mysticism* (New York, 1923); C. A. Bennet, *A Philosophical Study of Mysticism* (New Haven, 1923); Robert Hugh Benson, *Mysticism* (London-Edinburgh, 1907); Henri Bergson, *The Two Sources of Morality and Religion* (New York, 1935); Henry Browne, S.J., *Darkness or Light* (London, 1925); J. W. Buckham, *Mysticism and Modern Life* (New York, 1915); Cuthbert Butler, O.S.B., *Western Mysticism*, 2nd edition (London, 1926); A. Chandler, *Ara Caeli: An Essay in Mystical Theology*

(London, 1912); John Chapman, O.S.B., "Mysticism: Roman Catholic," in Hastings' *Encyclopaedia of Religion and Ethics,* IX, 90-101; W. F. Cobb, *Mysticism and the Creed* (London, 1914); J. Dalby, *Christian Mysticism and the Natural World* (London, 1950); Henri Delacroix, *Les grands mystiques chrétiens* (Paris, 1938); Hippolyte Delehaye, S.J., *Sanctus: Essai sur le culte des saints dans l'antiquité* (Brussels, 1927); Mary Anita Ewer, *A Survey of Mystical Symbolism* (New York-London, 1933); Ambrose Gardeil, O.P., *La structure de l'âme et l'expérience mystique* (Paris, 1927); Joseph de Guibert, S.J., *Leçons de théologie spiri- tuelle,* 2nd edition, Volume I (Toulouse, 1946); F. C. Happold, *Mysticism* (Baltimore, 1963); Franz Heiler, *Prayer* (New York, 1932); E. Herman, *The Meaning and Value of Mysticism* (Lon- don, 1915); W. E. Hocking, *The Meaning of God in Human Ex- perience* (New Haven, 1912); H. L. Hubbard, *Self-training in Mysticism* (New York, 1921); Friedrich von Hügel, *The Mystical Element in Religion* (New York, 1927); Aldous Huxley, *The Perennial Philosophy* (New York, 1945); W. R. Inge, *Christian Mysticism* (New York, 1899) and *Studies in English Mysticism* (New York, 1906); William James, *The Varieties of Religious Experience* (New York, 1902); Rufus M. Jones, *Studies in Mystical Religion* (London, 1909), *New Studies in Mystical Religion* (New York, 1929), and *Some Exponents of Mystical Religion* (New York, 1930); D. Joret, O.P., "L'élément fondamental de l'état mystique," *Vie spirituelle,* IV (1920), 283-302, 358-377, 449-464; Ronald A. Knox, *Enthusiasm* (New York, 1950); H. Kraemer, *The Christian Message in a Non-Christian World* (London, 1938); J. H. Leuba, *Psychology of Religious Mysticism* (New York, 1925); V. Lithard, "Mystique et contemplation: Etude de psychologie sur- naturelle," *Gregorianum,* XVI (1937), 584-595; Alois Mager, O.S.B., *Mystik als Lehre und Leben* (Innsbruck-Vienna-Munich, 1934) and *Mystik als seelische Wirklichkeit* (Graz-Salzburg, 1945); Joseph Maréchal, S.J., *Studies in the Psychology of the Mystics* (New York, 1927) and *Etudes sur la psychologie des mystiques,* 2nd edition, Volume I (Paris, 1938) and Volume II (Paris, 1937); J. de Marquette *Introduction to Comparative Mysticism* (New York, 1949); W. P. Montague, *The Ways of Knowing* (New York, 1925); Paul Elmer More, *The Catholic Faith* (Princeton, 1931) and *Christian Mysticism: A Critique* (London, 1932); Rudolf Otto, *Mysticism East and West* (New York, 1957); Paschale P. Parente, *Quaestiones de Mystica Terminologia* (Washington, 1941); Conrad Pepler, O.P., *The Three Degrees: A Study of Christian Mysticism* (St. Louis, 1958; particularly the chapter "What Is Mysticism?"); Auguste Poulain, S.J., *Les grâces d'oraison,* 11th edition (Paris, 1931); Léonce Reypens, S.J., "L'Ame: sa structure d'après les mystiques," *Dictionnaire de spiritualité,* I, 433-469; Karl Rickstätter, S.J., *Mystische Gebetsgnaden und Ignatianische Exerzitien* (Innsbruck, 1924); W. Riley, *The Meaning of Mysticism* (New York, 1930); Bertrand Russell, *Mysticism and Logic* (New York, 1918); A. Sharpe, *Mysticism: Its True Nature and Value* (London, 1910); Margaret Smith, *An Introduc- tion to the History of Mysticism* (London, 1930); Walter T.

Stace, *The Teachings of the Mystics* (New York, 1960); Maurice de la Taille, S.J., "L'oraison contemplative," *Recherches de science religieuse*, IX (1919), 273-292; Evelyn Underhill, *Mysticism*, 17th edition (London, 1949); A. E. Waite, *Studies in Mysticism* (London, 1906); E. I. Watkin, *The Philosophy of Mysticism* (London, 1920); Francis Younghusband, *Modern Mystics* (London, 1935); R. C. Zaehner, *Mysticism Sacred and Profane* (New York-London, 1961); and, various authors, "Contemplation," *Dictionnaire de spiritualité*, II, 1643-2193.

I

PLOTINUS

(204—270)

A CERTAIN wry justice may be seen to preside over the positioning of Plotinus here before Origen. Plotinus was magnificently contemptuous of time. What, then, could be more exquisitely just than that chronology be here defied and he be placed ahead of a man he comes after?

Yet I must confess to being rather less interested, at least at the moment, in justice to Plotinus than in justice to the reader. It would be less than fair to deny him the high advantage that comes from seeing at the outset all the characteristics, reputed or real, of mystic experience in their purest and most unequivocal form. He can see them all in Plotinus as in no other writer.

So Plotinus first. Had he lived not in the third century but in the thirteenth, I would still feel forced to place him first for that same sane pedagogical reason.

Plotinus was many things. He was a philosopher of singular intellectual probity. He was a psychologist to whom, it would seem, no areas of the spirit were foreign. He was not, it would seem, a mystic. He most desperately wanted to be one, and all the psychological analyses and the entire philosophy he structured upon them resulted from his abiding desire for mystical union. That complex fact, as much as anything, explains the hold his writings have had on the minds of men over the centuries. The desire for the eternal, resident in everyone, there finds eloquent expression. The most secret workings of the soul of man in search of a god, worthy or unworthy, is there described. And the *Enneads,* the posthumous compilation of his writings, have proved a storehouse of words at the disposal of all so that many a one, to the lasting confusion of just about everyone else, has been able to sound like a mystic without being a mystic.

As is only appropriate, Plotinus himself has caused the most confusion of all.

The experiences he describes as being strictly mystical, the experimental awareness of the presence of God, would seem to be one or other of two very different things. It could be, after the deliberate emptying of the mind which he both describes and prescribes, the residue—unrecognized—of symbolic imagery or of conceptual thought. Or it could quite easily be a state of momentary unconsciousness following hard upon a phase of severe inner concentration and, subsequently, interpreted in terms of the concentration. It seems to be the sort of experience that can be induced by anyone sufficiently patient and thorough going in his concentration. But, for all of that, so acute and accurate is the introspective psychology of Plotinus that authentic mystics, especially the introspective among them, use his language and use it gladly.

TEXTS [1]

THE GOOD OR THE ONE

As the soul advances towards the formless, unable to grasp what is without contour or to receive the imprint of reality so diffuse, it fears it will encounter nothingness, and it slips away. Its state is distressing. It seeks solace in retreating down to the sense realm, there to rest as upon a sure and firm set earth, just as the eye, wearied with looking at small objects, gladly turns to large ones. But when the soul seeks to know its own way— by coalescence and unification—it is prevented by that very unification from recognizing it has found The One for it is unable to distinguish knower and known. . . . Because what the soul seeks is The One and it would look upon the source of all reality, namely the Good and The One, it must not withdraw from the primal realm and sink down to the lowest realm. Rather must it withdraw from sense objects, of the lowest existence, and turn to those of the highest. It must free itself from all evil since it aspires to rise to the Good. It must rise to the principle possessed within itself; from the multiplicity

[1] *Enneads*, VI, 9. From *The Essential Plotinus*, edited and translated by Elmer O'Brien, S.J. (New York, 1964).

that it was it must again become one. Only thus can it contemplate the supreme principle, The One.

Having become The Intelligence, having entrusted itself to it, committed itself to it, having confided and established itself in it so that by alert concentration the soul may grasp all The Intelligence sees, it will, by The Intelligence, contemplate The One without employing the senses, without mingling perception with the activity of The Intelligence.[2]

The chief difficulty is this: awareness of The One comes to us neither by knowing nor by the pure thought which discovers the other intelligible things, but by a presence transcending knowledge. When the soul knows something, it loses its unity; it cannot remain simply one because knowledge implies discursive reason and discursive reason implies multiplicity. The soul then misses The One and falls into number and multiplicity.

Therefore we must go beyond knowledge and hold to unity. We must renounce knowing and knowable, every object of thought. . . . To obtain vision is solely the work of him who desires to obtain it. If he does not arrive at contemplation, if his soul does not achieve awareness of that life that is beyond, if the soul does not feel a rapture within it like that of the lover come to rest in his love, if, because of his closeness to The One he receives its true light—his whole soul made luminous—but is still weighted down and his vision frustrated, if he does not rise alone but still carrying within him something alien to The One, if he is not yet sufficiently unified, if he has not yet risen far but is still at a distance either because of the obstacles of which we have just spoken or because of the lack of such instruction as would have given him direction and faith in the existence of things beyond, he has no one to blame but himself and should try to become pure by detaching himself from everything.[3]

Do not let yourself be distracted by anything exterior, for The One is not in some one place, depriving all the rest of its presence. It is present to all those who can touch it and absent only to those who cannot. . . . Having freed itself of all externals, the soul must turn totally inward; not allowing itself to be wrested back towards the outer, it must forget everything, the subjective first and, finally, the objective. It must not even know that it is itself that is applying itself to contemplation of The One.[4]

As The One does not contain any difference, it is always

[2] VI, 9, 3; O'Brien, *op. cit.*, pp. 76-77.
[3] VI, 9, 4; *op. cit.*, pp. 78-79.
[4] VI, 9, 7; *op. cit.*, pp. 82-83.

present and we are present to it when we no longer contain difference. The One does not aspire to us, to move around us; we aspire to it, to move around it. Actually, we always move around it; but we do not always look. We are like a chorus grouped about a conductor who allow their attention to be distracted by the audience. If, however, they were to turn towards their conductor, they would sing as they should and would really be with him. We are always around The One. If we were not, we would dissolve and cease to exist. Yet our gaze does not remain fixed upon The One. When we look at it, we then attain the end of our desire and find rest. Then it is that, all discord past, we dance an inspired dance around it.

In this dance the soul looks upon the source of life, the source of The Intelligence, the origin of Being, the cause of the Good, the root of The Soul.

All these entities emanate from The One without any lessening, for it is not a material mass. If it were, the emanants would be perishable. But they are eternal because their originating principle always stays the same; not fragmenting itself in producing them, it remains entire. So they persist as well, just as light persists as long as sun shines.

We are not separated from The One, not distant from it, even though bodily nature has closed about us and drawn us to itself. It is because of The One that we breathe and have our being: it does not bestow its gifts at one moment only to leave us again; its giving is without cessation so long as it remains what it is. As we turn towards The One, we exist to a higher degree, while to withdraw from it is to fall. Our soul is delivered from evil by rising to that place which is free of all evils. There it knows. There it is immune. There it truly lives. Life not united with the divinity is shadow and mimicry of authentic life. Life there is the native act of The Intelligence, which, motionless in its contact with The One, gives birth to gods, beauty, justice, and virtue.

With all these The Soul, filled with divinity, is pregnant; this is its starting point and its goal. It is its starting point because it is from the world above that it proceeds. It is its goal because in the world above is the Good to which it aspires and by returning to it there its proper nature is regained. Life here below in the midst of sense objects is for the soul a degradation, an exile, a loss of wings.

Further proof that our good is in the realm above is the love innate in our souls; hence the coupling in picture and story of Eros with Psyche. The soul, different from the divinity but sprung from it, must needs love. When it is in the realm above, its love is heavenly; here below, only commonplace. The heavenly Aphrodite dwells in the realm above; here below, the vulgar, harlot Aphrodite.

Every soul is an Aphrodite, as is suggested in the myth of Aphrodite's birth at the same time as that of Eros. As long as soul stays true to itself, it loves the divinity and desires to be at one with it, as a daughter loves with a noble love a noble father. When, however, the soul has come down here to human birth, it exchanges (as if deceived by the false promises of an adulterous lover) its divine love for one that is mortal. And then, far from its begetter, the soul yields to all manner of excess.

But, when the soul begins to hate its shame and puts away evil and makes its return, it finds its peace.

How great, then, is its bliss can be conceived by those who have not tasted it if they but think of earthly unions in love, marking well the joy felt by the lover who succeeds in obtaining his desires. But this is love directed to the mortal and harmful—to shadows—and soon disappears because such is not the authentic object of our love nor the good we really seek. Only in the world beyond does the real object of our love exist, the only one with which we can unite ourselves, of which we can have a part and which we can intimately possess without being separated by the barriers of flesh.

Anyone who has had this experience will know what I am talking about. He will know that the soul lives another life as it advances towards The One, reaches it and shares in it. Thus restored, the soul recognizes the presence of the dispenser of the true life. It needs nothing more. On the contrary, it must renounce everything else and rest in it alone, become it alone, all earthiness gone, eager to be free, impatient of every fetter that binds below in order so to embrace the real object of its love with its entire being that no part of it does not touch The One.

Then of it and of itself the soul has all the vision that may be —of itself luminous now, filled with intellectual light, become pure light, subtle and weightless. It has become divine, is part of the eternal that is beyond becoming. It is like a flame. If later it is weighted down again by the realm of sense, it is like a flame extinguished.

Why does a soul that has risen to the realm above not stay there? Because it has not yet entirely detached itself from things here below. Yet a time will come when it will uninterruptedly have vision, when it will no longer be bothered by body. The part of us that sees is not troubled. It is the other part which, even when we cease from our vision, does not cease from its activity of demonstration, proof and dialectic. But the act and faculty of vision is not reason but something greater than, prior and superior to, reason. So also is the ob-

ject of the vision. When the contemplative looks upon himself
in the act of contemplation, he will see himself to be like its
object. He feels himself to be united to himself in the way that
the object is united to itself; that is to say, he will experience
himself as simple, just as it is simple.

Actually, we should not say, "He will see." What he sees (in
case it is still possible to distinguish here the seer and the seen,
to assert that the two are one would be indeed rash) is not seen,
not distinguished, not represented as a thing apart. The man
who obtains the vision becomes, as it were, another being. He
ceases to be himself, retains nothing of himself. Absorbed in
the beyond he is one with it, like a center coincident with another center. While the centers coincide, they are one. They
become two only when they separate. It is in this sense that we
can speak of The One as something separate.

Therefore it is so very difficult to describe this vision, for
how can we represent as different from us what seemed, while
we were contemplating it, not other than ourselves but perfect at-oneness with us?

This, doubtless, is what is back of the injunction of the mystery religions which prohibit revelation to the uninitiated. The
divine is not expressible, so the initiate is forbidden to speak of
it to anyone who has not been fortunate enough to have beheld
it himself.

The vision, in any case, did not imply duality; the man who
saw was identical with what he saw. Hence he did not "see" it
but rather was "oned" with it. If only he could preserve the
memory of what he was while thus absorbed into The One, he
would possess within himself an image of what it was.

In that state he had attained unity, nothing within him or
without effecting diversity. When he had made his ascent, there
was within him no disturbance, no anger, emotion, desire,
reason, or thought. Actually, he was no longer himself; but,
swept away and filled with the divine, he was still, solitary,
and at rest, not turning to this side or that or even towards
himself. In this state he busied himself no longer even with the
beautiful. He had risen above beauty, had passed beyond even
the choir of virtues.

He was like one who, penetrating the innermost sanctuary
of a temple, leaves temple images behind. They will be the first
objects to strike his view upon coming out of the sanctuary,
after his contemplation and communion there not with an
image or statue but with what they represent. They are but
lesser objects of contemplation.

Such experience is hardly a vision. It is a seeing of a quite
different kind, a self-transcendence, a simplification, self-
abandonment, a striving for union and a repose, an intentness

upon conformation. This is the way one sees in the sanctuary. Anyone who tries to see in any other way will see nothing.

By the use of these images, the wise among the soothsayers expressed in riddles how the divinity is seen. A wise priest, reading the riddle, will, once arrived in the realm beyond, achieve the true vision of the sanctuary. One who has not yet arrived there and knows the sanctuary is invisible, is the source and principle of everything, will also know that by hypostasis is hypostasis seen, and that like alone joins like. He will leave aside nothing of the divine the soul is capable of acquiring. If his vision is not yet complete, he will attend to its completion, which, for him who has risen above all, is The One that is above all. It is not the soul's nature to attain to utter nothingness. Falling into evil it falls, in this sense, into nothingness, but still not complete nothingness. And when it reverses direction, it arrives not at something different but at itself. Thus, when it is not in anything else, it is in nothing but itself. Yet, when it is in itself alone and not in being, it is in the supreme.

We as well transcend Being by virtue of The Soul with which we are united.

Now if you look upon yourself in this state, you find yourself an image of The One.

If you rise beyond yourself, an image rising to its model, you have reached the goal of your journey.

When you fall from this vision, you will, by arousing the virtue that is within yourself and by remembering the perfection that you possess, regain your likeness and through virtue rise to The Intelligence and through wisdom to The One.

Such is the life of the divinity and of divine and blessed men: detachment from all things here below, scorn of all earthly pleasures, the flight of the lone to the Alone.[5]

SELECTED BIBLIOGRAPHY

Editions

Plotini Opera Omnia, ed. G. H. Moser and F. Creuzer (Oxford, 1835), 3 volumes, is still of use and its index of Greek terms is well nigh indispensable. For a completely reliable edition of the original text, one will use the magisterial work-in-progress, *Plotini Opera,* ed. Paul Henry, S.J., and Hans-Rudolf Schwyzer (Paris, 1951-   ), of which two of the projected three volumes have so far (1963) appeared.

[5] VI, 9, 8-11; *op. cit.,* pp. 84-88.

Translations

The spirit of Plotinus is admirably captured in Stephen Mac-Kenna's *Plotinus: The Enneads,* 3rd edition revised by B. S. Page (London, 1962), but it lacks the literalness that alone can warm the scholar's heart. I have myself attempted to make up for that lack in my translation of ten of the chief treatises in *The Essential Plotinus* (New York, 1964).

Studies

The Philosophy of Plotinus by W. R. Inge (London, 3rd edition, 2 volumes, 1929) is still basic. A useful complement is provided by Emile Bréhier in his own *The Philosophy of Plotinus* (Chicago, 1958). The single best brief statement of the general doctrine of Plotinus together with an evaluative survey of Plotinus scholarship up to that time is to be found in H. R. Schwyzer's article "Plotinos," in *Paulys Realencyklopädie der classischen Altertumswissenschaft,* XXI (1951), 471-592. The place of Plotinus in the history of thought is discussed in his conventional learned and luminous fashion by Paul Henry in his Introduction to the MacKenna translation referred to above.

II

ORIGEN

(c. 185—253)

At much the same time that Plotinus, amid admiring pupils in Rome, was constructing his metaphysics of the soul's mystical return to The One, a fellow alumnus of the philosophical school of Alexandria, older than he and even better known, was being tortured in Caesarea for the Faith. They tortured him slowly and with exceeding care because they had received orders not to let him die under their hands. He did not die. And he did not deny his Faith. He seemed, most strangely, joyful and very much at home throughout the entire horrible business. To judge from Eusebius' account,[1] it was almost as if he had been through it all before. I would suggest that there lies the explanation: he had been through it before—often.

For the man was Origen and his mystical doctrine is everywhere marked with that same alarmingly realistic rubric which, towards the close of his life, came finally to mark his body: martyrdom. His mystic experience was, however one is to understand it, a '"martyrdom" experience.

That this could be so the reader will find a little less strange if he recalls that in Origen's day and long before it the central concept of Christian spirituality was the concept of martyrdom; martyrdom was considered the complete imitating of Christ and the most intimate conscious union with God that is possible on earth—the consummating perfection of the spiritual life—much as it has continued to be considered in traditional Christian spirituality right down to our own day.[2] The

---

[1] *Ecclesiastical History*, Book VI, Chapter 39.

[2] A brief exposition with references throughout to the relevant literature is provided by Marcel Viller, S.J., and Karl Rahner, S.J., *Aszese und Mystik in der Väterzeit* (Freiburg, 1939), pp. 29-40.

sole difference latterly (and by that I mean the last sixteen centuries) has been a widening of the concept for a purely practical reason: Perfection is obligatory for all at all times; but the chances of being martyred are dependent upon a steady flow of persecutors, which not every age has been able, or willing, to provide. A peacetime substitute had to be found, and so there came into being the concept of heroic virtue which, independent of historical fluctuations, has been the Church's norm in the canonization of Saints ever since.[3] But in Origen's day there was no need of a substitute; the real thing was all too readily at hand. One is not surprised, then, to find running throughout his writings that rich martyrdom-spirituality, in its purest and most primitive form, much as previous generations had known and lived it.

In that spirituality Christ was the luminous focal center. For the Christian, as for Christ, the complete act of love was achieved in the laying down of one's life for one's friend. But for the Christian, it became increasingly clear, the "friend" *par excellence* was Christ Himself, so that martyrdom was seen as both test and protest of one's love for Christ. It was, however, no isolated love but a love which was the central, cohesive, purifying principle of an act which was the constellation of all the virtues. It was "imitation" that was truly "union" with Christ, union hereafter but also union here in the very act of dying, an act in which many of the martyrs seemed to have experienced what by Faith they had already believed: the strengthening presence of Christ within them. One may, if so inclined, dub such experience "ecstasy." Yet it would seem better in obedience to the data to coin a barbarism and to call it "catastasy." It was not the rapture of the soul out of its native state (the basic idea of "ecstasy"), but *katastasis*— the firm, strong, rich repose and supernaturalizing of its native state.

For this day and for this experience the Christian prepared himself by self-denial, by prayer, by progressive withdrawal from what, then as now, was called "the world." It was in this spirituality that Origen was reared by his parents. A mere youngster, he was all for hieing off to martyrdom, too, the day his father was led out to his own death, and he would surely have done so had not his mother, resorting to that ageless maternal device for keeping little boys at home, taken his clothes and hidden them. When Clement of Alexandria retired to safety, it was Origen, eighteen years old and in full persecution, who reopened and headed the catechetical school. And so on. It is all in Eusebius.[4]

---

[3] See R. Hofmann, *Die heroische Tugend* (Munich, 1933).
[4] *Ecclesiastical History,* Book VI, Chapter 2.

If the reputed mystical experience of Plotinus fits into a pattern, a context, that of Origen—surely authentic—does as well. But its context is that of the third-century Church; the pattern, that of a life lived richly and adventurously. He reports it indirectly, within a coherent scriptural exposition, and does not speculate about it. There is, further, nothing of Plotinus' determinism. Actually, Origen's universe is a universe painted by Dali: everything, he was sure, had come apart with the first sin; Christ, with His coming, was the one solid reality; there alone reposed the twin freedoms of life, Christ's love of him and his love of Christ.

The necessity of purification is as strongly spelled out in his writings as it is in those of Plotinus. For him, as for Plotinus, it is a purification which is a "flight." For Plotinus, as for many a latter-day Christian, it is a flight from matter. For Origen, more sanely, it is a disengagement from sin. And, more so than in Plotinus, it is a flight *to*. This positive emphasis, so agreeably present in all his writings, is graphically illustrated in the origins of desert monasticism of which, in a later generation, he was to prove to be the great inspirational author: the great exodus to the desert came at a time when flight would seem to have been no longer necessary; the great persecutions ceased with the Edict of Milan in 313, precisely when the monastic movement began; seemingly it was a flight *to,* to the hard life, to the austere life of wayfarers on earth, which had disappeared from city life where Christianity was now tolerated.

Because the mystical doctrine of Origen is pretty well distributed throughout all his works and is expressed for the most part only incidentally in treatises which are polemical, dogmatic, scriptural, and never solely mystical, we must forgo the pattern of presentation that characterizes this volume generally. Instead of a brief introduction followed by extended extracts from the writings of the mystic concerned, here only an introduction, laced throughout with excerpts from his voluminous writings, is provided. Any other procedure, it seems, would be less than informative.

To achieve some kind of unity our exposition will follow the schema used by Origen himself in his *Homily XXVII on the Book of Numbers* and the *Commentary on the Song of Songs*.

The *Homily* affords its own special difficulties. To read aright the mystical itinerary it plots out, a map of the Near East in the time of Moses, with every last water hole properly identified, would be most helpful. And none is available.

It describes various stages. But, unlike those of Plotinus

and the early Augustine, none of them implies stability: he makes the point at length that these stages are nothing more than the perilous pitching of their tents by nomads, for, as has been previously remarked, there is no stability in the Origenist universe.

The first stage is self-knowledge. In common with all the early Fathers, Origen makes much of the Biblical doctrine that man was created to the image of God. In his *First Principles* he gives two connotations for "image." The first is the mystical connotation: knowing what one truly is, one knows God. The second is the less traditional moral connotation: the knowledge of one's weakness and sinfulness in contrast to the high dignity to which one is called precisely in being made to the image of God. It is not the mystical but the moral connotation which he exploits here; it is this knowledge that makes possible one's passage to the second stage.

Now is had the first purgation. As the Pillar of the Cloud, a figure of Christ, was what guided the Israelites out of Egypt and through the desert and to the Promised Land, so is it Christ here who takes the initiative in this spiritual exodus: "First of all, would we get out of Egypt, we must leave behind the cult of idols and of evil things and believe in Christ born of the Virgin Mary and the Holy Spirit who has come into the world in assuming our flesh."[5] It is a purgation, accordingly, effected by faith; there is no question here of asceticism, Plotinian or otherwise. It has two aspects. Negatively, it is withdrawal from sin:

Were I but able to be good, I would provide room within me for the Son of God, and then the Lord Jesus would build within me a place for His own sojourning. He would adorn it round about, and build walls and lofty towers that no enemy could scale so that there might be in me, did I but deserve it, a dwelling worthy of Him and of His Father. Thus would He, in adorning my soul, make it able to receive His wisdom, His knowledge, yes, and His sanctity in such wise He would have God the Father enter with Him and there they would be at home, there partake of the nourishment He had Himself provided. To obtain such graces, let us prepare within us a soul that is stainless to the end that the Lord Jesus will deign to accept the hospitality of our hearts.[6]

[5] *Homily XXVII on the Book of Numbers*, 3. This and all following translations from the works of Origen are my own and are based on the critical edition, *Origenes Werke* in "Die griechischen christlichen Schriftsteller."

[6] *Homily XXIV, In Librum Iesu Nave*, 2.

Positively, it is sorrow for sin:

> Christ is in His Passion so long as we continue to sin. If
> the Apostle wept at the plight of some who had sinned
> and not done penance for their sins (2 Corinthians
> 12:21), what will we say of Him who is called "the Son of
> Love" . . . ? How can we believe that the Apostle
> suffered for the impious and scourged himself for sinners
> and that my Lord Jesus is not in tears as He draws near
> the Father to offer for us a sacrifice of propitiation?[7]

The accent here is the same as that of Pascal in his *Le mystère
de Jésus*: "Jesus will be in agony until the end of time: We
cannot sleep in days such as these. . . . Jesus being in agony
and the greatest torment, let us pray the longer."[8]

It is rather easy to be put off by language such as this. Sentiment, never a particularly valuable commodity at best, seems
here to run ahead of reason. For how can Christ, now, really
suffer? Such is the impatient query put by many, including
even St. Bernard, forthright admirer of Origen though he was.
But Origen was ever acutely conscious of the Church; in the
Commentary on the Song of Songs, for example, it is question
equally of the relationship, in love, between Christ and the
soul and Christ and the Church. His happy theological awareness of the social, ecclesial dimensions of love had its necessary counterpart in an awareness of the social, ecclesial
dimensions of sin and of its consequence, suffering. It is not the
fleshly body of Christ but the Body of Christ which is the
Church that suffers and that, thus seen, induces in the soul a
purging, cleansing sorrow. All this, one need hardly point out,
is far removed from Plotinus' "flight of the lone to the Alone":
for Origen the mystic ascent is never, even at its earliest stage,
an individualistic and solitary enterprise.

The third stage is one of temptation, which Origen describes
rather dramatically with the image of the Israelites' progress to
the Red Sea with the Egyptians in full pursuit to make them
turn back and be subjected anew to slavery, for the soul's
progress towards sanctity is now threatened by multitudinous
temptations to turn back, not directly to sin, but to the com-
forts of inertia and an ending of its wayfarer's life.

Moderate penance marks the fourth stage and, once more,
self-knowledge, the better to see in the events of one's past the
consoling portents of progress in the future.

The fifth stage is the "new" Baptism. It is symbolized by the

---

[7] *Homily VII on Leviticus,* 2.
[8] *Pensées,* Brunschvicg, n. 553.

passage of the Chosen People through the Red Sea. There is the temptation, from which I find myself not wholly immune, to interpret what Origen says here as referring to that "second conversion" of which later mystical writers will treat. In any case, Origen does mean a period of especial difficulty and worth: solid earth is lacking to one's feet, the waters threateningly hurl themselves about, but one achieves the other shore if one continues to be guided by Moses, who is the symbol of the Law, the Commandments. At the very least he indicates thereby the essential ground of "second conversion." A deeper reformation of life, the "conversion" implies a new awareness under grace of the context of Christian living which is forever structured upon the total observance of the Commandments which are common to all Christians, no matter what the uncommon graces—mystical or otherwise—the individual Christian may receive.

The sixth stage is a purgative one, the "Bitter Waters" encountered by the Israelites in their own progress through the wilderness of Etham.[9] For, Origen says, just as doctors introduce bitter herbs into their medicines the better to effect the cure of bodies, so does God, the Physician of souls, introduce bitter trials for the cure of souls.

"Visions" mark the seventh stage. That Origen has in mind, not visions in the technical sense, but illusions is clear from the meaning (likely unjustified) he gives to the place where the Israelites now encamped: the Wilderness of Sin. In the Rabbinic interpretation of the time, the place name "Sin" meant "temptations." And here, as frequently elsewhere, Origen follows his advisers among the Rabbis. This, then, is a stage characterized by illusions which may well be temptations; the norms for determining whether they are or not he had provided earlier in the third book of his *First Principles* with his rule for the discernment of spirits.

The eighth is a purgative stage, subtly different from, and a progress upon, that of the sixth stage. It is marked by the more manifest intrusions of grace which involve (a paradox here!) "praiseworthy" temptations. Actually, in unfamiliar language and symbolism, Origen is striving to express the later, classical notion of the "night of the spirit," but, whereas in St. John of the Cross darkness will be emphasized, for him the night is always lightsome.

---

[9] The name Marah, which in Hebrew means "bitter," was given to the first source of water which the Israelites found after their journeying in the desert of Shur (or Etham). *See* Exodus 15:23 and Numbers 33:8. Origen throughout makes much of what the various place names mean or, at least, what he thinks they mean.

The ninth stage is "Terah," that of mystical union.[10] The discussion and analysis of this stage is provided in the *Commentary on the Song of Songs*. According to St. Jerome, "Origen surpassed all other writers in his other books; in his *Song of Songs* he surpassed himself."[11] To this eternal classic, therefore, we shall now direct our attention.

The soul is no longer in the desert wilderness. Not trial, but tranquillity, is now its lot:

> Why does He say to the soul, "Arise"? Why does He say to it, "Hurry"? "It is that for you I have borne the fury of the tempests. For you I have taken on Myself the storms which were meant for you. Because of you, My soul has been sorrowful unto death. On your account have I risen from the dead, and removed the sting of death and broken its bondage. That is why I say to you, 'Arise and come, My love, My beautiful one, because the winter is past and the rains are ended and flowers have reappeared in the land. In rising from the dead I have stilled the tempest and I have brought peace back to the land.' "[12]

The reader will not be slow to remark the admirable joining here of the seemingly merely poetic with basic dogmatic fact: the trials that were borne by the soul were able to be sustained because they were first sustained, and tempered, by the Spouse; something of the fruits of peace the soul can now taste because of the victory over the powers of evil won long ago by Him in His Resurrection.[13]

There are trials now, real enough trials in any case, but of a different sort. They consist in the occasional cessation of the

[10] In his Latin translation, Rufinus (c. 345-410) adds the remark that Terah would, in Greek, be "ecstasy" and thereby occasioned a bitter twentieth-century controversy about whether ecstasy and mystic experience, to which assuredly Origen here refers as the Terah stage, are one and the same thing. Somehow, the fact was lost sight of that the definition is not Origen's but a gloss by Rufinus. However, the erudite passage of arms was an engaging one; *see* W. Völker, *Das Vollkommenheitsideal des Origenes* (especially p. 135) and H. C. Puech, "Un livre récent sur la mystique d'Origène," *Revue d'histoire et de philosophie religieuses*, VI (1933), 508 ff.

[11] In the Preface to his translation of Origen's *Homilies on the Song of Songs*.

[12] This and the following quotation are not from the *Commentary* but from the second *Homily on the Song of Songs* because it gives in briefer, more easily quotable form the doctrine extensively presented in the *Commentary*.

[13] Origen here expresses a fundamental insight into Christian living that has only recently been recaptured by contemporary theology: the relevance, beyond its mere apologetic value, of the fact of the Resurrection.

Spouse's felt presence. For the soul has been made more spiritually sensitive by, has been cut open by, what Origen and many after him without any literary dependence upon him will be forced to call the "wound of love":

How good, how glorious it is to receive the wound of love. This man here suffers the ravaging of carnal love, and that one there is lacerated by earthly desires. But you, offer yourself defenseless, your limbs and your whole being, to this precious glowing dart for it is God who is the archer. Notice how Scripture speaks of this arrow. Or, better, to increase your marveling the more, listen as the Arrow Itself speaks and says: "He has set Me in reserve as the arrow of His choosing; and to Me has He said: 'Behold a great thing for Thee—You are My Son.'"[14] How happy is the lot of those who have been wounded by this arrow. This arrow was it that wounded the disciples while they conversed on the road to Emmaus, and they said, "Was not our heart burning within us the while He explained to us the Scriptures on the way?"

According to Origen mystical experience is the *sensed* presence of the Spouse. Even those who are not mystics he portrays as attracted to the life of virtue by the fragrance of Him who is all virtue. Not scent alone, but every spiritual sense is filled in the sensation of presence experienced by the mystic. For the Spouse, Christ, here

fills also the hearing, sight, touch, and taste, actuates each several sense in accord with its nature and its basic need. The eye in beholding the glory of the Son of God would see no other thing nor the ear attend any sound except this living Word. One who touches the living Word will touch henceforth nothing fleeting and mortal. Nor will one's taste, once it has savored the living Word (His Flesh, the Bread descended from Heaven), suffer thereafter the taste of anything else. After this sweetness, all else seems bitterness. . . . One who has deserved to be thus with Christ tastes and touches the exultant happiness[15] of the Lord. All his senses have their joy in the Word of God.[16]

[14] *Cf.* Isaiah 49:2-6.

[15] In the Latin version of Rufinus (which is being translated here because Origen's original Greek text is apparently no longer extant) some of the manuscripts read *voluntatem Domini*, "the Lord's will," instead of *voluptatem Domini*, "the happiness of the Lord." Either reading is consistent with Origen's thought, but the first is by far the more theologically profound and, critically, should be given the preference.

[16] *Commentary on the Song of Songs*, I, 4.

To this doctrine of the spiritual senses as the immediate vehicle of mystic experience we will return in a moment. First Origen's own explanation of the possibility of such experience (and, indeed, of the possibility of such senses) must be examined.

For him, as for many another whose background is Platonic, the truth of a being is its "Idea" and, secondly, the "place of the Ideas" is the spirit.[17] The higher one ascends the scale of beings, the less relative (and less material) is their truth. The truth which is proper to a material being is precisely that it be a shadow of the spiritual.[18] Material beings are not in themselves "true."[19] Yet he insists: "If nothing of what is perceived by the senses is true, it is not therefore false because the possibility remains that the sense object has an analogy with and towards the intelligible."[20] The existence of the sense object has not its center within the object; the object is accordingly relative in what is most interior and self-sufficient about it. To that degree, its existence is provisional: because it has not this interiority of existence on the Last Day it will pass away.[21] Sense objects are like the membrane which envelops the embryo (in this instance, the rational being) and makes it possible for it to grow.[22] Thus the total universe of sense is only sign and image. It is so, not by convention, but by its very essence.[23] Thus is it the precursor of absolute truth.[24]

The other Platonic datum, that spirit is the "place of the Ideas," initiates the following line of reasoning. Spirit possesses, by an intrinsic relation, its own proper truth, yet it will be truth solely in the measure that this relation is actualized. And its actualization is exclusively in the order of "idea"— and for Origen, the first Christian Platonist, the "Idea" is the Word made flesh: Christ had said, "I am the Truth," and Origen, to his profit, never forgot it. This movement of the soul beyond itself towards its Idea which is, however, immanent to it characterizes the spiritual life so fully that it is ever more prominent the better one is. It is, paradoxically enough (because Origen has been speaking not of will but of intellect), love.

The relative character of spirit does not disappear to the degree that its absolute character is consolidated in truth. It is

[17] *Homily V on Leviticus*, 2.
[18] *First Principles*, II, 16-17.
[19] *Commentary on the Song of Songs*, II, 5.
[20] *Commentary on John*, 1, 24.
[21] *First Principles*, III, 6.
[22] *Against Celsus*, IV, 74.
[23] *Homily IX on Genesis*, 1.
[24] *Commentary on the Song of Songs*, III, 12.

merely transformed. That is why, arguing with Celsus,[25] he will say that ectasy is demonic. The true going beyond oneself to what is immanent to oneself is catastasy, the luminous and rational actuation of the Word in our spirit.[26]

Much interest attaches to this explanation. Theologically, it inspires little conviction. Compared with the tough, solid, compact logic of Plotinus, it is singularly disorganized and weak. Yet in those deficiencies, theological and logical, lies its merit. Origen is not concerned, obviously, with rigorously plotting out how mystical experience must come about. He is providing incidental and partial insights into a mystical experience which did come about.

He uses three groups of symbols to cast further light on this mystery of the conscious compenetration of creature and Creator which is mystic experience: eating, marriage, the spiritual senses. There is even a compenetration of the three symbols themselves which does not make the task of explaining them briefly here any the easier.

The basic symbol is that of eating. It is in terms of the Eucharist[27] and provides one of the earliest examples of that parallelism between Sacraments and mysticism that will be exploited more fully by St. Gregory of Nyssa in the fourth century and, most fully of all, by Nicolas Cabasilas in the fourteenth.

The marriage symbol, of course, will be used even more widely in succeeding centuries. According to Origen, every soul is by its nature oriented towards its Idea as the espoused to the Spouse.[28] All the valencies of this concept are, one after another, explored in the multiple instances in which he comments upon his favorite Pauline verse, "Who cleaves to the Lord is one spirit."[29] He sees it as the spiritual counterpart of the "two in one flesh" of Genesis 2:24. Just as in marriage it is question of a new, higher personal oneness, a fusing of personality without a confusion of persons, so also is it in mysticism since "there is no possibility that what shares in life should become Life itself."[30]

The least basic symbol, theologically speaking, is the one which is descriptively the most informative—the spiritual senses. Here, again, Origen is a pioneer with a large following, particularly in the Middle Ages.[31] His followers are, I expect,

[25] *Against Celsus*, VII, 3.
[26] *Cf. Commentary on Psalm 4*, 4.
[27] See p. 38 for an instance.
[28] *Homily XLIII on Matthew*.
[29] 1 Corinthians 6:17.
[30] *Commentary on John*, 2, 4.
[31] Karl Rahner, S.J., "Le début d'une doctrine des cinq sens spirituels chez Origène," *Revue d'ascétique et de mystique*, XIII (1932), 113-145.

faithful in their fashion. But with St. Thomas Aquinas and St.
Bonaventure, who obviously have their own followers, the
spiritual senses become sensations; they are acts. Not so with
Origen. He insists, time and again, that they are faculties.[32]
He has, or thinks he has, good reason for this insistence.
Scripture itself describes them thus.[33] And, as such, they fit in
excellently with his doctrine of the bodily being the symbol of
the spiritual.[34] They are, he holds, possessed by all. In the non-
mystic, now one and now another will be actuated; in the
mystic, in the moment of mystic experience, all five of them
react. For St. Gregory of Nyssa, the experience is one of scent.
For St. Augustine, it is taste. For St. John of the Cross, it is
touch. For Origen, it is taste, touch, scent, sight, and hearing
—all five.[35]

Actually, there is no warranty in Scripture for this doctrine;
the texts which seem probative to Origen can be interpreted
most naturally in a nonmystical way. This, in effect, St. Augustine—himself a mystic—does in the famous Book X of *The
Confessions*.[36] And even Origen's fundamental doctrine of
sense as symbol of the spiritual does not provide sufficient
grounds for asserting the existence of such faculties. That doctrine, rather, provides grounds for a mysticism of a strictly
intellectual sort. All of which leads one to affirm once more
that the mystical experience discoverable in the writings of
Origen is not a theoretical conclusion but a reality.

Therefore, with a fair degree of reliability, it may be said
that this was the mystic experience of Origen: It was a
stability, a repose, an awareness of the presence of God in
Christ that was such a heightening of Faith that it was describ-
able only as like an experience which deploys itself through
the five bodily senses. It was rooted in what Origen called the
hégemonikon, borrowing the term from the Stoics but meaning
by it what St. Augustine later spoke of as the *cor spatiosum*
and Meister Eckhart as the *Seelengrund*—the pure essence of
the soul. In contrast to that of many a later mystic, at no stage
was his experience enveloped in darkness. In contrast to the
early stages of mystic experience in others (as, for instance,
St. Teresa), it was never ecstatic. It was comparable to that
experiential awareness of the presence of God which, it was
traditionally believed, some of the martyrs had in the moment
of their sacrifice: an awareness which did not in any way with-

[32] *First Principles*, I, 1, 9; *Against Celsus*, I, 48; *On Luke*, Fragment 9.
[33] *Cf. Commentary on the Song of Songs*, II, 11, and *passim*.
[34] See pp. 37-38.
[35] *Commentary on the Song of Songs*, I, 4; and see p. 38 above.
[36] See p. 62.

draw them from their normal rational condition but inten-sified it, purified it, and exalted it so that—in no trance, no stupor, no ecstasy—they were never more completely them-selves than at that moment when they were consciously at one with Another, with Christ in God.

Was it thus comparable in Origen's eyes? I know of no place in his voluminous writings where he makes the comparison.

However, grace builds on nature; it does not destroy it. The mystic experience of Origen may well have been just a further instance—however unusual—of the truth of that axiom, an experience which was of a piece with the martyrdom spiritu-ality he lived and which was fitted to the pattern of his lifelong desire for actual martyrdom. I am myself inclined to think it was just that.

SELECTED BIBLIOGRAPHY

Editions

The text of C. de la Rue (Paris, 1733-59) is reproduced, with helpful additions, in Migne, *Patrologia Graeca,* Volumes XI-XVII. Critical editions of the Scripture commentaries, one's chief source for the mystical doctrine of Origen, have been published by W. A. Baehrens, *Origines Werke* in "Die griechischen christlichen Schrift-steller," Volumes XXIX (1920) and XXXIII (1925).

Translations

Continuing the tradition of excellence that the series "Ancient Christian Writers" has long enjoyed, R. P. Lawson has provided an annotated version of the two most important mystical documents in his *Origen, The Song of Songs: Commentary and Homilies* (Westminster-London, 1957).

Studies

The pioneering work of W. Völker, *Das Vollkommenheitsideal des Origenes* (Tübingen, 1931), is of the utmost value, especially if complemented by the correctives of A. Lieske, S.J., *Die Theologie der Logosmystik bei Origenes* (Münster, 1938). *Origène et la "con-naissance mystique"* by Henri Crouzel, S.J. (Paris, 1961), is largely polemical yet contains many valid insights. A truly basic insight that has opened up a new rich vein in Origenist research is pro-vided by P. Nemeshegyi, *La paternité de Dieu chez Origène* (Paris,

1960). Origen and the long tradition he initiated of the mystical interpretation of the Song of Songs is studied by F. Ohley, *Hohelied-Studien: Grundzüge einer Geschichte der Hoheliedauslegung des Abendlandes bis zum 1200* (Wiesbaden, 1958).

III

ST. GREGORY OF NYSSA

(c. 330—p. 394)

ORIGEN lived in the early part of the third century; St. Gregory of Nyssa, in the latter part of the fourth.

Of the various things that happened in the meantime there are three in particular that the historian of religious ideas may ignore, it would seem, only at his not inconsiderable peril. Before ever Gregory was born he was, you might say, both exempted from the especial tensions of the Origenist era and destined to be exposed to heady philosophic and religious influences that Origen had never known; these events, so diverse in their nature and so disparate in their causes, effected a revolution in the climate of Christian living that was not without repercussions through the entire area of Christian thought.

The first of them, the promulgation of the Edict of Milan in 313, put an end to the general persecution of Christians. Therewith the prospect of martyrdom ceased to be what it had been for so long, an immediate imminency to every Christian whoever he was or wherever he might be, a sort of ubiquitous electrical charge presaging the storm which, frightening and exhilarating, filled the lowering atmosphere all about one. That now was gone. A factor so influential in shaping and deepening the thought of an Origen was no longer present to affect the thought of a Gregory.

Secondly, there was the general, if qualified, Christian acceptance of the teaching of Plotinus which had become widely current in the interval and was for centuries after to affect mystical writers of the most varied hue, whether basically with its philosophy or superficially with its mode of expression.

Gregory was introduced to it by his brother, St. Basil. What effect it had on him it will be one of our tasks to determine.

Finally, the years between had seen the monastic movement with all its precisions for the life of the spirit get fully under way, progressively clarifying insights inherited from Origen and exploiting their virtualities in the cooperative laboratory of community life to a degree quite impossible in Origen's time.

This influence, too, was brought home to Gregory (in an acutely literal sense) by Basil, the great organizer of monasticism in the East who eventually organized Gregory into it as well. For a while Gregory followed studies preparatory to the priesthood, but he gave up the idea before being ordained; he married and settled down (or so he thought) to a life as professor of rhetoric. But he had badly underestimated his brother's proselytizing abilities and before very long was himself a monk in a monastery, his wife, Theosebia, having been told in effect, "Get thee to a nunnery!"—which, it would seem, the poor thing did. It was during this monastic retirement (brief, because Basil next hailed him forth to become Bishop of Nyssa) that the thought of Gregory received its basic orientation.

It was a mystical orientation. Perhaps Gregory has fared so poorly at the hands of historians because his exceptional achievements as philosopher and as literary stylist have obscured from their eyes what fundamentally he was: a theologian of the mystical life. This he pre-eminently reveals himself to be in two works: *The Life of Moses* (which is subtitled "A Treatise on the Perfection of the Virtues") and the *Commentary on the Song of Songs*.

He describes the mystical ascent as taking place in three stages, symbolized by God's manifestation of Himself to Moses, first in light, then in the cloud, and finally in the dark. The first stage equals the Purgative Way of what became a traditional division ("Purgative," "Illuminative," "Unitive") in writings on the spiritual life; it is the time of active separation from error and evil. The stage of "the cloud"—again to use a later terminology—is the time of active contemplation when one progressively separates oneself from the world of appearances and of sense attractions. This stage, Gregory says, "the philosophers of this world" can achieve as well as anyone else. Only with the third and last stage, that of the divine dark, is it a question of the mystical, of that which no one can achieve, of that which must be divinely bestowed.

Several themes, by now familiar to the reader, make their appearance as Gregory attempts to convey some notion of the experiencing of the divine presence: the intoxication of the mind (as in Plotinus), the wound of love, and the spiritual senses—scent, sight, and taste (as in Origen, although Origen was forced to appeal to all five). What is distinctive about Gregory is the complex experience itself, made up of two chief experiences: the heightened sense of self-possession in the possession of God interior to one's soul and the sense of oneself into God transcendent. The term he uses to designate this enigmatic experience gives a clue for the solving of the seeming enigma. It is *epektasis*. It comes from a text of St. Paul that was one of his favorites.[1] It means for him, as it meant for Paul, a "straining" Godward that is bestowed upon one by God Himself. It is the *pondus ad sursum* of St. Augustine—but experienced. It is a continual movement, a continuous slaking of thirst where every assuagement awakens a deeper thirst, and every pleasure a more exquisite pain.

Did Gregory truly experience this? Or is he merely providing a doctrinal conclusion under the guise of the personal, much as, it seems, Plotinus does? He would appear to have experienced it. *Epektasis* is a concept wholly counter to the doctrines of the Stoics, of Philo, of Plotinus, and of Origen upon which he draws for many details of his own doctrinal system. And, further, one can see, throughout his writings, his system assuming its distinctive form in continuity with that early, basic experience.

TEXTS[2]

The path of those who rise to God is . . . unlimited. But how does the grace that the soul continually achieves become in turn the principle of a higher good? From the words spoken to the bride, we should have supposed that there would be a halt in her progress towards the heights. For after such an assurance of perfection, what could anyone hope for? But then we realize that she is still inside and has not yet gone out of doors; she does not yet enjoy that vision *face to face,* but is still making progress in her participation in good merely by the sounds she hears.

Now the lesson we are taught here is that for those who are ever advancing towards higher things there applies the saying of the Apostle: *If any man think that he knoweth any thing, he hath not yet known as he ought to know* (1 Corinthians 8:2). For up to this point, the soul is aware of only

[1] Philippians 3:13.
[2] From Jean Daniélou, S.J., ed., *From Glory to Glory,* translated by Herbert Musurillo, S.J. (New York-London, 1961-1963).

so much as she has understood. Yet what she still does not know is infinitely more than what she has comprehended. That is why, though the Bridegroom often reveals Himself to the soul, she never sees Him directly, though He keeps assuring the bride by His voice that she will.

To make this idea a little clearer, I shall illustrate it by a comparison. It is just as if you could see that spring which Scripture tells us rose from the earth at the beginning in such quantities that it watered the entire face of the earth (Genesis 2:10 ff.). As you came near the spring you would marvel, seeing that the water was endless, as it constantly gushed up and poured forth. Yet you could never say that you had seen all the water. How could you see what was still hidden in the bosom of the earth? Hence no matter how long you might stay at the spring, you would always be beginning to see the water. For the water never stops flowing, and it is always beginning to bubble up again.

It is the same with one who fixes his gaze on the infinite beauty of God. It is constantly being discovered anew, and it is always seen as something new and strange in comparison with what the mind has already understood. And as God continues to reveal Himself, man continues to wonder; and he never exhausts his desire to see more, since what he is waiting for is always more magnificent, more divine, than all that he has already seen. So too in our text the bride is in wonder and amazement at what she is beginning to see, yet she never, for all that, puts an end to her yearning for further vision.

Open to me, my sister, my love, my dove, my perfect one: for my head is full of dew, and my locks with the drops of night. Our interpretation will help you to grasp the meaning of this text. Moses' vision of God began with light; afterwards God spoke to him in a cloud. But when Moses rose higher and became more perfect, he saw God in the darkness.

Now the doctrine we are taught here is as follows. Our initial withdrawal from wrong and erroneous ideas of God is a transition from darkness to light. Next comes a closer awareness of hidden things, and by this the soul is guided through sense phenomena to the world of the invisible. And this awareness is a kind of cloud, which overshadows all appearances, and slowly guides and accustoms the soul to look towards what is hidden. Next the soul makes progress through all these stages and goes on higher, and as she leaves below all that human nature can attain, she enters within the secret chamber of the divine knowledge, and here she is cut off on all sides by the divine darkness. Now she leaves outside all that can be grasped by sense or by reason, and the only thing left for her contemplation is the invisible and the incomprehensible. And here

God is, as the Scriptures tell us in connection with Moses: *But Moses went to the dark cloud wherein God was.*[3]

But what now is the meaning of Moses' entry into the darkness and of the vision of God that he enjoyed in it? . . . The sacred text is here teaching us that . . . as the soul makes progress, and by a greater and more perfect concentration comes to appreciate what the knowledge of truth is, the more it approaches this vision, and so much the more does it see that the divine nature is invisible. It thus leaves all surface appearances, not only those that can be grasped by the senses but also those which the mind itself seems to see, and it keeps on going deeper until by the operation of the spirit it penetrates the invisible and incomprehensible, and it is there that it sees God. The true vision and the true knowledge of what we seek consists precisely in not seeing, in an awareness that our goal transcends all knowledge and is everywhere cut off from us by the darkness of incomprehensibility. Thus that profound evangelist, John, who penetrated into this luminous darkness, tells us that *no man hath seen God at any time* (John 1:18), teaching us by this negation that no man—indeed, no created intellect—can attain a knowledge of God.[4]

The soul that does see [God's beauty] by some divine gift and inspiration, retains his ecstasy unexpressed in the secret of his consciousness. . . . The great David rightly shows us how impossible this is. Lifted out of himself by the Spirit, he glimpsed in that blessed ecstasy God's infinite and incomprehensible beauty. . . . And though yearning to say something which would do justice to his vision, he can only cry out . . . : *Every man is a liar.*[5]

This is indeed a strange sleep and foreign to nature's custom. In natural sleep the sleeper is not wide awake, and he who is wide awake is not sleeping. Sleeping and waking are contraries, and they succeed and follow one another. But in this case there is a strange and contradictory fusion of opposites in the same state. For *I sleep and my heart watcheth.*

What meaning ought we to take from these words?

Sleep is the image of death. All the body's sensory perception is suspended: in sleep, sight, hearing, smell, taste, and touch do not perform their function. In sleep bodily tension is relaxed, a man's worries are forgotten and fears are put to rest, anger is calmed; so long as sleep has control over the

[3] *Commentary on the Song of Songs*, Sermon 11; Daniélou, *op. cit.*, pp. 245-247.
[4] *The Life of Moses*; *op. cit.*, p. 118.
[5] *On Virginity*; *op. cit.*, p. 34.

body, it relaxes the strain of those who are in grief and makes them unaware of any evil.

From what we have said, then, when the bride proudly declares, *I sleep and my heart watcheth,* we learn that she has risen higher than ever before. For indeed, so long as reason lives alone within itself and is undisturbed by the senses, it is as though the body were overcome with sleep and exhaustion. Then may it truly be said that the sight is inactive and asleep, when the soul despises such things as make an impression on the eyes of little children. . . . The contemplation of our true good makes us despise all these things; and so the eye of the body sleeps. Anything that the eye reveals does not attract the perfect soul, because by reason it looks only to those things which transcend the visible universe. So too the sense of hearing is dead and does not function, because the soul is absorbed in things that surpass speech. . . . When all of [the senses] have been lulled into inactivity by a kind of sleep, the heart's functioning becomes pure, the reason looks up to heaven, unshaken and unperturbed by the motion of the senses. . . . Thus the soul, enjoying alone the contemplation of Being, will not awake for anything that arouses sensual pleasure. After lulling to sleep every bodily motion, it receives the vision of God in a divine wakefulness with pure and naked intuition. May we make ourselves worthy of this vision, achieving by this sleep the awakening of the soul![6]

No created being can go out of itself by rational contemplation. Whatever it sees, it must see itself; and even if it thinks it is seeing beyond itself, it does not in fact possess a nature which can achieve this. And thus in its contemplation of Being it tries to force itself to transcend a spatial representation, but it never achieves it. For in every possible thought, the mind is surely aware of the spatial element which it perceives in addition to the thought content; and the spatial element is, of course, created. Yet the Good that we have learned to seek and to cherish is beyond all creation, and hence beyond all comprehension. Thus how can our mind, which always operates on a dimensional image, comprehend a nature that has no dimension, especially as our minds are constantly penetrating, by analysis, into things which are more and more profound. And though the mind in its restlessness ranges through all that is knowable, it has never yet discovered a way of comprehending eternity in such wise that it might place itself outside of it, and go beyond the idea of eternity itself and that Being which is above all being. It is like someone who finds himself on a

[6] *Commentary on the Song of Songs,* Sermon 10; *op. cit.,* pp. 40-41; 241-242.

mountain ridge. Imagine a sheer, steep crag, of reddish appearance below, extending into eternity; on top there is this ridge which looks down over a projecting rim into a bottomless chasm. Now imagine what a person would probably experience if he put his foot on the edge of this ridge which overlooks the chasm and found no solid footing nor anything to hold on to. This is what I think the soul experiences when it goes beyond its footing in material things, in its quest for that which has no dimension and which exists from all eternity. For here there is nothing it can take hold of, neither place nor time, neither measure nor anything else; it does not allow our minds to approach. And thus the soul, slipping at every point from what cannot be grasped, becomes dizzy and perplexed and returns once again to what is connatural to it.[7]

Along the seacoast you may often see mountains facing the sea, sheer and steep from top to bottom, while a projection at the top forms a cliff overhanging the depths. Now if someone suddenly looked down from such a cliff to the depths below he would become dizzy. So too is my soul seized with dizziness now as it is raised on high by this great saying of the Lord, *Blessed are the clean of heart, for they shall see God. . . .* But *no man hath seen God at any time,* says the great John. . . . This then is the steep and sheer rock that Moses taught us was inaccessible, so that our minds can in no way approach it. For every possibility of apprehension is excluded by the words: *No man can see the Lord and live.*[8]

In order to have us understand its profoundest doctrine, the Scriptures use as a symbol that which is the most violent of all our pleasurable inclinations, I mean the passion of love. Thus we are meant to understand that the soul that contemplates the inaccessible beauty of the divine nature falls in love with it in much the same way as the body is attracted towards things that are connatural to it. But here the entire disturbance of the soul has been transformed into impassibility, all carnal passion is extinguished in us and the soul burns with love by the sole flame of the Spirit.[9]

The soul, having gone out at the word of her Beloved, looks for Him but does not find Him. . . . In this way she is, in a certain sense, wounded and beaten because of the frustration of what she desires, now that she thinks that her yearning for the Other cannot be fulfilled or satisfied. But the veil of her grief is removed when she learns that the true satisfaction of her de-

[7] *Commentary on Ecclesiastes,* Sermon 7; *op. cit.,* pp. 127-128.
[8] *On the Beatitudes,* Sermon 6; *op. cit.,* pp. 42-43.
[9] *Commentary on the Song of Songs,* Sermon 1; *op. cit.,* p. 44.

sire consists in constantly going on in her quest and never ceasing in her ascent, seeing that every fulfillment of her desire continually generates a further desire for the Transcendent. Thus the veil of her despair is torn away and the bride realizes that she will always discover more and more of the incomprehensible and unhoped-for beauty of her Spouse throughout all eternity. Then she is torn by an even more urgent longing, and . . . she communicates to her Beloved the dispositions of her heart. For she has received within her God's special dart, she has been wounded in the heart by the point of faith, she has been mortally wounded by the arrow of love.[10]

SELECTED BIBLIOGRAPHY

Editions

The most generally available text is that of the complete works in Migne, *Patrologia Graeca,* Volumes XLIV-XLVI, but it is extremely faulty. An improved text of one of the most important of Gregory's mystical writings is given by Jean Daniélou, S.J., in his *Contemplation sur la vie de Moïse,* 2nd edition (Paris, 1955), and a strictly critical one of other relevant works by W. Jaeger, J. F. Cavarnos, V. W. Callahan, *Opera Ascetica,* Volume I (Leiden, 1952).

Translations

From Glory to Glory: Texts from Gregory of Nyssa's Mystical Writings by Jean Daniélou, S.J. (New York-London, 1961-1963) offers a Gregory expertly turned out in English dress by Herbert Musurillo, S.J.

Studies

The fundamental approach to Gregory's mystical doctrine is to contrast it with Platonism upon which, however, he was so largely dependent. Thus, with individual and informative differences, have proceeded Father Daniélou, *Platonisme et théologie mystique: Essai sur la doctrine spirituelle de saint Grégoire de Nysse* (Paris, 1944), Endre von Ivanka, "Von Platonismus zur Theorie der Mystik: zur Erkenntnislehre Gregors von Nyssa," *Scholastik,* XI (1936), 163-195, and H. Merki, O.S.B., *Homoiosis theo: Von der platonischen Angleichung an Gott zur Gottähnlichkeit bei Gregor von Nyssa* (Freiburg, 1952).

[10] *Commentary on the Song of Songs,* Sermon 12; *op. cit.,* p. 45.

IV

EVAGRIUS OF PONTUS

(346—399)

THE INFLUENCE, extended and deep, of Origen upon the mystical teaching of the centuries following his own has only of late come to be properly recognized. That it was not a wholly uniform influence and, in some significant instances, not altogether happy, many a scholar—however enamored of Origen —has begun reluctantly to suspect.

For our purposes it is sufficient to remark the different effect he had upon the Middle Ages in the West (upon William of St. Thierry, for instance, or St. Bernard or the Victorines) and upon the intervening monastic period in both East and West. To the monastic beginnings in the Egyptian deserts his doctrine came in a severely truncated form: little more than the philosophy it contained survived the passage. And, surviving, it soon acquired an independent vitality that surely would have dismayed Origen mightily had he been around to witness it. For rationalist implications that he had himself by constant recourse to Scripture and to experience kept carefully in check now burst forth full-blown.

One sole man would seem to have brought all this about: Evagrius of Ibora in Pontus, still—for reasons that will appear in a moment—largely a mystery man in the history of Christian ideas.

The first desert monk to write extensively of the spiritual life, Evagrius so clearly impressed readers with the Origenist inspiration of his doctrines that when Origenism was condemned by the Council of Alexandria a few months after his death he, as well as Origen, was considered condemned, and his writings thereafter went underground. Some, as his *On Prayer,* were circulated eventually under the name of Nilus of Ancyra.[1] Others, as the *Apology to the Caesareans,* moved about even more grandly under the imposing mantle of St. Basil the Great.[2] Still others were translated into Syriac and thus extended their influence throughout those sections of the Church which, less knowing, were less hostile.

And it was he, it now seems clear, who was really condemned in the condemnation of Origenism. Scholars had long been puzzled at the successive anathemas pronounced, not only by the local Council of Alexandria, but by the Provincial Council of Constantinople in 543 and by the Fifth Ecumenical Council itself, which was held there ten years later. For the characteristic doctrines of Origenism—the inequality of the Divine Persons, the pre-existence of souls, the immateriality of the body after the resurrection, the reabsorption of all intelligences into the One, and so on—are not to be found in the writings of Origen. Origenism seemed a phantom heresy. But it was no phantom. It shows its earthy face today in the rediscovered works of Evagrius.[3]

An altogether fascinating figure is this Evagrius and in many ways a beguiling one, as only history's proper scamps ever succeed in being. The high detection involved in his rediscovery by the heretic-hunters has its elements of romance, too, for us in our present rather more pacific and Christian enterprise. For the first time in over fifteen centuries one can look directly at the ambiguous giant whose shadow rests upon the thought of Cassian, of St. Benedict, of Gregory Palamas, of present-day theologians of Christian morality, of present-day theologians of asceticism.

It is not difficult to recognize the Origenist content in the doctrine of Evagrius. What is here in bloom was there (as we have already suggested) in seed. But, more than that, what

---

[1] It continues to be ascribed to Nilus in the *Patrologia Graeca* of Migne, Volume LXXIX, columns 1165-1200. Only with the dissertation of Irénée Hausherr, S.J., "Le traité de l'oraison d'Evagre le Pontique (Pseudo Nil)," *Revue d'ascétique et de mystique,* XV (1934), 34-93 and 113-170, especially 34-39, was its true author once more brought to light.

[2] Still ascribed to Basil as "Letter VIII" in Migne, Volume XXXII, columns 245-268, and in the Loeb Classical Library (Roy J. Deferrari, *Saint Basil: The Letters* [Cambridge, 1926], Volume I, pp. 47-93), its Evagrian authorship was simultaneously, but independently, recognized by R. Melcher, *Der achte Brief des Basilius, ein Werk des Evagrius Ponticus* (Münster, 1923), and W. Bousset, *Apophthegmata, Studien zur Geschichte des ältesten Mönchtums* (Tübingen, 1923), pp. 335-336.

[3] *Cf.* François Refoulé, O.P., "La christologie d'Evagre et l'origénisme," *Orientalia Christiana Periodica,* XXVII (1961), 221-266.

was there a garden of delights has here become a petrified forest. Rigidity is the mark of Evagrius. In this he reminds one of Plotinus. And he should. His borrowings from Plotinus are often meticulously effected, word for word. Thus, the introspection which he advocates as one's necessary beginning in the mystical ascent is that, metaphysical, of Plotinus and not that, moral, of Origen. Similarly, at the term of the ascent, the *locus* of experience is the *nous* of Plotinus, narrow and severely straitened, and not the spacious *hégemonikon* of Origen. Intellect, accordingly, chiefly in the exquisite operation of prayer, holds the primacy in Christian living—a characteristic doctrine which one must wait three centuries to see refuted, in isolation, by his otherwise faithful Maximus the Confessor.[4] The practice of virtue, quite logically, is proposed as a means of achieving the practice of prayer. And asceticism necessarily culminates in mysticism, a notion which has had its champions even in our own day, although one of Evagrius' own champions refuted it fourteen centuries ago.[5] But such subsequent insubordination in the ranks was rare. We shall have occasion to treat later of an entire mystical movement, Hesychasm, which grew out of total loyalty to Evagrius.

He was, like Origen, alertly aware of sin and its consequences. Indeed, it was he who first made a catalog of the capital sins, managing in his eagerness to discover eight of them while even the tradition which stems from him has never been able to find more than seven. But with Origen sin was beheld chiefly in the perspective of Christ. With Evagrius it is seen chiefly in the perspective of the individual Christian. From him, accordingly, as further inheritance came that preoccupation with sin and how to avoid it which characterizes the spirituality of the Fathers of the Desert centuries ago[6] and the recurrent Jansenism of centuries closer to our own.

"For three years I have not been troubled by fleshly desire after so long a life of toil and labor and unceasing prayer." So, dying, spoke Evagrius.

One can only rejoice that a spirituality so deadening as his finally dealt a deathblow to something, at least, that is better off dead.

[4] *Cf.* Marcel Viller, S.J., "Aux sources de la spiritualité de saint Maxime: les oeuvres d'Evagre le Pontique," *Revue d'ascétique et de mystique,* XI (1930), 239-268.

[5] I. Hausherr, S.J., "Contemplation et sainteté, une remarquable mise au point par Philoxène de Mabboug," *Revue d'ascétique et de mystique,* XIV (1933), 171-195.

[6] See the *Apophthegmata Patrum* (the "Sayings of the Fathers") in Migne, *Patrologia Graeca,* Volume LXV, columns 71-440, and F. Nau, "Histoires des solitaires égyptiens," *Revue de l'Orient chrétien,* XII (1907), 43-47, 171-189, 393-413.

TEXTS [7]

ON PRAYER

3. Prayer is a habitual commerce of the intelligence with God.

4. If, when he attempted to approach the burning bush, Moses could not do so until he had removed his shoes, how then will you, who wish to see Him who is beyond all intellection and all sensation, not remove all passionate thought? [8]

5. Above all pray to receive the gift of tears so as to soften with compunction the inherent hardness of your soul and, admitting against yourself your iniquity before the Lord, obtain His pardon.

7. When, in your prayer, you will have poured forth fountains of tears, be not proud: your prayer has simply obtained for you an aid to the full confession of your sins and the appeasement, by tears, of the Lord.

8. Therefore do not make a passion of the antidote to passion if you do not wish to irk the more the giver of grace; many who have wept over their sins have become deranged and deluded because they forgot the purpose of tears.

11. In time of prayer force yourself to make your intelligence deaf and dumb and you will be able to pray.

15. Prayer is a fruit of joy and thanksgiving.

16. Prayer is the exclusion of sorrow and discouragement.

17. Go sell all that you have and then take up the Cross; deny yourself so that you can pray without distraction.

18. If you would pray worthily, deny yourself continually; if you undergo trials of all sorts, accept your lot philosophically out of love for prayer.

19. All distress that you will have accepted philosophically, you will find to be fruitful in time of prayer.

20. If you would pray as you should, sadden no man; for if you do, you strive in vain.

[7] The translation is my own from the original Greek given in Migne, *Patrologia Graeca*, Volume LXXIX, columns 1165-1200, among the works ascribed to Nilus of Ancyra.

[8] His repudiation of "passionate thought" implies something basic and (fortunately) unusual in his doctrine, namely that virtue is a thought begotten by passion and hence an obstacle to contemplation.

31. Do not pray that your will be done for it does not necessarily agree with the will of God; pray rather as we have been taught and say, "Thy will be done" in me, and thus in all things ask Him that His will be done because He wishes what is good and useful to your soul. . . .

34. . . . Undistracted prayer is the intelligence's most lofty intellection.

36. If you would pray, renounce all to obtain all.

42. This is the proper character of prayer: a respectful gravity together with compunction and sorrow of soul in the avowal of faults made with inner groanings.

52. Prayer as a state is an attitude free of all feeling[9] which, by a lofty love, transports the intelligence to the sapient, spiritual, and intellectual heights.

55. It is not because one will have attained to unfeelingness that one thereby will truly pray, because one can continue in simple thoughts and distract oneself in meditating upon them and thus be far from God.

56. And, even if the intelligence does not dally in simple thoughts, it has not by that fact attained to the place of prayer. It is able to be occupied with the contemplation of objects and busy with their meanings. And they, although still simple expressions, nevertheless, as coming from objects, impress a form on the intelligence and remove it far from God.

57. Even if the intelligence raises itself above the contemplation of bodily nature, it has not yet perfect contemplation of God because it can still mingle with the intelligibles and share in their multiplicity.

58. If you would pray, you have need of God who gives the prayer to the one who prays; call upon Him then, saying, "Hallowed be Thy name, Thy kingdom come," that is to say, "the Holy Spirit and Thine only-begotten Son," because such is His teaching when He tells us to adore the Father in spirit and in truth.

60. If you are a mystic, you will truly pray; if you pray truly, you are a mystic.[10]

61. When, in ardent love of God, your intelligence goes out of the body and rejects all thoughts that come from sense and memory and bodily humors and is filled with awe and

---

[9] The truncation of Origen's doctrine by Evagrius is illustrated here: "Prayer as a state ('catastasy,' Origen's word) is an attitude free of all feeling ('apathetic,' a word Origen never used—except once in *Against Celsus*, VIII, 8—and a doctrine he was totally against)."

[10] The word translated "mystic" is *theologos*, which, for Evagrius as for the Pseudo-Dionysius later, connotes nothing so pedestrian as our "theologian."

joy, then it is allowable to think that you are close to the confines of prayer.

66. When you pray do not imagine divinity and do not allow your intelligence to be impressed by any form, but, immaterial, to the Immaterial go.[11]

69. Remain on guard, preserving your intelligence from all thought in time of prayer so that it be established in that tranquillity proper to it; then He that has compassion on the ignorant will come to you, too, and you will receive a most glorious gift of prayer.

70. You cannot have pure prayer if you are weighted down by material things and disturbed by constant cares because prayer is the suppression of thought.

84. Prayer is the appropriate activity of the intelligence or, what comes to the same thing, its best and perfect use.

117. I will say what I think, what I have said even to the youngest: Happy the intelligence which at time of prayer has achieved perfect emptiness.

118. Happy the intelligence which in undistracted prayer acquires ever new increases of the love of God.

119. Happy the intelligence which in time of prayer becomes immaterial and stripped of all.

120. Happy the intelligence which in time of prayer has achieved perfect insensibility.

142. You wish to pray? Depart from here below and have your dwelling continually on high, not in name only but by angelic practice[12] and by a knowledge more divine.

SELECTED BIBLIOGRAPHY

Editions

Several works are to be found in Migne, *Patrologia Graeca*, Volume XL, 1213-1286, and Volume LXXIX, 1165-1200. A Syriac version of the *Problemata Gnostica*, which is no longer extant in the original Greek, is given together with a French translation by A. Guillaumont in Graffin-Nau, *Patrologia Orientalis*, Volume XXVIII, pp. 16-257; six hundred pithy sayings on theological and ascetical subjects, they are of primary importance for the understanding of Evagrius.

[11] This variation on Plotinus' "lone to the Alone" could scarcely be improved upon by Plotinus himself.

[12] The awkward "angelic practice" is a literal translation. Insistence on the angelic destiny of humanity, to be achieved—even in time—during prayer, was one of the characteristics of Evagrius' Origenism.

Translations

A French version, complete with extended commentary, of *On Prayer* is provided by Irénée Hausherr, S.J., in his *Les leçons d'un contemplatif* (Paris, 1960).

Studies

The influence of Evagrius on monasticism has been brilliantly documented by René Draguet, "L'Histoire lausiaque: une oeuvre écrite dans l'esprit d'Evagre," *Revue d'histoire ecclésiastique*, XLI (1946), 321-364; XLII (1947), 5-49. But the absolute master in matters Evagrian is Irénée Hausherr. Aside from the translation-commentary mentioned above, one would signalize his "Les versions syriaque et arménienne d'Evagre le Pontique: leur valeur, leur relation, leur utilisation," *Orientalia Christiana*, 22 (n. 69) (1931), 69-118; 24 (n. 73) (1931), 38-40; "Par delà l'oraison pure grâce à une coquille. A propos d'un texte d'Evagre," *Revue d'ascétique et de mystique*, XIII (1932), 184-188; "Le De oratione de Nil et Evagre," *Revue d'ascétique et de mystique*, XIV (1933), 196-199; "Une énigme d'Evagre le Pontique, Centurie II, 50," *Recherches de science religieuse*, XXIII (1933), 21-38; "Comment priaient les Pères?" *Revue d'ascétique et de mystique*, XXXII (1956), 33-58, 284-296.

V

ST. AUGUSTINE

(354—430)

THE ESSENTIAL Augustine is hidden within an elemental mystery which he himself never wholly solved. Neither, it need hardly be said, will anyone else.

It is the stranger sort of mystery in that it deepens with every clarification that he, tireless student of his innermost reality, brings forward. It is as though every clarification were only a further progress into that incommunicable light which cloaks the Godhead Itself. That may well be so.

By remaining on the periphery of his introspective theology, one can easily be deceived. One can manage to sense no mystery at all. The language, the turns of thought, the very movement of his speculation, have long ago become part of the very fabric of the thinking of Western man so that we are at home with him as we could never be with Gregory of Nyssa, let us say, or even with Origen. We are at home with him quite as we are at home with ourselves, under the same conditions and liable to the same penalties of self-deception, conscious only of the surface consistencies, unaware of the mystery that reposes at the core of every man's existence.

The entire, gigantic intellectual effort of Augustine was directed solely, it is apparent now, to the probing of the mystery of Western man. Within that dynamic of the unfamiliar and the familiar, of the elemental, the individual, the existential, his theology is deployed. It is, one might say, situated within a magnetic field, between two polar tensions of which the positive is never clearly seen.

But the abiding desire of Augustine was that he should somehow *see*. There are, then, no grounds for surprise if in his earlier writings, as everywhere apparently in Plotinus, the wish is father to the speculation. For example, in his treatise *On the Grandeur of the Soul*,[1] which he wrote shortly after his baptism in 387, he asserts that by seven steps the ascent to Truth is possible. His understanding of the nature of the last four of them is particularly instructive. The fourth step is "Virtue," which he interprets as the effort, compounded of fear, to withdraw the soul from the tyranny of the senses, to purify it and adorn it with good habits. Then follows *necessarily* the fifth step, "Tranquillity." This for him means a relative peace of soul which makes one aspire, ardently and with confidence, for yet higher gifts. And from this *necessarily* comes the sixth step, the "Entrance into Light," or *Ingressio*, with which the soul, because of illuminations from on high, is able to rest its gaze upon Truth; but that inward eye, though truly seeing, is not yet sufficiently pure to sustain its gaze. The seventh and final step is "Habitation," or *Mansio*, the abiding contemplation of Truth.

There are here four points worthy of remark as exemplifying Augustine's early attitude towards mystical experience. That he was greatly dependent upon Plotinus in his first attempts to achieve a philosophic understanding of God, himself, and the universe is, of course, a fact recognized by all scholars. Here, in most significant fashion, the dependence is most marked. The necessity with which one step follows upon another in the ascent of Truth is of a piece with that necessity, wholly inexorable, with which in the Plotinian schema is achieved the ascent to The One. His terming the seventh step a *Mansio* should not distract the reader into thinking that here is the same reality that will later be termed "Mansion" by St. Teresa; the poor, dear man, in his longing, meant nothing more than "home" and "rest" and "journey's end." But "Tranquillity," the fifth step, seems another matter. It is the *hésuchia* of Plotinus before him, of the Desert Fathers of his own day, subsequently of an entire school of spirituality, appropriately called "Hesychasm," about which there will be occasion to say something in detail later; and of the eighteenth-century Quietists it will be the persistent *ignis fatuus*. Older and wiser, in his *Retractationes* four years before his death, Augustine would explicitly repudiate these early views.

But he repudiated them before that, almost imperceptibly and by implication, in the autobiographical asides in some of his sermons on the Psalms and, most notably, in the *Confes-*

[1] Chapter 33, nn. 70-76.

sions. What is there revealed is an experience of the divine presence which is not an inevitable consequence but rather is a visitation graciously and fleetingly accorded by Divinity Itself.

TEXTS

ON PSALM 41 [2]

Meditating day and night on this taunt ["Where is thy God?"], I have myself sought to find my God so that, if I could, I might not only believe but also somehow see. For I see the things which my God has made and my God Himself I do not see. . . . Having therefore sought to find my God in visible, bodily things and found Him not, having sought to find His substance in myself and found it not, I perceive my God to be higher than my soul. . . .

I have poured forth my soul above myself. No longer is there any being for me to touch save my God. The "house of my God" is there; there, above my soul, is His dwelling. From there He beholds me. From there He governs me and provides for me. From there He lures me and calls me and directs me, leads me in the way and to the end of my way.

But He, who has His house very high in a secret place, also has on earth a tabernacle. On earth His tabernacle is the Church. It is here that He is to be sought, for in the tabernacle is found the way by which we arrive at His house. . . . And, when I come to the "house of my God," I am struck speechless with astonishment. . . .

It was thus . . . [the Psalmist] was led on to the house of God: following the leadings of a certain delight, of inner mysterious and hidden pleasure, as if from the house of God some instrument was sweetly sounding, and he, while walking in the tabernacle, hearing a certain inward sound, led on by its sweetness, and following the guidance of the sound, withdrawing himself from all clamor of flesh and blood, made his way on even to the house of God. . . . In the house of God there is never-ending festival; the angel choir makes eternal holiday; the presence of God's face gives joy that never fails. And from that everlasting, perpetual festivity there sounds in the ears of the heart a strain, mysterious, melodious, sweet—provided the world does not drown it. As he walks in this

[2] I have based my translation on the text in Migne, *Patrologia Latina*, Volume XXXVI.

tabernacle and considers God's wonderful works for the redemption of the faithful, the sound of that festivity charms his ears and bears him away to the flowing waters.

But, seeing that the corruptible body weighs down the soul, even though we have in some way dispersed clouds by walking as longing leads us and for a brief while have come within reach of that sound so that by an effort we may catch something from that house of God, through the burden, so to say, of our infirmity we sink back to our usual level, relapse to our ordinary state.

THE CONFESSIONS[3]

It is with no doubtful knowledge, Lord, but with utter certainty that I love You. You have stricken my heart with Your word and I have loved You. And indeed heaven and earth and all that is in them tell me wherever I look that I should love You, and they cease not to tell it to all men, so that there is no excuse for them. For *You will have mercy on whom You will have mercy, and You will show mercy to whom You will show mercy:* otherwise heaven and earth cry their praise of You to deaf ears.

But what is it that I love when I love You? Not the beauty of any bodily thing, nor the order of seasons, not the brightness of light that rejoices the eye, nor the sweet melodies of all songs, nor the sweet fragrance of flowers and ointments and spices: not manna nor honey, not the limbs that carnal love embraces. None of these things do I love in loving my God. Yet in a sense I do love light and melody and fragrance and food and embrace when I love my God—the light and the voice and the fragrance and the food and embrace in the soul, when that light shines upon my soul which no place can contain, that voice sounds which no time can take from me, I breathe that fragrance which no wind scatters, I eat the food which is not lessened by eating, and I lie in the embrace which satiety never comes to sunder. This it is that I love, when I love my God.[4]

I shall mount beyond this power of my nature, still rising by degrees towards Him who made me. And so I come to the fields and vast palaces of memory.[5]

[3] From *The Confessions of St. Augustine* in the translation of F. J. Sheed, Copyright 1943, Sheed & Ward, Inc., New York: Sheed & Ward, Limited, London.

[4] X, vi; Sheed, *op. cit.,* pp. 215-216.
[5] X, viii; *op. cit.,* p. 218.

Great is the power of memory, a thing, O my God, to be in awe of, a profound and immeasurable multiplicity; and this thing is my mind, this thing am I. What then am I, O my God? What nature am I? A life powerfully various and manifold and immeasurable. In the innumerable fields and dens and caverns of my memory, innumerably full of innumerable kinds of things . . . in and through all these does my mind range, and I move swiftly from one to another and I penetrate them as deeply as I can, but find no end. So great is the force of memory, so great the force of life even while man lives under sentence of death here.

What am I to do now, O my true Life, my God? I shall mount beyond this my power of memory, I shall mount beyond it, to come to You, O lovely Light. What have You to say to me? In my ascent by the mind to You who abide above me, I shall mount up beyond that power of mine called memory, longing to attain to touch You at the point where that contact is possible and to cleave to You at the point where it is possible to cleave.[6]

So I must pass beyond memory to come to Him who separated me from the four-footed beasts and made me wiser than the birds of the air. I shall pass beyond memory to find You, O truly good and certain Loveliness, and where shall I find You? If I find You beyond my memory, then shall I be without memory of You. And how shall I find You if I am without memory of You?[7]

But where in my memory do You abide, Lord, where in my memory do You abide? What resting-place have You claimed as Your own, what sanctuary built for Yourself? . . . Why do I seek in what place of my memory You dwell as though there were places in my memory? Certain I am that You dwell in it, because I remember You since the time I first learned of You, and because I find You in it when I remember You. In what place then did I find You to learn of You? For You were not in my memory, before I learned of You. Where then did I find You to learn of You, save in Yourself, above myself? Place there is none, we go this way and that, and place there is none. You, who are Truth, reside everywhere. . . . Late have I loved Thee, O Beauty so ancient and so new; late have I loved Thee! For behold Thou wert within me, and I outside; and I sought Thee outside and in my unloveliness fell upon those lovely things that Thou hast made. Thou wert with me and I was not with Thee. I was kept from Thee by those things, yet had they not been in Thee, they would not have been at all.

[6] X, xvii; *op. cit.*, pp. 227-228.
[7] X, xvii; *op. cit.*, p. 228.

Thou didst call and cry to me and break open my deafness: and Thou didst send forth Thy beams and shine upon me and chase away my blindness: Thou didst breathe fragrance upon me, and I drew in my breath and do now pant for Thee: I tasted Thee, and now hunger and thirst for Thee: Thou didst touch me, and I have burned for Thy peace.[8]

SELECTED BIBLIOGRAPHY

Editions

The most generally faithful edition is still that of the Maurists, *Opera Omnia*, 11 volumes (Paris, 1679-1700); it is reproduced, with the usual incidence of error, in Migne, *Patrologia Latina*, Volumes XXXII-XLVII. The eighteen volumes of the *Corpus Scriptorum Ecclesiasticorum Latinorum* are singularly uneven in quality.

Translations

The Confessions of St. Augustine, translated by Frank Sheed (New York-London, 1943), is nothing short of uncanny in the accuracy and gracefulness with which it captures the distinctive nuances of Augustine's thought and expression. For the rest, the versions in the Oxford "Library of the Fathers" will serve the English reader well.

Studies

A pioneering work by a lifelong student of Augustine's mystical doctrine is *La contemplation augustinienne* by Fulbert Cayré, A.A. (Paris, 1927); the lineaments, however, of Augustine's own experience are perhaps unduly blurred by the author's efforts to make it of a piece with that of other mystics, notably St. Teresa. The entire discussion acquired new depth with the publication of *Augustins Verhältnis zur Mystik* by E. Hendrickx, O.E.S.A. (Würzburg, 1936), which, analyzing Augustine's relation to mysticism, concluded by denying flatly that there was any. A perceptive report of the innumerable studies, pro and con, that it occasioned in subsequent decades is given by André Mandouze, "Où en est la question de la mystique augustinienne?" *Augustinus Magister: Actes du Congrès International Augustinien* (Paris, n.d.), III, 103-163.

[8] X, xxv-xxvii; *op. cit.*, pp. 235-236.

VI

THE PSEUDO-DIONYSIUS

THE EXPRESSION on the face of St. Denis the Areopagite in the fresco by Bonnat in the Pantheon is singularly significant. Denis is there portrayed holding his head in his hands. He is doing so, however, not as a philosopher (he was a philosopher) who is a victim of distractions but as a martyr who was a victim of decapitation: he is picking his head up off the floor. And on his face, eyes closed but quite lively withal, is an enigmatic expression.

Bonnat was a realist so he made the expression enigmatic because this is not so much a picture of a man as a picture of a myth of an especially enigmatic sort. The hero of that myth is one Dionysius (or Denis) mentioned in the Acts of the Apostles as one of St. Paul's hearers on the Areopagus. According to Eusebius, he became the first Bishop of Athens; according to a tradition rather less easy to check, he subsequently became the first Bishop of Paris, the author of various works on mystical theology, and, at the age of one hundred and ten, a martyr.

However, the Dionysius who was converted by St. Paul lived in the first century; the St. Denis who was the first Bishop of Paris and was martyred there lived in the third century; the person who wrote the works on mystical theology lived in the sixth century.

Our interest is in the author of the works on mysticism. Who was he?

He says himself that he was a contemporary and intimate of the Apostles,[1] a witness of the eclipse at the time of the Crucifixion,[2] one who was present with Peter and James when the Virgin died,[3] a correspondent with St. John the Evangelist,

---

[1] *Divine Names*, II, 11; *Letter VII*, 3.
[2] *Letter VII*, 2.
[3] *Divine Names*, III, 2.

exiled and apparently eager for letters there on Patmos.[4] And that provides practically the only certainty we have: he was none of these things.

Conjectures about his identity, none of them lightly made, range these days all the way from Severus of Antioch, who was a sixth-century heretic, to Dionysius of Alexandria, who was a third-century saint, to alight briefly upon an unknown disciple of St. Basil the Great in the second half of the fourth century and various others, here and there, in between. The best-founded conjectures converge on the beginning of the sixth century as the time and on Syria as the place.[5]

Opinions about the value of his doctrine vary even more than those about his identity. They extend all the way from saying it is that of a pagan antagonist of Christianity, to that it is a Christian defense against pagan attacks; from assessing it as an otherwise evil thing permitted by God in order to strengthen a Christian spirituality which might otherwise have become overly sentimental, to canonizing it as heavenly wisdom. The truth, clearly, lies somewhere between.

Certainly it has long proved attractive to the Western mind. To the theologians of mediaeval Paris, Scotus Eriugena, the Victorines, St. Albert, St. Bonaventure, St. Thomas Aquinas, Meister Eckhart, there was the undeniable attraction that one feels for a local boy who has made good—they had no doubts that he was the Paris bishop and martyr. But for others, before their time and since, whose judgment could not be affected by chauvinism, there was the fascination of a cosmic vision which—of a piece with that of Plotinus—was expressed in a language that was Christian, liturgical, and gaudily oriental. Hans Urs von Balthasar describes it summarily thus:

> A vision in ecstasy of a sacral universe, pouring forth wave upon wave from out the unfathomable abyss of inaccessible divinity, spreading abroad in ever-lengthening undulations until it touches the shores themselves of Nothingness. . . . A cosmos gyrating in a dance of ceremonial liturgic adoration about the luminous darkness of that innermost mystery, aware of the awesome nearness of this center . . . and of the ever-widening distance from that One which is beyond essence and beyond inconceivability. This fascinating vision of the universe, which in its sacral and liturgic movement inebriates even

---

[4] *Letter X.*
[5] The time is indicated, negatively, by the absence of any reference to his writings before 533; positively, by the doctrinal dependencies of his writings on a variety of authors of the fifth century, most notably on Proclus (412-485). As to the place: the liturgy he describes is that of Syria.

while it clears the mind, has a purity about it that is discoverable neither in Alexandrian thought nor in Cap-
podocian, and much less in anything so austere as that
of Egypt or so earthbound as that of Antioch. What
then was better adapted than this to serve as canvas and
basic coloring for speculation whose goal will be completeness and harmony? . . . It is as though in the
sudden glare of a lightning bolt there was revealed the
existential compenetration of all the kingdoms of the cos-
mos, their hierarchies, their mutual relationship, the
ceaseless movement of ascension and descent from the
invisible summit to the base plunged in matter. Never before had the Christian world contemplated a vision of
such amplitude situated within the stable majesty of
peace.[6]

Because the doctrine of the Pseudo-Dionysius contains
much of the quite accurate psychological analysis of Plotinus,
it has had in almost every age a special attraction for authentic mystics such as Jan van Ruysbroek and John of the Cross.

The Dionysian analysis moves through three stages: by abstractive negation[7] (first stage) the intelligence achieves nescience (second stage) which effects union with God (third
stage).

The notion of abstractive negation corresponds, superficially, with the traditional idea of purification; but, basically,
the Pseudo-Dionysius separates himself at the very outset from
his Christian predecessors: with him there is no question of the
purification being, as it was with them, in the moral order.[8] It
is a question of multiple denials of all conceptual forms if one
would attain to the Deity. He gives neither source nor justification of this his fundamental doctrine; he simply asserts it, with
force. There seems no reason why one should expect to find
both source and justification in the personal experience of the
Pseudo-Dionysius.[9] His source would seem to be simply the
negative theology practiced by his predecessors, when they
would write about God, transposed without justification to the
area of experience. He does not simply say that thus one at-

---

[6] *Kosmische Liturgie* (Freiburg, 1941), p. 5.

[7] The term is that of J. Vanneste (see Selected Bibliography). It is an
attempt to translate what the Pseudo-Dionysius meant by ἀφαίρεσις
(*aphairesis*), which was used by Aristotle to convey the conventional
notion of philosophic abstraction by which, for instance, one arrives
at the universal idea "man." With the Pseudo-Dionysius it has its full
Plotinian meaning of "elimination," of "cutting away," as by a sculptor.

[8] *See* Irénée Hausherr, S.J., "Les grands courants de la spiritualité
orientale," *Orientalia Christiana Periodica*, I (1935), 124-126.

[9] As, at length, does Walther Völker. See Selected Bibliography.

tains to God; if he did, one might reasonably conjecture that he asserted it because he had himself experienced it. Instead, he insists that it *has* to happen; the verbs indicating necessity follow after one another pretty much as the δεῖ, χρή, ἀνάγκη of Plotinus. They are as little persuasive.

The nescience (second stage) achieved by the intelligence through abstractive negation is not, for him, ignorance. It is the seizure of the Unknowable; it is truly to know God. As justification of this doctrine he refers to previous works. But, so little credit for veracity does the poor man enjoy today, no one much believes that the works ever existed. It could be that the doctrine was only a latter-day application of the familiar Platonic notion that like is known by like. If it was that, it was an abandonment of Platonism at the very moment when it sounded most Platonic.

The third stage, union with God, is effected, too, by the abstractive negation which gave its precise character to nescience. The dynamism which propels the intelligence into the beyond of unknowable Transcendence is the dynamism of nescience and not of love.

It is difficult not to allow the mind to be seduced by the sheer flamboyance of thinking such as this. It is difficult, even, to convince oneself that one's mind should not for its own good be so seduced. But it is one thing to be strongly attracted by this thinking and quite another thing to subject one's mind to the mystical discipline it proposes. Many in succeeding generations would submit to the discipline gladly in the hope, wholly forlorn, of becoming mystics.

TEXTS [10]

THE MYSTICAL THEOLOGY

I.

The Divine Dark

1

O Trinity
    beyond essence and
    beyond divinity and
    beyond goodness
  guide of Christians in divine wisdom,
direct us towards mysticism's heights
    beyond unknowing
    beyond light
    beyond limit,
  there where the
    unmixed and
    unfettered and
    unchangeable
  mysteries of theology
    in the dazzling dark of the welcoming silence
lie hidden, in the intensity of their darkness
    all brilliance outshining,
  our intellects, blinded—overwhelming,
    with the intangible and
    with the invisible and
    with the illimitable.
Such is my prayer.
And you, beloved Timothy,
  in the earnest exercise of mystical contemplation abandon
    all sensation and
    all intellection and

[10] The translation I have made from the text in Migne, *Patrologia Graeca*, Volume III, 997-1073. I have arranged it colometrically because the text seems to demand it and the impression—wholly justified—of an incantation is better conveyed.

all objects
> or sensed
> or seen and

all being and
all nonbeing and

in unknowing, as much as may be, be
> one with the beyond being and knowing.

By the ceaseless and limitless going out of yourself and
> out of all things else

you will be led in utter pureness,
> rejecting all and
> released from all,

> aloft to the flashing forth,
> beyond all being,

of the divine dark.

2

Disclose not this
> to the uninitiated,
> to those, I say, who
>> clutch at essences and
>> fancy beyond essences nothing is and
>> dream they know by ordinary knowing

"Him that has made the dark His hiding place."[11]

If the unveiling of divine mystery is beyond their ken

what is to be said of those
> yet more profane who
>> to denote the loftiest Cause of all,
>> define It by the lowest of all and
>> deny It to be more lofty than the phantasies
>>> various and
>>> profane

they have formed of It,

the while to It must one,
> as to the Cause of all,

all modes of being

attribute and ascribe and,
> more truly still,

to It,
> as above them all,

deny them all.

[11] Psalm 18:11.

Think not
  that assertion and denial are here opposed
      but rather
  that, beyond the Yeas and Nays of modes, It
  is beyond all deprivations.

3

Thus the blessed Bartholomew says
  the theology is ample and yet small,
  the gospel is broad and long and yet narrow,
sublimely, I think, perceiving that one can be
      saying much of the Good, the Cause of all,
          and yet
      saying little
          and even
      saying nothing
  since for It nor word nor wit suffices,
because
      beyond essence transcendent,
      beyond seeing, truly hidden
          except for those alone who
      beyond foul and fair,
      beyond the holy heights,
          have made their way and
          left behind all divine
              illuminations and
              voices and
              words from heaven and
  have entered the dark where,
      as Scripture tells,[12]
He is who is
      beyond all.
For not without cause was blessed Moses told
  first to cleanse himself,
  then himself withdraw
      from those unclean,
      to hear, wholly cleansed, the many-tongued trumpets,
      to see the myriad lightnings—
          pure,
          diverse—
      flashing forth.

[12] Exodus 19:10, 20.

Then, from the throng withdrawn,
    he comes,
  the chosen priests his entourage,
  to the topmost peak of the divine ascent.
Yet he encounters God not,
  he sees God not
  (for God cannot be seen),
but sees alone the place on which He dwells.
This is the sign, I think, that
  the most divine
  the most sublime
    one can see or know
are symbols only,
    subordinate to Him
      who is Himself
      transcendent to them all; that
they are pointers to His presence
  who is beyond comprehending,
  who walks the holy heights the mind descries.
Moses then,
  going beyond where one sees and is seen,
enters the Dark—mystery wholly—of unknowing,
there stills all trying to understand and
attains entire the intangible and invisible and
achieves entire Him that is all-transcending
and he belongs himself no longer to himself nor any other
and, the more excellent way, is joined
  to Him all-unknowable
  in the stilling of all knowing.
By knowing naught, he
  —beyond knowing—
knows.

II. How One Must Be United to Him and Praise Him Who Is the Cause of All and Above All

Into this Dark beyond all light, we pray
  to come and,
    unseeing and unknowing,
  to see and
  to know
    Him that is
      beyond seeing and
      beyond knowing

precisely by not seeing,
     by not knowing.
For that is truly to see and
     to know and
     to hymn transcendently
       Him that transcends all.
That is, negating, to do as sculptors do,
  drawing [from marble]
    the statue latent there,
  removing all that
     hinders or
     hides
    the pure spectacle of the hidden form and
displaying, with this mere removal,
    the beauty hidden there.
One must, I think, hymn in
    negating and
    affirming
  for affirmations proceed
    from the topmost
    through the middlemost
    to the lowest.
But here,
    from the lowest
    to the topmost,
one denies them all, thus
    to lay bare the Unknowable who is
     by all known beings veiled,
    to see the transcendent Dark that is
     by the light of beings hid.

III. The Negative and the Affirmative Theologies

In our *Outlines of Theology* we have treated what is of the greatest importance in the theology of affirmation; that is, how God's holy nature is called both one and three; what, in this nature, is fatherhood and filiation and what is the theology of the Spirit; how from immaterial and invisible Good have flowed the illuminations that have their source itself in Goodness and have abided there, in It and in themselves, existing co-eternally with their act of origin; how Jesus, beyond essence, took on essence among human realities. These and all other mysteries are celebrated in accord with Scripture in our *Outlines*.

In the *Divine Names* [we have treated] of the meaning of the Divine titles: Good, Being, Life, Wisdom, and Power, and all other titles the intelligence applies to Him.

In *The Symbolic Theology* [we have discussed] the metaphors which, drawn from the world of sense, are applied to God: what, in God, "form" and "figures" mean; what are His "part," "organs," the "places where He dwells," His "adornments"; what, in Him, is the meaning of "anger," "sorrow," "indignation"; His "intoxication," His "wrath," His "oath" and "curse"; His "sleeping" and "waking"—all the inspired symbolism in which the holiness of God is figuratively clad.

You will have noticed how more wordy are the latter than the former. Necessarily the *Outlines of Theology* and the explanations of the *Divine Names* use less words than *The Symbolic Theology* because the higher we soar aloft the more our language becomes restricted by that more synthesizing view we have of the intelligibles.

Now, however, that we are on the point of entering the Dark that is beyond intelligence, rational discourse will not merely become more brief; it will disappear in the total cessation of word and thought. In the theology of affirmation discourse descends by degrees from highest beings to lowest, embracing as it goes an ever-widening number of concepts. But here, as we ascend from lowest to The Highest, discourse diminishes as it goes, and at the end of the ascent it will be totally silent because totally united to Him that no words can describe.

But why, you will ask, do we make our start from the lowest with the negative theology after having begun from the highest in the affirmative theology? The reason is this: in affirming the existence of what transcends all affirmation, we were obliged to begin from what is most akin to It and then make the affirmation upon which all the rest depended; but to attain in the theology of negation what is beyond all negation we are obliged to begin by denying what are most disparate from It. For is not God "Life" or "Good" more than He is "air" or "stone"? And is it not truer to deny that drunkenness or rage pertain to Him than to deny that He speaks or that He thinks?

IV. The Pre-eminent Cause of All that Is Perceived by Sense Is Not Anything Perceived by Sense

This, then, we say of the Cause,
    beyond all things,
    of all things:

He is
  not essence-less,
  not life-less,
  not reason or unreason,
  not body,
  not figure or form,
  not possessor of quality or quantity or mass,
  not in space,
  not visible,
  not to be felt,
  not sense-endowed or by sense perceived,
  not prey to disorder and confusion
    as if subject to sense passions,
  not powerless
    as if subject to the stresses of the world of sense,
  not light-less,
  not changing or failing or divisible or capable of ebb and
    flow,
  not "this" or "that" of anything of sense.

V. The Pre-eminent Cause of All that Is Perceived by the Intelligence Is Not Anything Perceived by the Intelligence

Ascending higher, we say
  He is
  not soul or intelligence,
  not imagination or conjecture or reason or under-
    standing,
  not word, not intellection,
  not said, not thought,
  not number, not order,
  not magnitude, not littleness,
  not likeness, not unlikeness,
  not similarity, not dissimilarity,
  not unmoving, not moved,
  not powerful, not power,
  not light,
  not living, not life,
  not essence,
  not eon, not time,
  not understandable,
  not knowledge, not truth,
  not kingship, not wisdom,

not one, not unity,
not deity,
not goodness,
not spirit (as we know spirit),
not filiation,
not paternity,
not anything known by us or by anyone among us,
not a nonbeing,
not a being,
not known, as He is, by beings,
not knower of beings as they are,
not definable,
not nameable,
not knowable,
not dark, not light,
not untrue, not true,
not affirmable, not deniable,
    for
while we affirm or deny of those orders of beings
    that are akin to Him
we neither affirm nor deny Him
    that is beyond
        all affirmation as unique universal Cause and
        all negation as simple pre-eminent Cause,
free of all and
to all transcendent.

THE FIRST LETTER

To Gaius, servant of the light:

The Dark is invisible in light,
    and the more that the light is the stronger.
Unknowing is unknown to knowledge,
    and the more that the knowledge is the greater.
Know here "unknowing,"
    not as a less,
    but as a greater;
and this that is truer than truth affirm:
    the unknowableness of God is hidden
        to those who have of beings
            light and
            knowledge;
        the transcendent Dark is
            hidden to light,
            veiled to knowledge.

If someone
  having seen God
    has understood what he has seen
  he has not seen God;
  he has seen of God His known creatures.
He that is
  beyond intelligence and
  beyond essence
is
  in total
    unknowing and
    unbeing,
  beyond essence and
  beyond intelligence,
known.
Total unknowing, transcendent, is the knowing of Him who is
beyond all that is known.

THE FIFTH LETTER

To Dorotheus, the leiturgos:

The divine Dark
    is the inaccessible light
    where God is said to dwell.[13]
Because transcendent clarity,
  it is invisible.
Because from the heights comes its light,
  it is inaccessible.
All worthy are they who enter there
  to know and
  to look upon
God.
    Unseeing and
    unknowing
they attain in truth what is beyond
  all seeing and
  all knowing.
Knowing naught of Him, except He is
  beyond all sensing and
  beyond all understanding,
they cry out with the prophet:
  "Such knowledge is too marvelous for me;
  it is high; I cannot attain it."[14]

[13] Cf. 1 Timothy 6:16.
[14] Psalm 139:6.

So, they say, Saint Paul knew God
    for it was above all intellection and understanding
      he knew Him;
    for he says
      "incomprehensible are His ways and
      inscrutable His decrees"[15]
      "indescribable are His gifts"[16]
      "surpassing all understanding is His peace";[17]
    for he found Him that is
      beyond all he knew,
      beyond all understanding;
    for he found that God
      being Cause of all,
      beyond all dwells.

SELECTED BIBLIOGRAPHY

Editions

Various efforts of the past three decades to bring a reliable critical edition of the works into existence have all come to nothing. One is therefore forced to use the text established by Balthasar de Cordier, *Opera Omnia* (Antwerp, 1594), that is reproduced in the third volume of Migne, *Patrologia Graeca*.

Translations

Far from literal, yet acutely faithful to the central ideas, is the version of C. E. Rolt, *On the Divine Names and the Mystical Theology* (New York, 1920). A translation of five of the important "letters" is contained as well in Alan Watts, *Theologia Mystica* (West Park, 1944).

Studies

The basic work is still that of Hal Koch, *Pseudo-Dionysius Areopagita in seinen Beziehungen zum Neuplatonismus und Mysterienwesen* (Mainz, 1900). Walther Völker interprets the entire Dionysian *corpus* on the supposition that its author was an authentic mystic in *Kontemplation und Ekstase bei Pseudo-Dionysius Areopagita* (Wiesbaden, 1958); J. Vanneste, S.J., seeks to disengage the "structure interne" of Dionysius' theology and concludes there is no evidence of his having been a mystic, in *Le Mystère de Dieu: Essai sur la structure rationnelle de la doctrine mystique du Pseudo-Denys l'Aréopagite* (Paris, 1959); each study is an excellent complement to the other.

[15] *Cf.* Romans 11:33.
[16] *Cf.* 2 Corinthians 9:15.
[17] Philippians 4:7.

VII

ST. MAXIMUS
THE CONFESSOR

(c. 580—662)

AMONG the individual accomplishments of Maximus, the greatest Greek theologian of the seventh century, was his making the doctrine of one of his predecessors, Evagrius, into something rather more respectable than it had been and the doctrine of another predecessor, the Pseudo-Dionysius, at least seem more respectable. His major accomplishment, however, was to have provided a theology of the operations of the human will under divine grace which in succeeding centuries would serve equally well the theologian in his lecture hall and the mystic in his attempts to understand what God was doing to him. As the following texts make clear, he was able to write so knowingly of the will because he knew in his own mystic experience the plenitude of love.

Fairly in the teeth of his beloved Dionysius, who had so insisted that only in darkness is Divinity seen, Maximus' experience—as Origen's—was flooded with light. Unlike Origen's, his was had in rapture and alienation from the senses, much as St. Bernard's would be, but of an extreme severity. Human effort—on this he was adamant—does not bring it about.

TEXTS [1]

CENTURIES ON CHARITY

The man that truly loves God certainly prays completely undistracted; and he that certainly prays completely undistracted also truly loves God. But he that has his mind fastened on some earthly thing does not pray completely undistracted; he therefore who has his mind bound to some earthly thing does not love God.[2]

The mind that gives its time to some sensible thing certainly experiences some attachment in its regard, as desire or grief or anger or ill will; and unless he scorns that thing, he cannot be freed from that attachment.[3]

The work of the commandments is to make the thoughts of things mere thoughts; and of reading and contemplation, to render the mind clean of any material thing or form; and from this there comes undistracted prayer.[4]

An active way is not enough so perfectly to free the mind from the passions that it can pray undistracted, unless various spiritual contemplations succeed one another in it. Now the first-mentioned frees the mind only from incontinence and hate; the others take it away from forgetfulness and ignorance. And thus it will be able to pray as it ought.[5]

There are two supreme states of pure prayer: the one, for those of the active life; the other, for those of the contemplative. The one comes to the soul from fear of God and a good hope; the other, from burning divine love and maximum purification. The signs of the first kind are these: namely, when a man gathers his mind from all the thoughts of the world, to make his prayers, as though God Himself were at his side (as really He is present), without distraction and undis-

---

[1] From *St. Maximus the Confessor, The Ascetic Life* [and] *The Four Centuries on Charity*, translated by Polycarp Sherwood, O.S.B., "Ancient Christian Writers," Volume XXI (Westminster-London, 1955).
[2] *Century II*, 1; Sherwood, *op. cit.*, p. 152.
[3] *Century II*, 2; *op. cit.*, p. 152.
[4] *Century II*, 4; *op. cit.*, p. 152.
[5] *Century II*, 5; *op. cit.*, pp. 152-153.

turbed; of the second, however, that at the very onset of prayer the mind be rapt by the divine and infinite light and be conscious neither of itself nor of any other creature at all, save only of Him who through charity effects such brightness in it. Then indeed, being concerned with the properties of God, it receives impressions of Him, pure and limpid.[6]

What a man loves, that he assuredly clings to and everything that obstructs his way to it he despises, lest he be deprived of it; and the man that loves God is concerned for pure prayer and every passion that obstructs his way to it he casts out of himself.[7]

The virtues separate the mind from the passions; spiritual contemplations from simple representations; pure prayer then places it before God Himself.[8]

In time of prayer cast away from the mind the empty representations of human affairs and contemplations of all creatures, lest in imagining lesser things you be deprived of Him who incomparably exceeds all beings.[9]

That mind is perfect which, through true faith, in supreme ignorance supremely knows the supremely Unknowable; and which, in gazing upon the universe of His handiwork, has received from God comprehensive knowledge of His providence and judgment—but I speak after the manner of men.[10]

SELECTED BIBLIOGRAPHY

Editions

Until the critical text appears upon which Aldo Ceresa-Gastaldo is engaged, one must make do with that of Migne, *Patrologia Graeca,* Volume XC, columns 960-1080.

Translations

Besides the excellent English version of Dom Polycarp Sherwood from which our own selections above are drawn, the French ver-

[6] *Century II,* 6; *op. cit.,* p. 153.
[7] *Century II,* 7; *op. cit.,* p. 153.
[8] *Century III,* 44; *op. cit.,* p. 181.
[9] *Century III,* 49; *op. cit.,* p. 182.
[10] *Century III,* 99; *op. cit.,* pp. 191-192.

sion by J. Pegon, fortified too with judicious notes, is recommended: *Maxime le Confesseur: Centuries sur la charité* (Paris, 1945).

Studies

Much of the contemporary interest in Maximus comes from the trail-blazing articles of Marcel Viller, S.J., "Aux sources de la spiritualité de saint Maxime: les oeuvres d'Evagre le Pontique," *Revue d'ascétique et de mystique*, XI (1930), 156-184, 239-268, 331-336. The best general study is still that of Hans Urs von Balthasar, *Kosmische Liturgie: Maximus der Bekenner, Höhe und Krisis des griechischen Weltbild* (Freiburg, 1941). See also Irénée Hausherr, S.J., *Philautie, de la tendresse pour soi à la charité, selon saint Maxime le confesseur* (Rome, 1952).

VIII

HESYCHASM

OF HESYCHASM, whose longevity as a mystical movement (from the fourth century to the present) outdistances all others by far, it is not easy to speak with the simplicity that one would desire because simplicity was never its characteristic. Born of an excessive rationalism, resulting often in an excessive sentimentalism, arrogantly theological in one period and just as arrogantly untheological in another, now the inspiration of monks in their desert solitude and now a cause to be championed or opposed by ecclesiastical politicians, Hesychasm (for the historian at least) is rather a headache. The least painful way for the reader to achieve some understanding of this complex and important movement is to approach it through two texts, already seen, of Evagrius. In them are to be found all the essentials of Hesychasm. In them, indeed, given the influence of Evagrius, it is not unlikely that history found them too and that they are there formulated for the very first time.

When you pray do not imagine divinity and do not allow your intelligence to be impressed by any form, but, immaterial, to the Immaterial go.

Remain on guard, preserving your intelligence from all thought in time of prayer so that it be established in that tranquillity proper to it; then He that has compassion on the ignorant will come to you, too, and you will receive a most glorious gift of prayer.[1]

Hesychasm has always been remarkable for the emphasis, bordering on the absolutely technical, that it puts on particular words. It is pleasantly ironical, then, to have all the essentials

[1] On Prayer, nn. 66, 69.

noted here by words other than the traditional and technical ones, although they were currently available and are to be found elsewhere in Evagrius' writings. If the unavoidable use of the traditional Greek terms will be pardoned for a moment, in substance Hesychasm was the attaining to ἡσυχία (*hésuchia,* "quiet") by νῆψις (*népsis,* "watchfulness") which has two stages: φυγή (*phugé,* "flight") and σιγή (*sigé,* "silence").[2]

Phugé, "flight," was a technical word before ever it became a prominent element in the technical vocabulary of Hesychasm. It was used, quite generally, to designate the first and indispensable state of the philosophic enterprise, a "getting away from it all" that had little or nothing to do with the going from one place to another; it was, rather, the escaping of the prospective philosopher into the tower (perhaps ivory) of his own head. That *phugé* was now used to designate the first and indispensable stage of the mystical enterprise tells one, then, much about the basic nature of Hesychasm: it was, whatever its protestations to the contrary, philosophic rather than spiritual and religious.

With *sigé,* "silence," much more is meant than not talking to or listening to others. Any talking to or listening to oneself (a comforting practice to which the monk in the desert might easily be prone) was equally excluded. More than that, the very stuff of conversation—thought, desire, the interior interplay of concepts—was equally to be muted.

The term *népsis,* "watchfulness," had also a technical sense before it came to be applied to the technique of the Hesychasts. In Philo of Alexandria, for instance, one finds it used to indicate the "sobriety" (today we would say "self-control") thought to be necessary for the contemplative life. In Hesychasm the simple shift was made from the notion of *népsis* as a state one is in to the notion of *népsis* as a thing that one does. By keeping watch over oneself through *phugé* and *sigé, hésuchia* is achieved.[3] It is a *hésuchia,* a "quiet," that is a foretaste and a promise of the quiet of Heaven. And, as there, so also here one experiences the glory of the Godhead.

The following is a classic example of how the monk was advised to proceed:

[2] In the texts cited, Evagrius favors πρόσειμι (*proseimi,* literally "draw nigh to") over φυγή, φυλακή (*phulaké,* "guard") over νῆψις, and ἠρεμία (*éremia,* "tranquillity") over ἡδυχία. The interest of this last is that early translations of the *On Prayer*—the Arabic, for instance—attest to the word's having been perhaps ἐρημία (*erémia*) which, meaning "solitude," would excellently underline an essential of the Hesychast method.

[3] That this *hésuchia* was rather more an *erémia,* "solitude," than simply an *éremia,* "tranquillity," seems clear. Perhaps the Arabs had the correct reading.

Seated in a quiet cell, off in a corner . . . lift your intelligence beyond every vain and temporal object. Then, resting your beard upon your chest and turning your bodily eyes with all attentiveness upon the center of your stomach (which is to say, upon your navel), limit the air that passes through your nose so that you are breathing with difficulty and search with your mind the interior of your belly and there find the habitation of your heart[4]. . . . In the beginning you will find darkness and a stubborn density. But if you persevere and engage in this occupation day and night you will find—O wonder!— felicity unlimited. When the intelligence comes to the habitation of the heart, it sees immediately . . . the air there at the center of the heart and it sees itself wholly luminous and full of discernment. And afterwards, directly a thought stirs, before it so much as takes shape, the intelligence by invoking Jesus Christ pursues it and destroys it.[5]

This as a method of attaining to an experience of God's glory will seem to most readers unendurably crude and quaint. But at its center, scarcely emphasized in the passage just cited, is something that no one will take ill. I mean the "invoking Jesus Christ." For this is a technique, only recently rediscovered by the West, that has long been productive of great good in the Oriental Church: the "Jesus Prayer" or, as it is also called, the "Prayer of the Heart." Essentially, it consists in the repeated invocation of the name of Jesus. Usually it assumes this more developed form: "Jesus Christ, Son of God, have mercy on me a sinner." It is "prayer of the heart" chiefly in the sense that it is not the meaning of the words that is adverted to but the mood to which at the outset the meaning gives birth.[6]

One of the anomalies of Hesychasm is that precisely where it strove to remain theologically correct it went theologically awry. By the fourteenth century it was a heretical movement within the Oriental Church and its distinguishing tenet was that the *doxa*, or "glory," of God is Divine but distinct from

---

[4] This unusual locating of the heart depends less upon a knowledge of anatomy than a knowledge of Scripture. In the Bible the heart is "the central place in man to which God turns, where religious experience has its root, which determines conduct." F. Baumgärtel, *Theologisches Wörterbuch zum Neuen Testament*, III, 615.

[5] Text in Irénée Hausherr, S.J., "La méthode de l'oraison hésychaste," *Orientalia Christiana*, 9 (n. 36) (1927), 164-165.

[6] "Un moine de l'Eglise d'Orient," *La prière de Jésus*, 3rd edition (Chevetogne, 1959).

the Divine essence. The doctrine came from the theological caution of the early Hesychasts in speaking of their technique as attaining truly to God, but to His glory rather than to His essence.

The traditional theological teaching that the essence of God is beheld only in Heaven will cause no such embarrassment and no such heresy in Ruysbroek, in the West, in the same fourteenth century. For Ruysbroek, clearly, knew whereof he spoke. He was a mystic. He was a theologian of unusual sophistication.

There is, I am sure, a lesson here somewhere.

SELECTED BIBLIOGRAPHY

Studies

Irénée Hausherr, S.J., "La méthode de l'oraison hésychaste," *Orientalia Christiana,* 9 (n. 36) (1927), 97-209; "Les grands courants de la spiritualité orientale," *Orientalia Christiana Periodica,* I (1935), 114-138; "A propos de la spiritualité hésychaste," *Orientalia Christiana Periodica,* III (1937), 260-272; E. Behr-Sigel, "La prière de Jésus ou le mystère de la spiritualité monastique orthodoxe, *Dieu Vivant,* n. 8 (1947), 67-94; and I. Hausherr, "L'hésychasme, étude de vie spirituelle," *Orientalia Christiana Periodica,* XXII (1956), 5-40, 247-285.

IX

SUFISM

THE SIMILARITIES that exist between Hesychasm and Sufism are startling. Each was in the beginning a spiritual movement and a spirituality that grew out of the practice of a specific technique for attaining to mystical experience. Each of them was unorganized. Each of them came into a clash, on doctrinal grounds, with organized religion. Hesychasm had its "Jesus Prayer." Sufism, as we shall see in a moment, had its *dhikr* Each of them made much of its highly technical vocabulary.[1] Each of them flourished in much the same part of the world at much the same time.

It would be pleasant to be able to state that the similarities are not so very startling, that they are only what one would expect to find between parent and offspring, Hesychasm being the Christian father of Mohammedan Sufism. But the present scantiness of the historical data permits no such statement. It is certain that al-Ghazzālī, for one, drew much from his contacts with the desert monks; but by that time the distinctive lines of Sufism had long been established. It is also most intriguing that one of the earliest records of the members of the cult being called "Sufis" comes from that Alexandria of the year 814 about which Hesychasm was largely located. But even that, at the moment, is most intriguing and nothing more.

They were called "Sufis" because they wore ṣūf, "wool." They were at first criticized for this—for wearing wool, as it was said, in imitation of Jesus whereas Mohammed had been content with cotton. Yet the name became a popular one so

---

[1] As with the Greek terms of Hesychasm, so here with the Arabic terms of Sufism, the historian is forced to impose upon his readers' patience by transliterating them the better to prevent global misunderstanding. For the most part I follow here the system of transliteration adopted in the *Shorter Encyclopaedia of Islam* (Leiden, 1953).

that eventually any mystic was called a Sufi no matter what he—or she—wore.

One of the most enduringly charming of Sufis was a woman, Rābi'a al-'Adawīya (c. 713-801). She was so wrapped around with legend shortly after her death that one can penetrate through to the authentic person only if one has continued and sole recourse to her own writings. Fortunately, they are most revealing.

Unlike the majority of Sufis in her day, Rābi'a was not a Quietist: ascetic effort of the most traditional sort—as, for instance, the living in abject voluntary poverty—was one of her distinctive characteristics. And yet she was the eloquent champion of what is always the will-o'-the-wisp of your Quietist: the "pure" love of God. Her notion of this disinterested love she expressed variously: "I have not served God from fear of Hell; I would be a wretched hireling if I served Him from fear. Nor have I served Him from the desire for Paradise; I would be a bad servant if I served for the sake of what was given to me. I have served Him only because I love Him and desire Him." Or, again, "O my Lord, if I worship You from fear of Hell, burn me in Hell; and if I worship You in hope of Paradise, exclude me from Paradise; but if I worship You for Your own sake, then do not withhold from me Your eternal loveliness." And she had about her a sort of peasant logic that is quite endearing and that served excellently to keep her feet firmly on the ground: when it was suggested to her that she ask help of her kinsmen in order to lessen the poverty of her existence, she replied, "I would be ashamed to ask for the things of this world from Him to whom the world belongs. How then can I ask for them from those to whom it does not belong?"

Her verses on the love of God are justly famous. Here is my attempt to translate two of them.

> With two loves have I loved You,
>   With a love that is selfish
>   And a love that is worthy of You:
>
> In the love that is selfish
>   I busy myself with You
>   And others exclude.
>
> In the love that is worthy of You
>   You raise the veil
>   That I may see.
>
> Yet not to me is the praise in this or that,
>   But, in that and this, is the praise to You.

O Beloved of hearts
I have no other like You.
Pity then this day this sinner that comes to You.

My Hope,
My Rest,
My Delight,
The heart can love no other than only You.

This love has its origin in *tawba*, "repentance," the turning
(actually the word means "returning") wholly to God and
away from sin. Almost all Sufis taught this. Few expressed it
with the theological accuracy of Rābi‘a. "How," she asked,
"can anyone repent unless his Lord gives him repentance and
accepts him repentant? If He turns towards you, you will turn
towards Him." The next generation would distinguish between
repentance of return (*tawbat al-ināba*) and repentance of
shame (*tawbat al-istihyā'*) and explain it thus: "The repentance of return is that due to your fear of God because of His
power over you, but the repentance of shame is due to your
shame before God because of His nearness to you." This, of
her followers, was quite in the authentic traditon of Rābi‘a.

Like many a Sufi saint, Rābi‘a was a leader with numerous
followers. Abū Yazīd al-Bistami (d. 874) had even more numerous followers; but he was not a leader. He took precau-
tions that he would not be, hiding himself for almost his whole
life long in the mountain recesses of Tabaristan, Persia. He
wrote nothing. The ascetic effort expended by his followers
seems chiefly to have been in following him into ever new and
more inaccessible retreats, there to glean from him what small
wisdom they could. We know our man, accordingly, from
what they learned by word of mouth from him and (with
unexpected reliability) recorded.

Historians, in general, do not like al-Bistami. I cannot
fathom why. He sounds a quite good man even when speaking
most foolishly. He did cry out one day, "Glory to Me! How
great is My majesty!" He was convinced that he had become
God or, perhaps, God had become him. Of this he was convinced because of the prior conviction that God was not only
One but the Only One. We may deplore the theology here but
it is difficult not to approve the heart from which it came.
"At the beginning," he once said, "I was mistaken in four
different ways. I made it my concern to remember God, to
know Him, to love Him, and to seek Him. And when I came
to the end, I saw that He had remembered me before ever I
remembered Him, that He knew me before ever I knew Him,

He loved me before ever I loved Him, and He had sought me before ever I went looking for Him." This idea of God's loving and seeking His own before they loved or sought Him goes far beyond the doctrine of early Sufism. It has, further, an additional distinction once one asks why, in al-Bistami's view, God would seek him out. He remarked one day that he once heard a voice that said to him, "O Bāyazīd, Our treasure-house is filled to overflowing with the acts of adoration and devotion that are offered by men. Do you bring Us something that is not in Our treasury." "But what shall I bring, O Lord?" he said; and the voice answered him, "Bring Me sorrow of heart and humility and contrition."

It is true that the poor man in his attempt to reach the Only One strove to slough off his personality like a snake its skin. It is also true that his followers imitated him chiefly in this improbable exercise and, in the delusive stresses it induced, would cry out, as he had, that they were God and, unlike him, be promptly put to death for their trouble.

Rather more the academic than al-Bistami, Dhu 'l-Nūn al-Misrī (c. 796-859) was the first to distinguish "stages" (makāmāt) and "states" (aḥwāl) in the Sufi way to God: of this enduring contribution to Sufism we will treat later. He was also the first to introduce elements from the doctrine of the Pseudo-Dionysius into Sufism. They would exercise a profound influence upon the doctrine and practice of later Sufis but seem to have affected al-Misrī himself precious little. For him, heart rather than head was the area of mystic encounter. Thus, asked to define uns (mystic experience), he answered, "It is the joy of the lover in his Beloved." Thus could he pray:

O my God, who is more merciful than Yourself to all my shortcomings, for You have created me weak? And who is more forgiving than You, for Your knowledge of me was before I was? Your command to me is all-encompassing: I have resisted You only by Your permission, and You have reproached me with it; I have disobeyed You, and You were aware of it and have proved me in the wrong. I ask You for the mercy that I need and the acceptance of my pleading. For I am poor towards You, and You are bounteous towards me.

And, perhaps because he was more academically inclined than his contemporary al-Bistami, he spoke with greater theological propriety of the identification with God experienced by the Sufi:

Mystics see without knowledge and without sight, without information received and without contemplation, without description, without veiling and without veil. They are not themselves. They exist not through themselves. Insofar as they exist at all, they exist in God. Their movements are caused by God, and their words are the words of God which are spoken by their tongues, and their sight is the sight of God which has entered into their eyes. Thus God Most High has said, "When I love a servant, I, the Lord, am his ear so that by Me he hears; I am his eye so that by Me he sees: I am his tongue so that by Me he speaks; and I am his hand so that by Me does he grasp."

The reader will not be slow to detect the Dionysian overtones of the first part of this passage, but it was the same al-Misrī who defined "ecstasy" in this quite un-Dionysian and excellent fashion: "the bewilderment of discovery."

Abū 't Kāsim al-Djunaid (d. 910) was, again, a proponent of a Sufism doctrinally better founded than that of al-Bistami. He was perhaps the greatest champion of the "sober" type of Sufism, and it is a large irony that he should have been the spiritual director of *shaikh* of al-Hallādj, who was put to death in 922 for statements *à la* al-Bistami.

The influence, through the Pseudo-Dionysius, of Plotinian doctrine upon al-Djunaid is clear: since all things have their origin in God they must finally return, after their dispersion, to live again in Him, and this return the mystic achieves in the state of *fanā'*. He thus described *fanā'*: "At that time you will be addressed, yourself addressing; questioned concerning your tidings, yourself questioning; with abundant flow of benefits and interchange of attestations; with constant increase of faith and uninterrupted favors." This sounds not at all unpleasant, but of his own experience he wrote:

What I say comes from the continuance of calamity and the consequence of misery, from a heart which is stirred from its foundations and is tortured in its ceaseless conflagrations, by itself within itself: admitting no perception, no utterance, no sensation, no emotion, no repose, no effort, no familiar image, but constant in the calamity of its ceaseless torment, unimaginable, indescribable, unlimited, unbearable in its fierce onslaughts.

The most academic of Sufi mystics was Abū Hāmid al-Ghazzālī (1058-1111). His life was an intellectual odyssey through successive areas of influence which, affecting him deeply, would in turn affect by way of his writings all later

Sufism. There was the influence of Plotinus which he encountered in the so-called *Theology of Aristotle,* an interpretative Arabic translation of extracts from the *Enneads.* There was, too, the influence of Jewish tradition concerning David and the Prophets. There was, finally, the influence of the books of the New Testament as well as that, through personal contact, of the flourishing Christian monasticism in Syria, Palestine, and Egypt. Yet all such disparate influences did not result in a doctrine that was disparate and disjointed because al-Ghazzālī's constant nourishment through it all was the Koran.

The influence of his doctrine upon his successors moved in two directions, the one popular and the other intellectual. The popular influence culminated in the establishment of religious confraternities. The intellectual influence ended in a mysticism that might be termed "metaphysical" or even "gnostic." The most eloquent inheritor of this metaphysical mysticism of al-Ghazzālī was Djalāl al-Dīn Rūmī (1207-1273).

Perhaps unfortunately, Rūmī was guilty of one flamboyancy which has long lodged in the popular imagination pretty much to the exclusion of everything else. To perpetuate the memory of his *shaikh,* Shams al-Dīn Tabrīzī (d. 1247), Rūmī founded a confraternity of dervishes (the *Mawlawīs*) who were chiefly distinguished by their practice of the circular sacred dance, hence the name of "whirling dervishes." But it is in his poetry, in which with forgivable poetic license he expresses a highly metaphysical Sufism, that he is today most worthy of note. For example:

I am a mote from the sun, I am the sun's circuit; to the mote I say, Hither! and to the sun I say, Hence!

I am the glimmer of dawn, I am the air of eventide; I am the rustling of the branch, the roar of the sea.

I am mast, rudder, steersman, ship; and I the reef on which the ship founders.

I am bird-catcher, bird, net; I am face and mirror, voice and its echo.

I am the tree of life, and the parrot in its branches; I am silence and thought, tongue and talking.

I am the breath of the flute, I am the spirit of man; I am the spark from the stone, the sheen of metals.

I am drunkenness, I am vine, I am winepress, I am must;
   toper and tavern, the crystal of the cup;

The candle and the moth that circles round it; the rose
   and the rose-drunk nightingale.

I am physician and sickness, poison and antidote; sweet
   and bitter, honey and gall.

I am war and peace, battlefield and victory; the town and
   its besiegers, the stormers and the wall.

I am the plaster and the trowel, the builder and the plan;
   cornerstone and rooftree, the building and its ruin.

I am hart and lion, lamb and wolf; I am the shepherd
   who gathers all into one fold.

I am the chain of being, I am the ring of the worlds; the
   ladder of creation, mounting and fall.

I am what is and is not. I am—O you who know, Djalāl
   al-Dīn, say it—I am the soul in the All.

So much for individual Sufis. What follows applies to Sufism
in general.

Traditionally, in at least verbal dependence on al-Misrī, distinctions were made between the "stages" (*makāmāt*) and
"states" (*aḥwāl*). The *makāmāt* were recognized as the result
of personal effort. Their most conventional listing is the following: *tawba*, repentance; *wara'*, delicacy of conscience;
zuhd, total renouncement of worldly goods; *fakr*, poverty of
spirit; *ṣabr*, patience in all adversity; *tawakkul*, confidence in
God; and *riḍā*, acceptance of all that occurs.

But Sufism, at least in theory, was never an Operation Boot-
strap: correlative to *makāmāt* one finds *aḥwāl*, the result of the
Divine mercy; *murākiba*, continual recollection; *kurb*, prox-
imity; *maḥabba*, love; *khawf*, fear; *radjā'*, hope; *shawq*, desire;
uns, intimacy; *tuma'nīna*, peace in tranquillity; *mushāhada*,
contemplation; and *yakīn*, certitude.

In all its variations and through all its degrees, Sufism as the
way to mystical union was initiated and sustained by the practice of a technique strikingly similar to the Jesus Prayer. Of
itself meaning simply "remembrance," *dhikr* as a religious
technical term meant the glorifying of God with certain fixed
phrases that were repeated in a ritual order, either aloud or
in the mind, with special breathings and physical movements.

When pronounced aloud, it is *dhikr djalī;* when inwardly, a *dhikr khafī*; and there has been no agreement, at any time, as to which is the more estimable, while in the Jesus Prayer preference has always been given to the interior practice.

Sufism was at no time a normal development of Islam as a whole, but something marginal and incidental.

In the ninth century, when divine union came to be conceived of as conjunction (*ittiṣal*) or as inhabitation (*ḥulūl*) in the soul of the mystic, official Islam admitted only *ittiṣal* and rejected with violence the idea of *ḥulūl* which—mistakenly —was thought to be equivalent to the Christian doctrine of the Incarnation. For the assertion of *ḥulūl*, al-Ḥallādj and others were put to death. Scholarly opinion today is almost equally divided on whether they were, therefore, heretics or martyrs.

SELECTED BIBLIOGRAPHY

The surest general guide through the entire area of Sufi studies is R. A. Nicholson, particularly in his *The Mystics of Islam* (London, 1914), *Studies in Islamic Mysticism* (Cambridge, 1921), and *The Idea of Personality in Sufism* (Cambridge, 1923). The conclusions of more recent scholarship, much of it the authors' own, will be found in *Mystique musulmane* by G. C. Anawati, O.P., and Louis Gardet (Paris, 1961). Although at times overly given to the exclamatory, Professor A. J. Arberry is a popularizer better than most in his *An Introduction to the History of Sufism* (London, 1942) and *Sufism* (London-New York, 1956). And every interested student should at least look briefly into the epochal study by Louis Massignon, *Essai sur les origines du lexique technique de la mystique musulmane,* 2nd edition (Paris, 1954).

Individual studies: Margaret Smith, *Rābi'a the Mystic and her Fellow Saints in Islām* (Cambridge, 1928); for al-Bistami, see R.A. Nicholson, *Eastern Poetry and Prose* (London, 1922); for al-Misrī, Massignon, *Essai,* pp. 187-191; for al-Djunaid, see Ali Abdel Kader in *The Islamic Quarterly,* I (1954), 71-89; the definitive studies on al-Ghazzālī are those of Miguel Asín Palacios, *Algazel* (Saragossa, 1901) and *La espiritualidad de Algazal y su sentido cristiano* (Madrid-Granada, 1934-1941), 4 volumes; R. A. Nicholson, *Rumi: Poet and Mystic* (London-New York, 1950).

X

WILLIAM OF ST. THIERRY

(c. 1085–1148)

ALTHOUGH they were contemporaries, indeed the closest of friends, William, the Abbot of St. Thierry, is best considered in the history of mysticism as if he were a predecessor of St. Bernard.[1] For not only has his expression of the mystical life the same quality—largely Origenist—but he effects even more clearly than Bernard the doctrinal fusion of knowledge with love. Man, for him, is "in the image and likeness of God" in the sense that as "image" he is capable of receiving the imprint of the Trinity and as "likeness" actually receives it. The reception of the "likeness" is an experiential knowledge of the Trinity accorded by the Holy Spirit thus: "memory," the imprint of the Father, produces "reason" as the Father begets the Son; "memory" and "reason" produce "will" as the Holy Spirit proceeds from Father and Son; this knowledge, initially "in a glass darkly," becomes clarified to a seeing "face to face." [2]

In his *The Mirror of Faith,* before ever the nature-super-nature theme had been properly worked out by mediaeval theologians, he managed to make excellently clear that this experienced reception of the "likeness" is supernatural. The modalities of love he analyzed in his *On the Nature and Dig-*

[1] *Cf.* Jacques Hourlier, O.S.B., "Saint Bernard et Guillaume de Saint-Thierry dans le 'Liber de amore Dei,'" in the symposium, *Saint Bernard théologien* (Rome, 1953), pp. 223-233.

[2] *Cf.* O. Brooke, O.S.B., "The Trinitarian Aspect of the Ascent of the Soul to God in the Theology of William of St. Thierry," *Recherches de théologie ancienne et médiévale,* XXVI (1959), 85-127.

nity of Love. The whole of this lofty doctrine he accorded a lowly and sure foundation in *The Epistle to the Brethren of Mont Dieu.* But nowhere did he present his doctrine—and himself—better than in his *On Contemplating God.* Hence the selection made here.

TEXTS [3]

ON CONTEMPLATING GOD

Come, let us climb the mountain of the Lord to the dwelling of the God of Jacob and He will teach us His ways. Come with me, my thoughts, my desires, my wishes, my understandings, my affections, and all within me, come let us climb the mountain to where the Lord sees and is seen. Cares, worries, anxieties, toils, the pains of my slavery, await me here below with the ass, my body, until the boy and I—my reason, I mean, and understanding—hasten aloft. We shall return to you after we have adored.

Indeed we shall return. Alas, how soon it will be! The love of truth leads us far from you but the truth of love does not suffer us, because of the brethren, to abandon you, to reject you. But, although our need of you must draw us back, there is no need that, because of you, we miss this sweetness wholly.

Lord God of hosts, turn to us and show us Your face and we will be saved. But alas, alas, O Lord, how forward, how rash, how unfitting, how presumptuous, how alien to the rule of Your truth and wisdom is it for the unclean heart to wish to look upon God! O highest good, my sum of goodness, life of the heart, light of the inner eye, have pity, Lord, in Your goodness. For this is my cleansing, this is my hope, this is justice, the contemplation of Your goodness, good Lord. Therefore, O Lord my God, who say to my soul as only You know how, "I am your salvation," Rabboni, best of teachers, sole preceptor of the sights I long to see, say to Your blind man, to Your suppliant: "What do you wish that I do for you?"

And You know, because You have already granted the request, what my heart will say to You. It will reject from the most profound of its recesses all the wonders of this world, its beauties, its attractions, and all that can stir the concupiscence of the flesh or of the eyes or awaken the pride of spirit and

---

[3] I translate from the Latin text as critically established by Dom Hourlier. *See* Selected Bibliography.

has in the past done so. My heart will cry out to You, "My face has sought You; Your face, Lord, will I seek. Turn it not away from me; go not in anger away from me, Your servant."

Impudent, certainly, am I. I know it. Wretch am I, O my helper of old and my unwearying protector, but see how it is out of love of Your love that I act as I do. See it as You see me who do not see You. You it is who have given me the desire of You. You are the reason if there is anything in me that pleases You. Pardon, soon, this blind man of Yours who comes running to You. If he stumbles over something as he comes, put out Your hand to Him.

Within me, in my soul, in my mind, may the voice of Your witnessing—tumultuous, buffeting all that is in me—speak in response. May my inner eye be overwhelmed by the lightnings of Your truth telling me, no man can look upon you and live. I, wholly in my sins until now, have been unable to die to myself and thus live for You.

Yet, in accord with the command You have given and the gift You have bestowed, I stand in You upon the rock of Faith, the Christian Faith, there where it is close to You. There, as much as I can, I suffer patiently as I wait. I kiss Your hand lying protectively upon me. And sometimes when I am in contemplation and strain to see, I perceive the back[4] of Him who looks on me. I perceive, as passing, the lowliness of the human dispensation of Christ, Your Son. But when I strive to draw close to Him or, like the woman with the issue of blood, I try to steal, as it were, healthiness for my sickly and ailing soul by touching the hem of His garment; or when, like Thomas, that man of desires, I desire to see Him completely and to touch Him and, not only that, but to approach the sacred wound in His side, the gateway that was made in His side, not only that I might put my finger there or my whole hand but go in myself completely to the very heart of Jesus, into that holy of holies, into that ark of the covenant, even to the urn of gold, to the soul of our humanity which contains within it the manna of the divinity—alas, is said to me then, "Touch me not," or that sentence of the Apocalypse, "There is no room here for dogs."

And so, as is only right, when my conscience expels me and drives me outside, I have to pay the penalty of my forwardness and presumption. And once again I return to my rock, like a

---

[4] *Cf.* Exodus 33:21-23, "And the Lord said, 'See, here is a place by Me where you shall stand upon the rock; and . . . I will cover you with My hand until I have passed by; then will I take away My hand and you shall see My back.'" And long before William, this text was considered in the mystical tradition to express the religious, nonmystical knowledge of God.

hedgehog creeping back to its hiding place, except that I am covered not with thorns but with sins. So once more I grasp, once more I kiss Your hand lying protectively upon me. That I should have had the experience, even so fleetingly, and seen, inflames my desire the more. And, almost with impatience, I await the day when You will remove Your protecting hand and pour forth the grace which will enlighten me so that finally there will be the day when, in accord with the response of Your truth and dead to myself and living for You and Your face unveiled, I begin to see Your face itself and to be changed unto You by the vision of Your face. O face, face of my soul, how blessed a face that it deserve to be "changed" unto You in seeing You,[5] building in its heart a tabernacle of the God of Jacob, effecting all according to the model shown it on the mountain. Here with truth and by right it sings, "To You my heart has said: My face has sought You; Your face, Lord, will I seek."

SELECTED BIBLIOGRAPHY

Editions

La contemplation de Dieu, an introduction, critical Latin text and French version by Dom Jacques Hourlier, O.S.B. (Paris, 1959); *Exposé sur le Cantique des cantiques,* critical Latin text, introduction and notes by Dom. J. M. Déchanet, O.S.B., and a French version by M. Dumontier, O.C.S.O. (Paris, 1962).

Translations

The Epistle to the Brethren of Mont Dieu, translated by Walter Shewring and edited by Dom Justin McCann, O.S.B. (London, 1930); the English versions by Messrs. Geoffrey Webb and Adrian Walker, although rather free, admirably catch the man's characteristic fire: *On Contemplating God* (London, 1955), *On the Nature and Dignity of Love* (London, 1956), and *The Mirror of Faith* (London, 1959).

Studies

The pioneering work, which attracted the attention of the scholarly world to Abbot William, was that of Léopold Malevez, S.J.,

[5] This is one of William's briefest descriptions of the reception of the likeness of the Trinity I mentioned above.

"La doctrine de l'image et de la connaissance mystique chez Guillaume de Saint-Thierry," *Recherches de science religieuse*, XXII (1932), 178-205, 257-279. Since that time the task of magisterial analysis has been almost equally divided between Dom Déchanet and Mlle. M. M. Davy. Of the first, one will wish to consult *Aux sources de la spiritualité de Guillaume de Saint-Thierry* (Bruges, 1940) and *Guillaume de Saint-Thierry, l'homme et son oeuvre* (Bruges-Paris, 1942); of the second, *Théologie et mystique de Guillaume de Saint-Thierry* (Paris, 1954).

XI

ST. BERNARD OF CLAIRVAUX

(1090—1153)

IF AS LITTLE were known about St. Bernard as is known about
the Pseudo-Dionysius and one had only his writings to judge
by, one would never doubt that they were the work of a very
young man—learned, a realist to his fingertips, wise with the
wisdom that is usually born of experience, but young. For if it
is true, as Origen was so acutely aware, that children are incapable of knowing the passion of love, it is equally true that
young men and women know it well and (literature is witness)
express it best. And few men have ever expressed it better
than Bernard.

Here, then, one would say is a young man revealed, a pleasantly eloquent young man obviously in love for the first time.
First love, it is not puppy love. It is the strong love of young
manhood, a new fresh fire.

However, we know much about St. Bernard. We know with
an absolute accuracy the dates of most of his writings. And
we know that the writings most filled with the fresh ardors
of youth are those he wrote in his sixties.

The seeming paradox one may explain as one will, but
eventually one must come to this: the love that fills the writings of Bernard is the love for that God who, as Augustine
said long ago, is beauty ever ancient, ever new; it is the love for
that Christ who, as Irenaeus pointed out even longer ago,
is Himself Newness Itself, *Ipsa Novitas;* the experience in love
which is there expressed is of that depthless Godhead where,
St. Gregory knew, every assuagement awakens a new fresh
thirst. That was why Bernard's love grew younger as Bernard

grew older. In this he was not exceptional. Every saint has engaged in an identical reversal of time in his earthly love affair with Eternity. Bernard was exceptional only for the degree in which, in him, it showed.

"Love is itself a knowing." This dictum of St. Gregory the Great, *amor ipse notitia est,* Bernard made particularly his own. It is the perfect, capsule expression of his mystic experience.

Good Platonist that he was, he held that like is known by like. But man is "like" God in that man was made in His image and likeness. For Bernard, human free will is the image; its proper exercise is the likeness. As all knowledge consists in the transformation of the knowing subject into the likeness of the object known, so here the virtuous exercise of the will, by the transformation it effects, is a knowing of God. But God is love (1 John 4:8). So the transforming of the knowing subject into the likeness of the object here known is—and can only be, Bernard insisted—by love.

Can there be, on grounds such as these, any question of an experiential awareness of the presence of God?

Bernard affirms it. The soul then loves as it is loved. Experiencing its own love, it experiences God's love for it. And God's love for it is the communication of Himself who is love.

But hear Bernard himself, who speaks of this far better than I could ever pretend to.

TEXTS [1]

Man's love of himself for his own sake:
Fleshly Love

Love is a natural affection, one of the four.[2] But it is only right that what is natural should serve the Maker of nature before all others. Hence the first and greatest commandment: "Thou shalt love the Lord thy God. . . ."[3]

But nature is weak and it is feeble; it is impelled by a sort of inner need to look to itself first, and so there is that fleshly love by which before all else, man loves himself for his own

---

[1] I translate the Latin text of Migne, *Patrologia Latina,* Volumes CLXXXII, CLXXXIII.
[2] That is, love, fear, joy, sorrow.
[3] Matthew 22:37.

sake. . . . It is imposed by no command. It is implanted in our very nature, for whoever hated his own flesh?[4]

Yet, truly, if this love, as is its custom, begins to be too precipitate or too lavish—if it is not at all content within the riverbed of necessity and overflows, it will invade the fields of pleasure. Then, at once, its overflow is blocked by the commandment that opposes it: "Thou shalt love thy neighbor as thyself."[5]

Man's love of God for his own sake: Mercenary Love

Man, therefore, loves God. But still for a while he loves Him for his own sake and not for Himself.

It is, however, a sort of prudence to know what one can do all alone and what one can do with God's help, to keep oneself unoffending before Him who keeps us unharmed. But if troubles assail a man again and again, and if on this account he turns often to God and as often finds deliverance, is it not the truth that even though breast were of iron and heart were of stone, in one so many times rescued there must of necessity be a melting within at the grace of the Rescuer so that the man then can love God not merely for his own sake, but for God's own sake?

That situation arises from frequent need.

Thereafter it is necessary that one should, frequently and in repeated exchange, go to God, who is tasted in such exchange. By tasting is it seen how sweet is the Lord.[6] And thus it happens that, once tasted, His sweetness draws us to the pure love of Him more powerfully than our need impels.[7]

Man's love of God for the sake of God: Filial Love

The young also love. But the young always keep their inheritance in mind. Afraid that they may in some way or other lose it, they show him from whom they expect their inheritance rather more respect than ever they do love.[8]

---

[4] Cf. 1 Corinthians 15:46.
[5] Matthew 22:39; Love of God, Chapter VIII.
[6] Cf. Psalm 33:9.
[7] Love of God, Chapter IX.
[8] Sermon LXXXIII on the Song of Songs, v.

Man does not love even himself except for the sake of God: Nuptial Love

A great thing is love. But there are degrees in it. The espoused dwells in the highest.[9]

Happy is he who has deserved to attain as high as the fourth degree, where a man does not love even himself except for the sake of God. . . . Flesh and blood, body of death, when will you attain to this? When will mind know such an experience, be drunk with the love of God, be disregarding of itself, be in its own eyes a "vessel that is destroyed,"[10] that it may go clean out to God and, joined to God, be one spirit with Him?[11] . . . Happy is he to whom it has been given to know such an experience in this earthly life at rare intervals or even once, and even then abruptly and scarcely for the space of a single moment. . . . To lose yourself so that you are as though you were not,[12] to be unaware of yourself and emptied to yourself, to be, as it were, brought to nothing—this pertains to heavenly exchanges, not to human affection.[13]

The soul's return is her conversion to the Word, to be reformed through Him and to be conformed to Him. In what respect? In love. . . . Such conformity joins the soul in marriage to the Word, when, being already like Him in nature [as image, free will], it shows itself no less like Him in will [resemblance, exercise of will], loving in the same way that it is itself loved. If then it loves perfectly, it has become His bride. . . . Truly spiritual and a contract of holy matrimony is a relation such as this. It is less than understatement to call it a contract. It is an embrace (*amplexus*)—an embrace surely, where to will and not to will the same thing makes one spirit out of two. . . . When love comes into the soul it changes everything else into itself and takes the affections captive. The soul therefore that loves, loves, and knows nothing else. . . . They are bride and Bridegroom. . . . But this Bridegroom, remember, is not only loving; He is Love itself. . . .

Of all the movements of the soul, feelings and affections, in love alone can the creature make a return to the Creator, al-

[9] *Loc. cit.*
[10] Psalm 30:13.
[11] *Cf.* 1 Corinthians 6:17.
[12] Galatians 2:20.
[13] *Love of God,* Chapter X.

though it is hardly on equal terms that he does it. For example, if God were angry with me, could I, in like manner, grow angry with Him in return? Certainly not. I would tremble and shake with fear and beg forgiveness. Similarly, if He rebukes me, I shall not rebuke Him in return; I shall justify Him. If He condemns me, I shall not condemn Him; I shall adore Him. . . . If He wields His power as my Lord and master, I must act as His servant. If He commands, I must obey. But how different it is with love. When God loves, He seeks nothing but love in return; He loves for no other reason than that He be loved . . . knowing that those who love Him become by that love itself most blessed. . . . He seeks for nothing else. The soul has nothing else. Therefore is it that He is a Bridegroom and the soul is a bride, for this belongs only to a wedded pair. To it no other ever attains, not even a son. . . . The love of the Bridegroom—rather, the Bridegroom who is Love—asks only a return of love and fidelity. Let the bride, then, return love for love.

With good reason, then, renouncing all other affections the bride gives herself wholly to love alone. In reciprocating love she is forced to make a return of love to Him who is Love itself. Yet when she has poured out her whole being in love, what is it in comparison with the unceasing flood from the source of Love? The waters of love do not flow with equal copiousness from the lover and from Him who is Love, from the bride and the Bridegroom, from the creature and the Creator. You might as well compare one who is thirsty and the fountain from which he drinks. What then? Will hope cease on this account and become empty simply because the soul is unable to compete with a giant in the race, to dispute the palm of sweetness with honey, of gentleness with the lamb, of brilliance with the sun, of love with Him who is Love? Assuredly not. A creature loves less because a creature is less. Yet, if it loves with its entire being, there can be nothing lacking. So, as I have said, to love thus is to have been joined in marriage because it is impossible thus to love and not be greatly loved. In the mutual consent of the two parties consists the integrity and perfection of every marriage. . . .

Happy the soul to whom it is given to experience this embrace for it is nothing else than love which here joins two together, not in one flesh, but in one spirit, and makes the two no longer two, but one. As St. Paul says: "He who is joined to the Lord is one spirit." [14]

But now bear with my foolishness for a moment. I want to tell you, as I have promised you I would, how such events

[14] 1 Corinthians 6:17; *Sermon LXXXIII on the Song of Songs.*

have taken place in me. I know it to be a matter of no importance. But I put myself forward only that I may be of help to you. If you derive any profit, I shall be consoled for my forwardness; if you do not, I shall simply have displayed my foolishness.

I confess, then, though I say it in my foolishness, that the Word has visited me, and has even done so very often. Yet although He has often entered into my soul, I have never at any time been aware of the precise moment of His coming. I have felt that He was present; I remember later that He has been with me; I have sometimes even had a presentiment that He would come; but I have never felt His coming or His leaving. For whence He came in entering my soul, and where He went upon leaving it, by what means He has made either entrance or departure, I confess that I do not know even to this day. . . .

You will ask, then, how, since the ways of His access are thus incapable of being discovered, I could really know that He was present.

He is living and full of energy. As soon as He has entered into me He has awakened my sleeping soul. He has stirred and softened and wounded my heart which was torpid and as hard as a rock. He has started to pluck up and to destroy, to plant and to build, to water areas that were arid and dry, to cast light into areas that were dark with shadow, to throw open those that were shut close, to warm with His flame those that were cold, and to straighten the crooked paths of my heart and make its rough places smooth, so that my soul might bless the Lord and all that is within me might praise His Holy Name. . . .

The Bridegroom-Word, although He has several times entered into me, has never made His coming apparent to sight, hearing, or touch. . . . Not by His movements was He recognized by me. I could not tell by any of my senses that He had penetrated to the depths of my being. It was, as I said, only by the movement of my heart (*tantum ex motu cordis*) that I was able to recognize His presence, to know the might of His power by the sudden departure of vices and the strong restraint placed upon all carnal affections. From the discovery and conviction of secret faults I have had good reason to be astonished at the depths of His wisdom. His goodness and kindness I have known in the amending, whatever it may amount to, of my life, while in the reformation and renewal of the spirit of my mind, of, that is, my inward man, I have perceived in some degree the loveliness of His beauty. And I have been filled with wonderment at the magnitude of His greatness as I meditated on all this. . . .

But when the Word withdrew Himself, all spiritual powers

and faculties began to droop and to languish. It was as though the fire had been removed from under a bubbling kettle. Such, to me, is the sign of His departure.[15]

The mind is drawn along by the ineffable sweetness of the Word and, as it were, it is stolen from itself or, better, it is rapt and remains out of itself there to enjoy the Word. . . .

It has been permitted to me to have had that experience. It is not at all permitted to me to express it in speech. In the reference I made to it just now, I adapted my words so as to speak only to those of you who are able to receive what I say. O you who are full of curiosity to know what it is to enjoy the Word, prepare your mind for it, not your ear. The tongue cannot teach it; it is taught only by grace.[16]

SELECTED BIBLIOGRAPHY

Editions

A critical edition is in process of being constituted under the editorship of Dom Jean Leclercq, O.S.B. Until its appearance, one is not badly served by texts provided in Migne, *Patrologia Latina*, Volumes CLXXXII-CLXXXV, and *Select Treatises of Saint Bernard of Clairvaux*, edited by W. W. Williams and B. R. V. Mills (Cambridge, 1926).

Translations

Wholly admirable is the version of T. I. Connelly, S.J., *St. Bernard on the Love of God* (New York, 1937); translated selections from the *Commentary on the Song of Songs* are included.

Studies

The two fundamental essays at interpretation are those of Etienne Gilson, *The Mystical Theology of St. Bernard* (New York, 1940) and Dom A. Le Bail, "S. Bernard," *Dictionnaire de spiritualité*, I (1938), 1454-1499. For major matters of detail, the researches of Dom Jean Leclercq, O.S.B., are indispensable; particularly to be recommended are his *Etudes sur saint Bernard et le texte de ses écrits* (Rome, 1953) and "Recherches sur les sermons sur les Cantiques de Saint Bernard," *Revue Bénédictine*, LXIV

[15] *Sermon LXXIV on the Song of Songs*, v-vi.
[16] *Sermon LXXXV on the Song of Songs*.

(1954), 208-223; LXV (1955), 71-89, 228-258; LXVI (1956), 63-91; LXIX (1959), 237-257. A singularly perceptive interpretation, largely counter to the one I have provided in these pages, is given by Jean Mouroux, "Sur les critères de l'expérience spirituelle d'après les Sermons sur la Cantique des cantiques," in *Saint Bernard théologien* (Rome, 1953), pp. 253-267.

XII

RICHARD OF ST. VICTOR

(d. 1173)

IN 1108, William of Champeaux established the Monastery of St. Victor at Paris. The chop-logic adversary of Abelard, he could hardly foresee the center of mystical theology it was to become a short generation later. One man, Hugh the Saxon, effected that quite unexpected development. Hugh was himself a mystic, but his fame as the greatest theologian of his day has succeeded in blinding historians to that fact, so it is to others of the Victorines that attention in this respect is given. Among them the poet, Adam of St. Victor, is receiving due regard these days. But the lion's share of contemporary scholarship on the Victorine School is devoted to Richard of St. Victor, and rightly so.

Less the theologian than Hugh, Richard was yet more the theologian than either William of St. Thierry or St. Bernard: he does not confuse love and knowledge. For him, love is born of knowledge. Contemplation is the consequence of two intellectual operations, cogitation and meditation. This he distinguishes from mystical experience, which he believes to be dependent upon no less than four quite disparate factors: the Beatific Vision, the concurrence of God's grace, human effort, and knowledge of the Scriptures.

TEXTS [1]

It now remains to be shown . . . how the human mind may fall into ecstasy and transcend itself through intensity of joy and exultation. This kind of going forth seems to be sufficiently well expressed in those very words which we quoted from the Song of Songs, in the second mode. "Who is she," saith the Scripture, "that cometh up from the desert, flowing with delights, leaning upon her beloved?"[2] If we rightly interpret the desert as being the human heart, what is this rising up from the desert, but the passing of the human mind into ecstasy? The human soul rises up from the desert when it passes beyond itself by ecstasy of the mind, when leaving itself altogether and passing up into the heavens, by contemplation and devotion it is immersed in divine things. But the cause of this ascension is allied to and follows upon what is described as "rising up, flowing with delights. . . ." There is no other source from which we may have and possess this flowing of delights and abundance of true joys but that deep joyfulness of the soul, filled with sweetness by the gift of God. It does not say "having delights" but "flowing with delights." So that it is not every experience of these delights, but only that fullness thereof which creates and perfects the ascent made from the desert. It is manifest that however much we progress, we cannot have these delights continually in this mere earthly life. Therefore when the soul lacks this kind of overflow she is not able to rise up to this ascent of which we speak, for she must be "flowing with delights" for this ascent. I think, too, that it is one thing to ascend while flowing with delight and another to flow or abound while ascending, and yet another for the abundance to be the cause of the flowing. The abundance of delights, therefore, is the cause of the ascent when, by that infusion of divine sweetness, the holy soul does not understand what she feels in her inmost heart, inasmuch as the greatness of her exultation and joy casts her out of herself and ravishes her above herself. Thus indeed the ardent and immense happiness, as it grows beyond human measure, bears a man away above himself, and raising him up beyond human things, supports him in divine regions.

We may see daily an example of this in the life of animals. Sometimes in their play they leap up and their bodies remain

[1] From *Richard of Saint-Victor, Selected Writings on Contemplation*, edited and translated by Clare Kirchberger (New York-London, 1957).
[2] Song of Songs 8:5.

for a short time in the air. So often fish, playing in the waters, rise up above the water and go beyond the bounds of their native dwelling place, supporting themselves for a short time in the void. So also the holy soul, when by the inward excitement of its fervor it is cut off from itself, when it is moved by ecstasy of mind to rise up above itself, when it is carried away altogether and rests in a celestial world, when it is wholly immersed in angelic visions, seems to have transcended the limitations of its native powers. . . .

If we rightly understand contemplative men by the mountains and speculative men by the hills, see how correctly the mountains are said to rejoice like rams and the hills like the lambs. For sometimes contemplation and speculation are used as equivalent terms and thus often the true meaning of Scripture is obscured and confused. But we define speculation aptly and expressly when we say that we see through a glass (*speculum*) but contemplation is when we see the truth in its purity, without any hindrance or veil of shadows. So the hills rejoice like the lambs when that exalted rite of solemn and secret movements lifts them up beyond themselves that they may be worthy to see the hidden mysteries of heaven as in a glass and darkly. But the mountains rejoice like rams when the higher spirits in the exultation of their ecstasy contemplate in the purity and simplicity of truth that which the lower spirits can hardly behold even in a glass and darkly.

Let nobody presume upon his own powers for such exaltation or uplifting of the heart or ascribe it to his own merits. For it is certain that this comes not from human deserving but is a divine gift. So that soul, however she may be, who is described as ascending from the desert, is said to lean upon her beloved. She leans when she is moved by his strength and not by her own power. And, I say, to rely upon her beloved, means that she does not presume at all upon her own strength in this matter. As far as I can see, she is right in not counting at all upon her own effort, nor on her own abilities, especially in that place where she comes up from the desert, nor even in the desert, when she goes through it. And this beloved of hers knows it well, and therefore leads her on in a cloud by day and all night by the light of fire. How indeed could she bear the burden and heat of the day, but under the shadow of him whom her soul loveth? And what safe place would she find from the fears of the night, especially in that region of terror and vast solitude, unless he sent forth his light and his truth? Moreover she would have nothing whereby to temper the heat of desire unless the power of the Most High overshadowed her. And again, she would be without enlightenment in the darkness of her ignorance, unless she saw light in his light. And this is the meaning of what she says to him: "For thou lightest my lamp, O Lord: O my God, enlighten my darkness."[3] Therefore the beloved, by the gift of her beloved and the generosity of her bridegroom, receives two remedies for the two chief evils, the cooling cloud for the concupiscence of the flesh and the light of revelation for ignorance of the mind. How often a man knows the way of truth but does not take it, being drawn away and enticed by his desire, and so he has a day of knowledge but not the cloud of cooling grace. And how many have a zeal for God but not according to knowledge, and these perchance feel no heat of desire and for a time breathe quietly in the coolness of the night. And these men seem to have the night but have not the fire of illuminating grace. Therefore it is good to hope in the Lord and not presume upon oneself. How blessed are they to whom he is as a covering by day and as the light of stars by night, spreading the cloud over them for protection and sending the fire to lighten them by night. But then "it is not of him that willeth nor of him that runneth, but of God that sheweth mercy." [4] The beloved knows this and therefore leans on her beloved, for rightly is it written of her: "Who is she that cometh up from the desert, flowing with delights, leaning upon her beloved?" [5]

To sleep is one thing, to pass away another. It is one thing to recollect one's spirit wholly within oneself, another to rise up and leave oneself behind. It is one thing to control the appetites, to cut out the care of external things from the heart, another to arrive at complete forgetfulness of oneself. For it is necessary before one is able to go into that hidden place of inner quietness, the sanctuary of the highest tranquillity, it is necessary, I say, that this most grave and truly wonderful thing take place, not the dissolution of body and soul which is the type of that more wonderful and glorious separation, which must be suffered, but the division of the soul and the spirit. This, according to the Apostle, is worked in us by the living and powerful word of God, sharper and more penetrating than any two-edged sword and piercing even to the dividing asunder of soul and spirit.[6]

What can any creature perceive more marvelous than this separation where that which is essentially one and individual is divided and that which is single and without parts is divided and disjoined within itself? Nor is there in one man an essence

[3] Psalm 18:28.
[4] Romans 9:16.
[5] *Benjamin Major*, Book V, Chapters XIV-XV; Kirchberger, *op. cit.*, pp. 203-206.
[6] *Cf.* Hebrews 4:12.

which is spirit and something else which is soul, but rather he is one and the same substance of one single nature. Nor must we understand a twofold substance by these two words, but when we distinguish between the twin powers of the same essence, the higher is called spirit, the lower soul. In this division the soul and that which is animal remains below, but the spirit and that which is spiritual flies upwards. That which is of the body and subject to corruption, perishes and as a dead body falls back into itself and below its nature. That which is subtle and purified ascends upward like a breath of air, rises above and transcends itself. O that high quiet, that sublime peace where all man's usual movement loses its mobility, where any movement made, is through the divine power and passes into God.[7]

SELECTED BIBLIOGRAPHY

Editions

Professor Jean Châtillon is engaged in bringing out a critical edition of Richard's writings; only the volume *Sermons et opuscules spirituels inédits* (Bruges, 1951) has appeared thus far. The text established long ago of what was believed to be the complete works is reproduced in Migne, *Patrologia Latina*, Volume CXCVI.

Translations

Besides the English version, wholly admirable, of Miss Clare Kirchberger, from which the selections in this book are drawn, the translation of the *De Trinitate* by Gaston Salet, S.J. (*Richard de Saint-Victor: La Trinité* [Paris, 1959]), will be found most helpful.

Studies

The great name here is that of Jean Châtillon. All but indispensable to the student are his *Les Degrés de la Contemplation et de l'Amour dans l'Oeuvre de Richard de Saint-Victor* (Toulouse, 1939); "Les quatres degrés de la charité d'après Richard de Saint-Victor," *Revue d'ascétique et de mystique*, XX (1939), 237-266; "Les trois modes de la contemplation de Richard de Saint-Victor," *Bulletin de littérature ecclésiastique*, XLI (1940), 3-26. Still basic is J. Ebner's *Die Erkenntnislehre Richards von Saint-Viktor* (Münster, 1917).

[7] *De Exterminatione Mali*, Part III, Chapter XVIII; *op. cit.*, pp. 246-247.

XIII

ST. EDMUND RICH

(c. 1180—1240)

WITH ST. EDMUND, Archbishop of Canterbury, the doctrine of Richard of St. Victor came to the British Isles. In crossing the Channel, it suffered a sea change and acquired Pseudo-Dionysian qualities that were to prove, for whatever reason, especially congenial to the English mentality.

In his *Mirror of Holy Church* Edmund does not hesitate to give the most exigent mystical doctrine to what must have been spiritual illiterates. But he had no doubt that it was the thing to do; dying, he said, "Lord, I have believed in You, preached You, taught You; and You are my witness that here on earth I have sought nothing else than You." He may not have made any mystics; no one other than God does that. But he may—so good a man was he—have managed to make things easier for those who were mystics.

Recurrently one encounters in the history of religion periods and places especially distinguished by writings about or by mystics. The explanation I suggested earlier was that mystical experience which, to a degree, is everywhere always has in these periods or places an atmosphere congenial to its unembarrassed expression.

Such a period was the fourteenth century. Such a place was England. Perhaps it was St. Edmund of the thirteenth century with his *Mirror of Holy Church* who introduced the atmospheric change.

TEXTS[1]

THE MIRROR OF HOLY CHURCH

There are two things, only two, which make a man holy, knowledge and love: knowledge of truth and love of goodness. But the truth is the knowledge of God, and you can never come to that except through knowledge of yourselves: nor can you ever come to the love of God, which is goodness, except through the love of your neighbour. You can come to know yourselves as you practise the highest forms of meditation: you can come to know God through pure contemplation.[2]

If you say that you love your father and mother because you were born of their flesh and blood—so now are the worms that feed on them every day.[3]

When in this way you have looked at God in His creatures, lift your heart up to your Creator, and think of the great power with which everything was made out of nothing and given its existence, of the great wisdom which ordered them in such great beauty, of the great goodness with which they are multiplied every day for our use. Ah, God, have mercy on us, who so undo our own nature. We destroy all these creatures which He has created, we confuse what He has governed, we lay waste what He has multiplied.[4]

Every hour in which you have not thought of God has been an hour lost.[5]

The first step in contemplation is for the soul to retreat within itself and there completely to recollect itself. The second step in contemplation is for the soul to see what it is when it is so recollected. The third step is for the soul to raise itself beyond itself and to strive to see two things: its Creator, and His own nature. But the soul can never attain to this until it has learned to subdue every image, corporeal, earthly and celestial, to reject whatever may come to it through sight or

[1] From *The Mediaeval Mystics of England*, edited and translated by Eric Colledge (New York-London, 1961-1962).
[2] Colledge, *op. cit.*, p. 126.
[3] *Op. cit.*, p. 127.
[4] *Op. cit.*, p. 131.
[5] *Op. cit.*, p. 126.

hearing or touch or taste or any other bodily sensation, and to tread it down, so that the soul may see what it itself is outside of its body. To do this, see what a wonderful thing the soul is in itself: how in its nature it is single, and none the less made of so many different things, for it is the soul itself which sees with the eyes, hears with the ears, tastes with the mouth, smells with the nose, touches with the hands and other members.

Then, next, think how great is the soul which in one single thought could comprehend heaven and earth and everything in them, even if they were a thousand times greater than they are. If man's soul is a thing so great and so noble that no created being can perfectly understand it, how great and how noble is He Who made something so noble out of nothing. For He is above all things and beneath all things and within all things and without all things. He is the highest and the deepest, the innermost and the widest: the highest, ruling all things, the deepest, supporting all things, the innermost, fulfilling all things, the widest, encompassing all things. This kind of contemplation engenders in men firm faith and great devotion.

After this you must understand how great He is; and this you can see in many ways. First, see how generous He is with temporal goods, how He gives His wealth to evil men as well as to good in all things which you can see upon earth: and then how generous He is in forgiving, for if there were a man who had committed as many sins as all the men on earth, still He would be a hundred times more ready to forgive than that wretch would be to ask for forgiveness. Then you should think how generous He is with spiritual goods, that is to say with the six virtues, for whoever has one has all of them. Fourthly, you should think how generous He is with material goods to all those who are willing to ask for them as they should: for how can He deny you what He admonished you to pray for? Furthermore, He is willing, if we ask Him for something, to grant us even more. "Ask me," He says, "to give you the joy of heaven, and I will give you all temporal goods without your having asked." This contemplation of His power and His generosity engenders in man true hope.

After this you ought to recognise and think of His goodness and His sweetness and His beauty. To do this you should well consider the great beauty and the great goodness and the great sweetness which there is in earthly creatures. How many things there are which delight our earthly eyes by their beauty and our taste by their sweetness and our touch by their smoothness and so all our other senses! See then how great goodness, sweetness and beauty there must be in a spiritual creature which is everlasting, when there is so much beauty and sweetness and goodness in a thing which exists today and tomorrow will have passed away. On the other hand, if there is so much beauty, sweetness and goodness in every created thing, how much beauty must there be in its Creator, Who made all this and every thing, and out of nothing! You know well how great, beyond measure, the difference must be. This kind of contemplation engenders in man love towards his Creator.

After this, when you have in this way looked at your Creator and His creatures, put every corporeal image outside your heart, and let your naked intention fly up above all human reasoning and there you shall find such great sweetness and such great secrets that without special grace there is no-one who can think of it except only him who has experienced it. And if you wish to know by instruction, go to him who has experienced it. And even though I, wretch that I am, might have experienced it, still I cannot tell of it: for how could I tell with my lips what I cannot think of in my heart? This is a thing so great and so secret that it surpasses every thought, and therefore I keep silence. And it is right that I should do so, for the tongue cannot teach this, but only divine grace.[6]

SELECTED BIBLIOGRAPHY

Editions

The Mirror, in the original Anglo-Norman, has been edited by H. W. Robbins, *Le Merure de Seinte Eglise* (Lewisburg, Pa., 1925).

Translations

The entire *Mirror,* St. Edmund's devotional interpolations excluded, has been translated by Eric Colledge alone in recent times. From that acute version, accordingly, the passages above were drawn.

Studies

Edmund, at least as a mystical author, has been much neglected. See, however, Dom Wilfred Wallace, O.S.B., *The Life of St. Edmund of Canterbury* (London, 1893).

[6] *Op. cit.,* pp. 137-139.

XIV

ST. MECHTILDE
OF MAGDEBURG

(1210—1295)

AN ASTONISHING series of events occurred in German Benedictine convents in the twelfth and thirteenth centuries. They were of a sort to induce dismay into the hearts of historians and a distress even more acute into the hearts, usually so at peace, of theologians. Historically, no categories exist in which to insert these events. Theologically, there are no principles at hand to explain them. So, admitting at the outset its twofold inadequacy, I shall here provide a report as simply and soberly as ever I may of what happened and let it go at that.

St. Hildegarde of Bingen (1098–1179) and St. Elizabeth of Schönau (1129–1164) and St. Gertrude of Helfta (1256–1302) and St. Mechtilde of Hackeborn (1241–1299) and St. Mechtilde of Magdeburg (1210–1295) were all recipients of extraordinary, curiously similar, mystical experiences. They were all ecstatics and visionaries—a fact which is hardly in their favor. They were all of them saints—a fact which is much in their favor and provides the reason, really, for any-one's bothering to talk about them at all. Because, if the visionary and the ecstatic usually means psychological imbalance and a general psychic unhealthiness, canonizable sanctity always means the opposite. And each of these women was as uncomplicatedly normal as a new potato. There is no evidence of their making a cult of contemplation or of their seeking the experiences which were accorded them. Indeed, the ecstasies were clearly unwanted and, to the extent possible, actively resisted.

Psychologically balanced, psychically healthy, they were (the misogynist reader will not be slow to point out) women and so inevitably given to emotionalism and vivid imaginings however much they might not want to be so afflicted. In answer to the difficulty of assessment which that pat observation seemingly suggests, one need merely point out that theirs was a "mysticism of essence"—intellectualist, accordingly, in the extreme. Yet they *were* women. And that raises a difficulty which I have no hope of solving in this book. It is this: Why is it that, among the greatest mystical writers, only the women (one sole exception comes to mind[1]) are ever visionaries? Besides this notable quintet, one thinks of St. Catherine of Siena, Julian of Norwich, St. Catherine of Genoa, St. Teresa, and Marie of the Incarnation. And, so thinking, one does not know what to think.

There seems no reason for believing that the poems of St. Mechtilde of Magdeburg are simply transcripts of the visions she had; their highly complex metrical form suggests that literary artifice had much to do with their character. To the symbols of nuptial mysticism, inherited from St. Bernard, are added the devices of courtly love, borrowed from the Minnesingers, to express experiences akin to those of Ruysbroek in the century following.

TEXTS[2]

Ah! Lord! seeing Thou hast taken from me all that I had of Thee, give me of Thy grace, the gift every dog has by nature, that of being true to my Master in my need, when deprived of all consolation.[3]

That prayer has great power which a person makes with all his might. It makes a sour heart sweet, a sad heart merry, a poor heart rich, a foolish heart wise, a timid heart brave, a sick heart well, a blind heart full of sight, a cold heart ardent. It draws down the great God into the little heart, it drives the hungry soul up into the fullness of God, it brings together two lovers, God and the soul in a wondrous place where they speak much of love.

Alas for me, unworthy . . . that I cannot die![4]

---

[1] See pp. 194-208.
[2] From *The Revelations of Mechtild of Magdeburg*, translated by Lucy Menzies (New York-London, 1953).
[3] II, 25; Menzies, *op. cit.*, p. 55.
[4] V, 13; *op. cit.*, p. 136; the text is here obscure, hence the dots.

Love without Knowledge
Is darkness to the wise soul.
Knowledge without revelation
Is as the pain of Hell.
Revelation without death,
Cannot be endured.[5]

Soul

Ah dearest Love, for how long
Hast thou lain in wait for me!
What, O what can I do?
I am hunted, captured, bound,
Wounded so terribly
That never can I be healed.
Cunning blows hast thou dealt,
Shall I ever recover from thee?
Would it not have been well
That I had never known thee?

Love

I hunted thee for my pleasure,
I caught thee for my desire,
I bound thee for my joy,
Thy wounds have made us one,
My cunning blows, me thine.
I drove Almighty God
From Heaven and it was I
Who took His human life
And gave Him back again
With honour to His Father—
How couldst thou hope, poor worm,
To save thyself from me?

Soul

But Queen, I fear I might
Through one small gift of God,
Through food and drink, escape thee?

Love

That prisoners may not die
One gives them bread and water
And God has given thee these

[5] I, 21; *op. cit.*, p. 12.

Mere respites for a time.
But when thy death-blow falls,
And when thy Easter comes,
I shall be all around thee
I shall be through and through thee,
And I shall steal thy body
And give thee to thy Love.

Soul

Love! I have been thy scribe,
Seal those words with thy sign.

Love

Who loves God more than self
Knows where to find the seal
It lies between us twain.—
The seal is there, thine Easter come
And God, thy glorious grave, thy Home.[6]

Thus speaks the Bride of God who has dwelt in the enclosed sanctuary of the Holy Trinity—"Away from me all ye creatures! Ye pain me and cannot comfort me!" And the creatures ask, "Why?" The Bride says, "My Love has left me while I rested beside him and slept." But the creatures ask, "Can this beautiful world and all your blessings not comfort you?" "Nay," says the Bride, "I see the serpent of falsehood and false wisdom creeping in to all the joy of this world. I see also the hook of covetousness in the bait of ignoble sweetness by which it ensnares many."

"Can even the Kingdom of Heaven not comfort you?" ask the creatures. "Nay! it were dead in itself were the living God not there!" "Now, O Bride, can the saints not comfort thee?"

"Nay! for were they separated from the living Godhead which flows through them, they would weep more bitterly than I for they have risen higher than I and live more deeply in God."

"Can the Son of God not comfort thee?"
Yea! I ask Him when we shall go
Into the flowery meadows of heavenly knowledge
And pray Him fervently,
That He unlock for me
The swirling flood which plays about the Holy Trinity,
For the soul lives on that alone.
  If I am to be comforted
According to the merit to which God has raised me,

[6] I, 3; *op. cit.*, pp. 7-9.

Then His breath must draw me effortlessly into Himself.
For the sun which plays upon the living Godhead
Irradiates the clear waters of a joyful humanity;
And the sweet desire of the Holy Spirit
Comes to us from both. . . .
Nothing can satisfy me save God alone,
Without Him I am as dead.
Yet would I gladly sacrifice the joy of His presence
Could He be greatly honoured thereby.
For if I, unworthy, cannot praise God with all my might,
Then I send all creatures to the Court of Heaven
And bid them praise God for me,
With all their wisdom, their love,
Their beauty; all their desires,
As they were created, sinless by God,
To sing with all the sweetness of their voices
As they now sing.
Could I but witness this praise
I would sorrow no more.[7]

SELECTED BIBLIOGRAPHY

Editions

The original of *The Flowing Light* in Low German apparently no longer exists. One works accordingly from a version in High German by Heinrich of Nördlingen and a Basel group of the Friends of God as edited by G. Morel, *Das fliessende Licht der Gottheit* (Regensburg, 1869).

Translations

That of Miss Lucy Menzies is both the best and most complete. It was made directly from *MS Einsiedeln 277*, upon which Dom Morel's edition was based.

Studies

The fundamental work is that of Mme. Jeanne Ancelet-Hustache, *Mechtilde de Magdebourg: Etude de psychologie religieuse* (Paris, 1926). For complementary matters of detail, see G. Lübers, *Die Sprache der deutschen Mystik des Mittelalters im Werke der Mech-*

[7] IV, 12; *op. cit.*, pp. 104-105.

tilds von Magdeburg (Munich, 1926) and H. Tillmann, *Studien zum Dialog bei Mechtilde von Magdeburg* (Marburg, 1933). On Mechtilde's use of the poetic forms current in her day consult R. Kayser, "Minne und Mystik im Werke Mechtilds von Magdeburg," *Germanic Review*, XIX (1944), 3-15.

XV

MEISTER ECKHART

(1260—a. 1329)

THERE ARE few figures in the entire history of mysticism as fascinating or, at times, as downright puzzling as Meister Eckhart of Hochheim. The exquisite fascination he exercises, especially upon the minds of intellectuals of the more rootless sort, will doubtless continue without abatement. But there are rather good prospects now that he will shortly cease being such a puzzle: reliable editions of most of his writings are available today and the research of the last few decades has largely reconstructed the doctrinal background against which his writings can be placed for a proper understanding and assessment.

That background is one in which the Pseudo-Dionysius looms large—a much less tractable Dionysius than the one Eckhart's fellow Dominicans, St. Albert the Great and St. Thomas Aquinas, had known. For the air was heavy by now with Plotinian doctrine that brought out the worst, some might say, of Dionysius.[1]

And he captured Eckhart early.

The cyclic view of the universe, common to such other me-

[1] The doctrine of Plotinus, at its most rigid, had by now become current in the Latin Middle Ages through translations of the works of Ibn Sīnā, the *Book of the Twenty-four Philosophers* by the Pseudo-Hermes Trismegistus, the *Liber de Causis* of al-Fārābī, the *Elements of Theology* of Proclus, the *De Anima* of Gundisalvi, and so on.

diaeval mystical theologians as Scotus Eriugena and Hugh of
St. Victor, assumed in Eckhart a new, extreme quality: origin
and term of the cyclic rhythm of reality is the "wilderness of
the Godhead," the "nothingness that is beyond existence," the
"formless abyss and desert stillness" where there is "no willing, no need, no act, no generation," but only "an eternal
silent undifferentiated One-ness."

This "eternal silent undifferentiated One-ness" is not God
because God and Godhead are "as different as Heaven and
earth."[2] It is "beyond and above God." It is "the motionless
peace from which the Blessed Trinity and all else comes." The
Trinity, God, is distinct from, and revelatory of, the Godhead.
Eckhart's notion of the Divine simplicity is such that the
Trinity is necessarily distinguished from it and external to it.

And, good Plotinian, he plots out all the rest of reality—
descending according to degrees of increased multiplicity to
the lowest—with the consequence that for him the existence
of the Trinity can be proved by unaided natural reason because the Trinity is closest to the natural realities man most
immediately knows.[3]

Perhaps a diagram will be helpful here.

As the process of reality is emanation from Godhead to Un-
spoken Word (the Father), to Spoken Word (the Son), to
Love (the Spirit), to ideal creation, to phenomenal creation,
so also is the return for man through these same stages, in-
versely, to the wilderness of the Godhead.

The practical spiritual doctrine of Eckhart is in perfect
correspondence with his theory. The first stage of the soul's
return is regression from phenomena, that is, from creatures in
their actual state because they are not merely nothing, they are
annihilating.[4] The second stage is the beholding of the un-
creaturely in creatures, that is, of creatures in their ideal state.
The third stage is introspective: one meditates upon the purely
spiritual faculties of the soul, the trinity of memory, understanding, and will.

But the soul's destiny, quite as the destiny of all creation, is
not the Trinity but what is beyond the Trinity—the Godhead.
Therefore there is a complex fourth stage. Positively, it consists in passing beyond memory-understanding-will to the deli-

[2] This is his conventional expression whenever he wishes to indicate
complete contrast.

[3] It is the same sort of logic, which seems really an abuse of logic, that
allows him to conclude that were there no creatures there would be no
God (Trinity).

[4] Doctrine condemned by Pope John XXII (March 27, 1329) as
"ill-sounding, rash, and suspect of heresy."

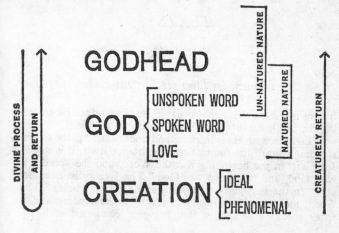

"The un-natured nature natures nothing. The Father natures His Son in the un-natured nature, and the Father is as close to the un-natured nature as He is to the natured nature because He is one with it. The Father is alone in the un-natured nature and also the first in the natured nature. And the son is with the Father in the natured nature naturing. . . ."[5]

cate simplicity of the soul's pure nature, to a oneness so rarefied that, Eckhart says, "it is almost as though it were not in man at all." Negatively, it consists in stripping all residual multiplicity from the soul both from within and from without. Within, all willing and knowing are eliminated. Without, one is liberated from all creatures and from the multiplicity which is God: "We pray to God," he says, "to be free from God."

Thus is the circle completed, the mystic return achieved, its term and modalities directly corresponding to the origin and modalities of egress.

The soul, hereafter and here, is "buried in the Godhead" and "is God Himself" enjoying all things, disposing all things as does God. Thus, seemingly, is to be understood Eckhart's repeated insistence on the identification of the operations of the just man with the operations of the Divine Persons. The just man wills as God, thinks as God, proceeds as the Son, is principle of procession as the Father, is Providence, is Creator, and so on.

[5] *Treatise 15.* The original German is in *Meister Eckhart*, edited by Franz Pfeiffer (Göttingen, 1857), p. 537.

TEXTS [6]

SERMONS

Utrum in Deo sit Unum Esse

It does not seem to me that because He is therefore He understands, but because He understands therefore He is, in such wise that, because He is intellect and understanding, the understanding is itself the foundation of existence itself. It is said in John 1: "In the beginning was the Word, and the Word was with God, and the Word was God." The Evangelist does not say: "In the beginning was being and God was being." The Word, moreover, is wholly ordered to understanding and is either speaking or spoken, not being or composed of being.

Quasi stella matutina

I said one day in class that the intellect was more noble than the will. . . . On the contrary, a teacher in another class held that the will was more noble than the intellect "because the will," said he, "grasps things as they are in themselves while the intellect grasps them as they are in itself, that is, in the intellect." That perhaps is true: an eye in itself is more noble than an eye that is painted on a wall. None the less, I say that the intellect is more noble than the will. The will in fact seizes God clothed in goodness; the intellect seizes Him stripped, such as He is, despoiled of goodness and of being.

Intravit Iesus

A man would never grow old were his spirit always united to God in this faculty. For the instant when God makes the first man, and the instant when the last man disappears, and the instant in which I am speaking, are all alike in God, for there exists [for God] only the present instant. But this man abides in that same light with God. That is why there is in him

[6] I translate from the Stuttgart edition. See Selected Bibliography. It is the convention to refer to Eckhart's sermons by the initial words of the Scriptural text, in Latin, on which they are based.

neither suffering nor succession [of events], but an eternity ever the same. This man, in truth, is able to be astonished at nothing; in him all things are in their [eternal] essence. Thus is he the recipient of nothing new nor of any accident whatsoever, for he abides in a Now which, always and without end, is itself new. Such is the divine splendor which resides in this faculty.

In hoc apparuit

What is a pure heart? It is a detached heart, isolated from creatures. For creatures, all of them, are able to do nothing else than stain those who use them. To use creatures is a fault which stains the soul. All creatures are a pure nothingness. Creatures like the angels are absolutely nothing. They are able only to soil for they are made of nothing. They were nothing and they are nothing. To make use of them is therefore to go against their nature. If I hold a burning coal in my hand, it will hurt me. That is all that we can derive from the use of creatures. If we do not succeed in ridding ourselves of them we shall never be pure.

Iusti autem

To God is honor due. Who are they that honor Him? Those who are completely gone out of themselves and no longer seek their own interest in any thing be it little or great, who seek for nothing either beneath them or above them or on either side of them, who pursue neither good, nor glory, nor approbation, nor pleasure, nor profit, nor interior devotion, nor sanctity, nor recompense, nor the Kingdom of Heaven, but are separated from all of that, separated from all that pertains to them; it is from them that God receives glory, they glorify God in giving Him His due.

Expedit vobis

So long as any thing is still object of our gaze we are not yet one with The One. For there where is only The One, only The One is beheld. . . .

Every creature is as a "beam" in the soul's eye since, by its very nature as creature, it is an obstacle to union with God.

Thus, so long as anything creaturely remains in the soul, it must get outside of itself. Nay more, it should reject even the saints and angels, yes, and the Blessed Virgin, for they are all creatures. The soul should remain in nakedness, without any needs, for God is thus in nakedness and without any need. In other words, it is stripped of matter that the soul attains to God. It is only thus that it succeeds in uniting itself to the Blessed Trinity. But its happiness can become even greater yet if the soul search out the naked Godhead, for the Trinity is only the manifestation of the Godhead. In the pure Godhead there is absolutely no activity. The soul attains to perfect beatitude only in throwing itself into the desert of the Godhead there where there are neither operations nor forms, to bury itself there and lose itself there in that wilderness where its ego is annihilated and where it has no more care than it had in the days before it existed. Then only is it dead to itself and alive only to God. The Godhead is its sepulcher. This it is that St. Paul said: "You are dead and your life is hidden in God with Christ. . . ."

Listen now to how one can know that he is inserted in the Trinity. By this, first of all: the contemplation of the Holy Ghost purifies the soul of all fault, in such a way that it forgets itself and all things else. Then, what it receives from the Godhead is the eternal Wisdom of the Father, the knowledge and understanding of all things. In this way the soul is no longer reduced to appearance, to conjecture, to faith, for it has arrived at the Truth. Finally, the noble soul, which in union with the Word is inserted into the Holy Trinity, obtains, in an instant, some of the fortitude and power of the Father, so that it will be possible for it to do all things.

Nolite timere

Listen attentively. All creatures direct their course towards their highest perfection. All feel the need to raise themselves from their existence to their essence. All creatures are congregated within my intellect. I alone prepare them to return to God. You, all of you, look to what you are doing. Listen to me, this I beg of you by the eternal Truth and my immortal soul.

Godhead and God are realities as distinct as Heaven and earth; God appears when all creatures speak of Him. All creatures do speak of God. Why do they not then speak of the Godhead? Because all that is in the Godhead is unity, and one can say nothing of it. God operates; the Godhead does not.

God and Godhead differ as differ operation and nonoperation. . . .

When I have returned into the Godhead . . . no one has perceived my absence because it is there that God disappears.

Happy are they who have understood this sermon. Had there been no one here I should have preached it to the poor box.

THE TALKS OF INSTRUCTION II

It is necessary to pray with such energy that one would wish that all one's members and all one's strength, one's eyes, ears, mouth, heart, and all one's senses were straining within one. One should not cease before having had the impression that one has become one with Him who is present and to whom one prays, that is, God.

SELECTED BIBLIOGRAPHY

Editions

The first complete, genuinely critical edition is *Meister Eckhart: Die deutschen und lateinischen Werke,* Herausgegeben im Auftrage der Deutschen Forschungsgemeinschaft (Stuttgart, 1936, etc.); it supersedes all previous efforts.

Translations

H. Blackney, *Eckhart* (New York, 1949) is still useful. James M. Clark, in his *Meister Eckhart: An Introduction to the Study of His Works with an Anthology of His Sermons* (Edinburgh-New York-Toronto, 1957) and—with John V. Skinner—his *Treatises and Sermons of Meister Eckhart* (New York, 1958) provides more competent versions.

Studies

Much of Eckhartian scholarship continues to be passionately argumentative, divided almost equally between proponents of his orthodoxy or self-appointed prosecutors of his heterodoxy. Among the best who think well of him, one may profitably consult Otto Karrer, *Meister Eckhart: Das System seiner religiösen Lehre und Lebensweisheit* (Munich, 1926), and Herma Piesch, *Meister Eck-*

hart: Eine Einführung (Vienna, 1946). Prosecutors of the better sort are Frank Pelster, S.J., "Ein Gutachten aus dem Eckhart-Prozess in Avignon" (in the symposium, *Aus der Geisteswelt des Mittelalters* [Münster, 1936], pp. 1099-1124) and G. Della Volpe, *Eckhart o della Filosofia Mistica* (Rome, 1952). Grinding no axes of any sort, Benno Schmoldt discusses most illuminatingly Eckhart's Middle High German vocabulary in his *Die deutsche Begriffssprache Meister Eckhart* (Heidelberg, 1954).

XVI

RICHARD ROLLE

(d. 1349)

ST. EDMUND RICH is the portent of a change in the religious atmosphere of Britain.[1] Richard Rolle is initial evidence that the change took place.

He would have preferred, poor man, to have ended up something better than a human barometer from which a later age might learn what the weather was like in England's soul in the fourteenth century. For he, as many another before his time and since, seems desperately to have wished to be a mystic. And he thought he was. And he said he was. But no one believes him.

He describes, as in the third selection below, an experience in prayer of *calor, dulcor,* and *canor,* that is, of fire, sweetness, and song. The experience, he says, became habitual to him. Many a mystic has felt the same but as an overflowing into the senses of an experience which was centered in the soul. And most mystics have learned early to distinguish between these bodily reflexes and the essential reality of their profound, lived awareness of God. Rolle seems to have known nothing more than the feelings which, not essential to mystical experience, can be most easily self-induced by the honestly pious and by those, pious to a fault (I will not say dishonest), like himself.

TEXTS

In searching the scriptures as best I could I have found and realized that the highest love of Christ consists of three things —fire, song and sweetness. . . . I call that heat, when the mind is truly set on fire with divine love and the heart is felt similarly

[1] See p. 113.

to burn with a love, not in imagination but really. For a heart turned into fire gives the feeling of the fire of love. Song I call it when now the sweetness of eternal praising is received in the soul with abundant heat, and thought is turned into song, and the mind dwells upon sweet melody.[2]

If you will begin today to meditate, you shall discover a sweetness which will draw your heart up to heaven, and which will make you weep and long greatly for Jesus. And all your thoughts shall be of Jesus, and so they shall be received above all earthly things, above the firmament and the stars, so that the eye of your heart may look into heaven.

And then you enter into the third degree of love, in which you shall have great comfort and delight, if you may obtain the grace to come to it. For I do not say that you or any one else who reads this shall accomplish it all; for it is according to the will of God whom He chooses to do what is said here, whom He wishes to do other things in other ways, as He gives grace to men to have their salvation. For different men obtain different graces from our Lord Jesus Christ, and all shall be placed in the joy of heaven who end their life in love. Whoever is in this degree has wisdom and discretion to love according to the will of God.

This degree is called contemplative life, the life which loves to be solitary, not clamoring or making a noise, not singing or crying aloud. At the beginning, when you come to this degree, the eye of your spirit is taken up into the bliss of heaven, and there it is illumined with grace and kindled with the fire of Christ's love, so that you shall truly feel love burning in your heart more and more, raising your thoughts to God, and feeling such great love and joy and sweetness that no sickness or anguish or shame or penance may afflict you, but all your life shall be turned into joy; and then, because your heart is so exalted, your prayers shall turn into joyful song and your meditations into melody. Then Jesus shall be all your desire, all your delight, all your joy, all your solace, all your comfort; I know that all your song shall be about Him and all your rest shall be within Him. Then you may say:

> I sleep and my heart wakes:
> Who shall to my lover say
> I long for His love for aye?

All who love the vanities and the darlings of this earth, and who set their hearts on anything else than the things of God,

[2] *The Fire of Love*, I, xiv. From David Knowles, *The English Mystical Tradition* (New York-London, 1961), pp. 66-67.

shall never come to this degree, nor to the second degree of love which I named before. And therefore you must forsake all worldly solace, so that your heart is not inclined to the love of any created thing or to any earthly concerns, so that you may be in silence, so that your heart may always be steadfastly and valiantly fixed upon the love and the fear of God. Our Lord does not give beauty and riches and delights to men so that they should set their hearts on them and waste them in sin, but so that they shall know Him and love Him and thank Him for all His gifts.[3]

I was sitting in a certain chapel, and while I was taking pleasure in the delight of some prayer or meditation, I suddenly felt within me an unwonted and pleasant fire. When I had for long doubted whence it came, I learned by experience that it came from the Creator and not from creature, since I found it ever more pleasing and full of heat. Now from the beginning of that fiery warmth, inestimably sweet, till the infusion of the heavenly, spiritual harmony, the song of eternal praise, and the sweetness of unheard melody, which can be heard and experienced only by one who has received it, and who must be purified and separated from the earth, nine months and some weeks passed away.

For when I was sitting in the same chapel, and was reciting psalms as well as I might before supper, I heard above me the noise of harpers, or rather of singers. And when with all my heart I attended to heavenly things in prayer, I perceived within me, I know not how, a melody and a most delightful harmony from heaven, which abode in my mind. For my thought was straightway changed into a song, and even when praying and singing psalms I gave forth the selfsame sound. Thenceforth I broke out within my soul into singing what previously I had said, for abundance of sweetness, but in secret, for it must be in the presence of my Maker alone. I was not recognized by those who saw me, lest if they had known me they would have honored me beyond measure, and so I would have lost part of the fairest flower and would have fallen into desolation. Meanwhile wonder seized me that I was taken up into such joy, and that God should have given me gifts which I knew not how to ask for, nor had thought that any, even the most holy, would receive such in this life. Certainly I think that this is granted to none as a thing merited, but freely to whom Christ has willed it. Yet I think that no one will receive it, unless he love specially the name of Jesus, and

[3] *I Sleep and My Heart Wakes.* From *The Mediaeval Mystics of England,* edited and translated by Eric Colledge (New York-London, 1961-1962), pp. 151-152.

honor it so that he never allow it to fall from his memory save in sleep. He to whom this is given will, I think, achieve that other. So, from the beginning of my conversion to the highest degree of the love of Christ that I could attain by God's gift, the degree in which I sang the divine praises with joyful melody, was four years and about three months. This state, together with the former ones that prepared for it, remains to the end of my life. After death it shall be more perfect, because here the joy of love and the fire of charity begins, and in the heavenly kingdom it will receive most glorious consummation. And indeed he who is set upon these degrees or this life goes forward not a little, but does not rise to another state, nay rather, as it were confirmed in grace he is at peace so far as mortal man may be. Wherefore I long to return thanks and praises to God without ceasing.[4]

SELECTED BIBLIOGRAPHY

Editions

The Middle English text of the *Meditations, Lyrics,* and the *Epistles,* together with a selection from other writings, has been edited by Hope Emily Allen, *English Writings of Richard Rolle* (Oxford, 1931). The Latin original of *The Fire of Love* has been edited by Margaret Deanesly, *The "Incendium Amoris" of Richard Rolle of Hampole* (Manchester, 1915).

Translations

G. C. Heseltine, *Selected Works of Richard Rolle* (London, 1930), provides versions in modern English of the *Epistles,* the *Mending of Life,* and some commentaries on Scripture.

Studies

James Gilmour, "Notes on the Vocabulary of Richard Rolle," *Notes and Queries,* Number 201 (1956), 94-95; Gabriel M. Liegy, "Richard Rolle's *Carmen Prosaicum,* an Edition and Commentary," *Mediaeval Studies,* XIX (1957), 15-36, and "The 'Canticum amoris' of Richard Rolle," *Traditio,* XII (1956), 369-391. David Knowles, *The English Mystical Tradition* (New York-London, 1961-1962), pp. 48-66, provides the balanced, learned, gracious statement one would expect of him.

4 *The Fire of Love,* I, xv; Knowles, *op. cit.,* pp. 69-72.

XVII

"A FRIEND OF GOD"

(fl. 1350)

THROUGHOUT the Rhineland provinces in the fourteenth century were to be found people who called themselves, and were called by others, "The Friends of God." Not a religious community, much less a sect, their numbers were made up from every class of society and included both ecclesiastics and laity. Their splendidly honorific title was honestly and simply come by. Amid the encompassing moral degradation of both ecclesiastics and laymen, they sought by an intense spiritual life to draw close to, to be "the friends" of God. Amid laxity, they sought severity, and the deeper and more intimately they could work it into the fabric of their interior lives the better.

A spirituality excellently tailored to such a purpose was at hand in the sermons which, rightly or wrongly, circulated about under the name of Meister Eckhart.

The anonymous author of the selections given below could be thought to have done little more than provide an extended development of a short sermon of Eckhart on poverty of spirit. He could also be thought to have done little more than provide a development in Christian terms of an *Ennead* of Plotinus. The interior stripping to the point of absolute poverty of spirit appears in no way unlike the purification advised by Plotinus. Inevitably with all three—Eckhart, Plotinus, and our author here—the contemplation of the Divinity is the consequence. But as Plotinian doctrine came to St. Augustine in the morally fetid air of Carthage as a first, liberative blessing, so may it have been for the Friends of God in their not dissimilar place and time.

TEXTS[1]

THE BOOK OF THE POOR IN SPIRIT

There is a speaking of God in the core of the soul where no creature can enter or speak, for only God lives there and only He speaks. God speaks there when the soul puts aside all that is created, when she silences her powers and gains a vision into the foundation of her pure essence.

In this pure and silent soul God the Father speaks and she hears His voice. And this hearing is simply an inner feeling of God in the centre of the soul, a feeling which overflows into all her powers and with such a joy that she would gladly forgo her action and allow God alone to act, only attending to His leadings. The more she withholds from action, the more God acts in her.[2]

Some negate natural knowledge and others affirm it. Yet it must be both negated and affirmed. It is to be negated, for, though man's mind may penetrate all knowledge and distinction, and though man may have a real distinction of all truth in himself, still he must forgo all distinction and carry himself towards his centre with unity and into unity. And he should remain in this unity and contemplate it with a simple and single urge. Then all natural knowledge should leave, for it consists in images and forms, and man can never really know God through images. Since he must finally know Him without them, the spirit must be stripped of all images. . . . Knowledge seeks that which is stripped, namely, the naked truth, and it is never satisfied until it enters in complete nakedness and sees God and knows Him without medium. When it comes into Nothing all natural marks disappear and the soul becomes unoccupied and rests in pure peace. It is then that the spirit arrives at the source from which it flowed. In this way natural knowledge is negated, and in this way it is necessary that one should become empty of his natural knowledge if he desires true spiritual poverty. His knowledge is so magnified with divine charity in this nakedness and poverty of spirit that nothing remains of the knowledge that belongs to him only naturally.[3]

[1] From *The Book of the Poor in Spirit* by A Friend of God, edited and translated by C. F. Kelley (New York-London, 1955).
[2] Kelley, *op. cit.*, p. 134.
[3] *Op. cit.*, p. 82.

Man should draw in his senses and attend to the inner man because man's best part is within. And it is right that one should serve the best and forgo the worst. To favour the senses is to act like a man who forsakes his best friend in favour of a foe.[4]

The man who really desires divine love must so control his passion and silence his faculties as to be able to hear what God speaks in the soul.[5]

The source of divine love is in the eternal Word that God utters in the soul and he who ignores this fails in the foundation of divine love. Man should, then, turn all his senses and powers towards the eternal Word in order to attain to the source of divine love.[6]

He who wants to receive something from another must be with him from whom he would receive. And all that is in man should be inwardly with God, since that is where God is. In this way only can divine love be received.

One should draw in his senses because each time he turns to the exterior, the senses contact something impure, carry it with them and spoil the soul. He who wishes to remain pure should keep his senses within and not allow them to wander, and in this way his heart will stay at peace. Should one wander too much towards external things even for the sake of good works, he will not have true peace of heart, for this peace of God is beyond the senses.[7]

To illustrate this [*sc.* how the mind loses itself in God], let us consider a man who throws a stone into a bottomless sea. As the stone must continually sink, yet never reach ground nor be brought out again unless it rests somewhere (and this is impossible since the sea is unfathomable), so it happens with the mind which has thrown itself into the unfathomable Godhead. He sinks continually, but finds no stopping place. No one can bring him out again and he has no final ground where he can stop and rest. He has broken away from the created; hence no creature can reach him and he thus lives for ever in God. He can no more come out of the Godhead than the stone can rise again to the surface by its own force.

Because sensuous men cannot understand this, they say: As long as a man lives in time he can always fall. This is quite

[4] *Op. cit.*, pp. 262-263.
[5] *Op. cit.*, p. 259.
[6] *Op. cit.*, p. 259.
[7] *Op. cit.*, pp. 263-264.

true. But the men we have spoken of do not live in time, for their "dwelling-place is in heaven," as St. Paul says.[8] He who enters this dwelling must remain there. For example, if a man is bound by bonds so strong that he cannot break them, he cannot, people will say, become free unless he is helped. It is in this way that the mind is bound by God. Even if all creatures united their strength, they could not break this bond. And the mind has become so powerless over itself that it is unable of itself to break the bond.

One will immediately say: If this is so, then the freedom of the will is taken away. My answer is that the freedom of the will is not taken away from but given to it, for the will is quite free when it cannot endure anything except what God wills. We say that a king is free who conquers all his enemies and rules mightily in his kingdom.[9]

SELECTED BIBLIOGRAPHY

Editions

Long thought to be the work of John Tauler, *The Book* has often been published as his *Nachfolgung des Armen Lebens Christi* (for instance, at Frankfurt in 1833 and Regensburg in 1855). The first critical edition was provided by the man who first successfully disputed its ascription to Tauler, Heinrich Seuso Denifle, O.P., *Das Buch von geistlicher Armuth* (Munich, 1877).

Translations

The Following of Christ by J. R. Morell (London, 1886) is a literal translation into an antiquated English. Felicitous throughout is C. F. Kelley's version, *The Book of the Poor in Spirit* (New York-London, 1955), as the passages selected above indicate.

Studies

The religious atmosphere, of which *The Book* is simply a distillation, has been magisterially discussed by W. Zippel, *Die Mystiker und die deutsche Gesellschaft des 13. und 14. Jahrhunderts* (Düren, 1935). See, as well, Maurice de Grandillac, "Tradition et développement de la mystique rhénan," *Mélanges de science religieuse,* III (1946), 37-82, and Rufus M. Jones, *The Flowering of Mysticism: The Friends of God in the Fourteenth Century* (New York, 1939).

[8] Philippians 3:20.
[9] *Op. cit.,* pp. 166-167.

XVIII

TAULER

(c. 1300—1361)

FOR CENTURIES, actually up until the latter part of the nineteenth century, *The Book of the Poor in Spirit* was thought to have been written by John Tauler, Dominican, the Rhineland's most influential preacher and spiritual guide in the days of its mystical flowering. This false ascription can serve to remind one of three important characteristics of the man and his doctrine.

Some of the Friends of God became suspect of heresy, and rightly so; what better way, then, to assure currency to this quite orthodox work than to send it about under the name of the quite orthodox Tauler. This sort of pious deception, which we saw to have successfully preserved the most important writings of Evagrius, was liberally engaged in during the Middle Ages.

Again, the doctrine of *The Book* is very much that of Eckhart, and such, too, is the doctrine of Tauler in his authentic works.

Finally, the comparative restraint which recommended *The Book* to so many generations of readers is one of Tauler's distinctions as a writer on mystical subjects.

It is not difficult to imagine the attraction that Tauler's teaching would have for the Friends. They very much *wanted* to be good, and he emphasized the will. This emphasis provides the chief difference between Eckhart and himself. Eckhart's writings are shot through with intellectualism: the seat of mystical experience is *Vernunft,* "reason." For Tauler it is *Gemüt,* which to judge by the contexts in which it is used would be perhaps best translated by something like "root-will."

However, as is clear from the selected texts that follow, it is a *Gemüt* which is directed to an Eckhartian—and Plotinian—task.

TEXTS [1]

SERMONS

However pure and noble the visual impressions may be, they still form an obstacle for the perfect vision, God himself. If the soul wants to reflect the Sun, it must be bare and free from all other impressions, because even one will obstruct the reflection.[2]

Visual impressions, whatever they may be, only hinder you because there is the danger that they may blur your true self. If you were to rid yourself of them and their characteristics, though you possessed a kingdom, it could do you no harm.[3]

Moses said: "Verily thou art a hidden God." He is far deeper hidden in all things than the pith of the soul is hidden from man. He is utterly hidden in the ground of truth, incomprehensible to man. That is wherein you should penetrate, using your entire strength to leave far behind every thought of your worldliness, which is as remote and alien to the inner self as only an animal can be, living, as it does, without knowledge, perception or awareness of anything except its senses. Sink down and hide in the seclusion from all worldly influences, from everything foreign and not attuned to the Essence of all things. But this is not meant to be said for the sake of mere metaphors and mental reflections, it should be done really and truly, stretching your will to the utmost and longing to rise above the senses. Then man may witness the uniqueness of divine solitude within a silent seclusion where never a word is spoken—the essential meaning of the Word is not put into language—nor one single action performed. It is utterly still, hidden and lonesome, nothing but God in his purity reigns there, nothing alien or creaturely, no image or sound have ever reached thus far.

[1] From *Signposts to Perfection, A Selection from the Sermons of Johann Tauler,* edited and translated by Elizabeth Strakosch (St. Louis-London, 1958).
[2] Strakosch, *op. cit.,* p. 24.
[3] *Op. cit.,* p. 24.

Our Lord spoke of this solitude when he bade the prophet Joel speak thus: "I will lead my own into the wilderness and I will speak to their hearts." [4] This wilderness is his silent, lonesome Godhead to which he wants to lead all those who are to be taught to respond to his whisper, now and in all eternity. Take your vain and lonely ground, which is filled with weeds and devoid of all goodness, and where the wild beasts of your animal senses and forces reign supreme, into God's solitary, still and free ground.

Then you will contemplate the divine darkness, which by its blinding clearness appears dark to human and even to the angels' understanding, just as the resplendent orb of the sun appears dark to the weak eye; for it is in the nature of all created understanding that, compared with the divine clarity, it is as small as a swallow's eye when compared with the size of the sun and as far as this understanding is merely of the natural order it must be beaten back into unconsciousness so that it can do no more harm.

You should, however, endure your abysmal darkness, devoid and in need of the true light as it is, and leave the deep gulf of divine darkness to be known only to itself, unknown to all creatures and things. This gulf, unaware, unnamed and blessed, inspires more love and sets more souls aflame than all the understanding of the divine Being which can be gained in eternal bliss.[5]

SELECTED BIBLIOGRAPHY

Editions

Standard is the text established by Ferdinand Vetter, *Die Predigten Taulers* (Berlin, 1911); but it is somewhat less than ideal, because of omissions and false ascriptions (on which see P. Strauch, *Zu Taulers Predigten,* Number 44 in "Beiträge zur Geschichte der deutschen Sprache und Literatur" [Halle, 1920]).

Translations

Sermons of John Tauler, translated by Walter Elliott, C.S.P. (Washington, 1910); *The History and Life of the Revd Dr John Tauler of Strasbourg* by Susanna Winkworth (London, 1857) contains translations of a number of the sermons, not all of which are authentic any more than they are in the Elliott version. The trans-

[4] Actually the reference is to Hosea 2:14.
[5] *Op. cit.,* pp. 131-132.

lation by Elizabeth Strakosch, used above, contains only genuine writings.

Studies

A detailed treatment of Tauler's influence upon Martin Luther is provided in Julius Köstlin, *Luthers Theologie in ihrer Geschichtlichen Entwicklung dargestellt* (Stuttgart, 1863). Tauler the preacher is studied in Dick Helander, *Johann Tauler als Prediger* (Lund, 1923); Tauler the theologian, in F. W. Wentzlaff-Eggebert, *Studien zur Lebenslehre Taulers* (Berlin, 1939).

XIX

BLESSED HENRY SUSO

(c. 1296—1366)

LIKE TAULER, Suso began to write only after the condemnation of Eckhart, their common teacher; so his doctrine is, as Tauler's, a comparatively restrained version of Eckhart. Like St. Mechtilde, he was a poet whose language was that of courtly love (the which, by then in decadence, he restored to respectability) and whose verse forms were those of the Minnesingers.

Yet he was also very much his own man.

In his own person he effected the unlikely marriage of the Plotinian doctrine found in the Pseudo-Dionysius with the Franciscan doctrine of the following of Christ. More than that, he set his face firmly against a doctrine that had a long and noble history before ever it was popularized anew by Eckhart, that of the birth of Christ in the souls of believers.[1] He described, as did Eckhart, the transformation of the Christian as a "being born." But unlike Eckhart he held that it was the Christian who then came to birth, not Christ. And for him, unlike Eckhart, there was nothing in the least mystical to be claimed for it.

Historians are pretty generally agreed that Suso knew what mystical experience was personally and not merely—as Eckhart or Tauler—from the people he directed. The experience he described himself as having had seems to have been much

[1] Its history has been engagingly related by Hugo Rahner, S.J., "Die Gottesgeburt: Die Lehre der Kirchenväter von der Geburt Christi im Herzen des Gläubigen," *Zeitschrift für katholische Theologie*, LIX (1935), 333-418.

like that of St. Bernard—rapturous yet of the homiest quality, like Bernard's kettle a-bubble on the hearth.

TEXTS[2]

LITTLE BOOK OF TRUTH

There came over the Disciple a desire to know whether in any country there lived a self-abandoned man so noble that he had been rapt into God through Christ. If so, he asked God to help him to become acquainted with this man, that he might have confidential converse with him. Once, when his heart was full of longing, he began to sink into himself, his senses were dimmed, and it seemed to him that he was transported to a spiritual land. There he saw in mid-air an image, benign of aspect, hovering over a cross, as if it were the image of a man. There were two kinds of men thronging round this image, but they could not reach it. One kind of them contemplated the image only from within, and not from without, the others only from without, and not from within; but both faced the image, as if in opposition and obduracy. Then it seemed to him that the image came down to the ground like a real man, sat down beside him, and said that if he asked what he wanted to know, his questions would be answered.

He began speaking and sighing from the depths of his heart: "Ah, Eternal Truth, what is it, and what does this wonderful vision mean?" Then the answer came, and a voice spoke within him thus: "This image which thou hast seen, means the only-begotten Son of God, in the form in which He received human nature. Thou sawest only one image, and yet the image was endlessly diversified: this signifies the men who are His limbs, and are like the many members of a body. His head shone thus transcendent: this meant that He is the first and only-begotten Son, in accordance with the all-surpassing glory of being taken up into the self-hood of the Divine Person, but the others are only taken up into the transcendent unity of this image. The cross means that a truly self-abandoned man, in his outer and inner man, must at all times continue to be resigned to everything that God wills that he should suffer, from whatever direction it comes, so that he may be bowed down as in death, to accept it all to the glory of the heavenly Father. And such men are inwardly ennobled and outwardly armed.

[2] From Henry Suso, *Little Book of Eternal Wisdom* and *Little Book of Truth*, edited and translated by James M. Clark (New York-London, 1953).

If the image near the cross was so benign, that denotes that they despise all their sufferings, however great they may be, because of their own self-abandonment. In whatever way or direction the head turned, the body turned also: this signifies the uniformity with which they faithfully follow the mirror of His pure life and His good doctrine towards which they vigorously turn, and to which they conform themselves.

The first kind of men, who look at Him from within and not from without, denote those persons who only consider Christ's life intellectually, who are only contemplative, not active, whereas they should break through their own natures and practise the imitation of this image. They drag down everything the image suggests to the lusts of their own nature, and to reinforce their inordinate freedom, and everyone who does not agree with them in this seems to them to be coarse and unintelligent.

Some men, on the other hand, consider the image only from without, and not from within, and they seem to be hard and strict; moreover, they also exercise themselves severely, live carefully and display before men an honourable, holy exterior, but they overlook the inner Christ. Although His life was gentle and meek, these men are very quarrelsome; they condemn others, and everyone who does not live their way seems to them to be in error. The conduct of these persons is not like the life of Him whom they claim to follow, and this is to be seen in the fact that, if one observes them, they do not persevere in self-abandonment, in dying to their own natures, and moreover in giving up those desires, such as likes or dislikes and so forth, which strengthen self-will. Hence, their self-will is retained and increased, so that they do not attain the Divine virtues, such as obedience, patience in suffering, renunciation, and so on, which virtues, after all, lead men to the image of Christ.

The Disciple asked again forthwith, and said: Tell me, what dost thou call the manner in which a man attains his blessedness?

Answer: It may be called a birth, as it is written in Saint John's Gospel, that He gave also might and power to all who were born of nothing else than God, to become children of God.[3] And that takes place in the same way as birth is understood in common or general language. For that which gives birth to something else, forms it according to itself and in itself, and gives it a similar essence and activity. Therefore, the eyes of a self-abandoned man, whose Father is God alone, and in whom nothing temporal is born of the flesh, are opened, so that he understands himself, and then he receives

[3] John 1:12-13.

His precious essence and life, and is one with Him, for all things are one in the One.[4]

At this time a great change took place in him. It happened occasionally, in the course of ten weeks, more or less, that he was so powerfully rapt away that either in the presence of others, or when alone, his senses used to fade away, and ceased to perform their functions, so that everywhere in all things only One replied to him and all things were in One, without any diversity of this or that.

The Word began and spoke to him: How now, how are things now? Was I right?

He said: Yes.[5]

SELECTED BIBLIOGRAPHY

Editions

The most reliable text of the German writings is still that established by Karl Bihlmeyer, *Heinrich Seuse: Deutsche Schriften* (Stuttgart, 1907); of the *Horologe of Wisdom*—the most durably popular and influential of his writings—the best text is *Colloquia Dominicana . . . a Beato Henrico Susone dictata* (Munich, 1923).

Translations

Professor James M. Clark is Suso's authoritative English translator: *The Life of the Servant* (London, 1952); *Little Book of Eternal Wisdom* and *Little Book of Truth* (London, 1953).

Studies

Critical problems relative to the biography of Suso and the authenticity of works ascribed to him are faced in a fresh, often subjective, always stimulating fashion by C. Gröber, *Der Mystiker Heinrich Seuse* (Freiburg, 1941). J. A. Bizet situates Suso in his historical context with *Henri Suso et le déclin de la scolastique* (Paris, 1946) and in his literary context with *Suso et le Minnesang* (Paris, 1944).

[4] Clark, *op. cit.*, pp. 188-190.
[5] *Op. cit.*, p. 191.

XX

ST. CATHERINE OF SIENA

(1347—1380)

MORE PROBLEMS than he deserves stand in the way of the student who would learn of St. Catherine, the mystic.

The extraordinary public career that was hers in her attempt to restore unity to the Church tends to obscure all except St. Catherine, the politician. The eagerness of her followers that she make an impressive showing in the eyes of posterity has led to the introduction of the preposterous, as well as the unnervingly pious, into writings ascribed to her.

Fortunately, of late, literary sleuths have been devoting close attention to the *corpus Catherinum* and have so sorted out the authentic from the fictive that it is now possible, by basing oneself solely on the authentic writings, to make at least a few hesitant statements about the nature of her mystic experience.

First of all, she was a mystic. That fact stands out, not only in what she said about her experience, but also in the highly unsystematic way she said it. Not even the extensive editing zealously engaged in by her admiring contemporaries (for she could herself neither read nor write) succeeded in impressing doctrinal and literary consistency upon her statements.

In *The Dialogue* she dictated between December, 1377, and October, 1378, there is expressed a meeting with God under a variety of conflicting symbols: the interior home of the heart; herself outside herself, in the commerce of Christians; in

Christ; through Christ, and in the Father; Christ as Bridge;
Christ as Door; God as "Sea Pacific." And so on.

The most informative of the symbols is that, recurrent and
complex, of passage upon the Bridge which arches over the
threatening waters of this world, to—not dry land!—the Sea
Pacific. The student will find it helpful to give full advertence
(as later he must with Marie of the Incarnation) to what is
said of inundation in that Sea.

TEXTS [1]

THE DIALOGUE

The soul, who is lifted by a very great and yearning desire for
the honour of God and the salvation of souls, begins by exercising herself, for a certain space of time, in the ordinary
virtues, remaining in the cell of self-knowledge, in order to
know better the goodness of God towards her. This she does
because knowledge must precede love, and only when she has
attained love, can she strive to follow and to clothe herself
with the truth. But, in no way does the creature receive such a
taste of truth, or so brilliant a light therefrom, as by means of
humble and continuous prayer, founded on knowledge of herself and of God; because prayer, exercising her in the above
way, unites with God the soul that follows the footprints of
Christ crucified, and thus, by desire and affection, and union
of love, makes her another Himself. Christ would seem to have
meant this, when He said: *To him who will love Me and will
observe My commandment, will I manifest Myself; and he
shall be one thing with Me and I with him.*[2] In several places
we find similar words, by which we can see that it is, indeed,
through the effect of love, that the soul becomes another
Himself.[3]

Thou askest Me, then, for pains, so that I may receive satisfaction for the offences, which are done against Me by My
Creatures, and thou further askest the will to know and love
Me, who am the Supreme Truth. Wherefore I reply that this
is the way, if thou wilt arrive at a perfect knowledge and enjoyment of Me, the Eternal Truth, that thou shouldst never

---

[1] From *The Dialogue of St. Catherine of Siena,* translated by Algar
Thorold, new and abridged edition (London-Westminster, 1925-1943).

[2] Hardly an exact quotation. Compare, however, Chapter 14 of the
Gospel According to John.

[3] Thorold, *op. cit.,* pp. 26-27.

go outside the knowledge of thyself, and, by humbling thyself in the valley of humility, thou wilt know Me and thyself, from which knowledge thou wilt draw all that is necessary.[4]

Wishing to remedy your great evils, I have given you the Bridge of My Son, in order that, passing across the flood, you may not be drowned, which flood is the tempestuous sea of this dark life. . . . I say that this Bridge reaches from Heaven to earth, and constitutes the union which I have made with man. . . . Now learn that this Bridge, My only-begotten Son, has three steps. . . . On the first step, lifting her feet from the affections of the earth, the soul strips herself of vice; on the second she fills herself with love and virtue; and on the third she tastes peace. So the Bridge has three steps, in order that, climbing past the first and the second, you may reach the last, which is lifted on high, so that the water, running beneath, may not touch it.[5]

"Having climbed the three steps, [man] finds that the three powers of the soul have been gathered together by his reason in My Name. And his soul, having gathered together the two commandments, that is love of Me and of the neighbour, finds herself accompanied by Me, who am her strength and security, and walks safely because I am in the midst of her. Wherefore then he follows on with anxious desire, thirsting after the way of Truth, in which way he finds the Fountain of the Water of Life, through his thirst for My honour and his own salvation and that of his neighbour, without which thirst he would not be able to arrive at the Fountain. He walks on, carrying the vessel of the heart, emptied of every affection and disordinate love of the world, but filled immediately it is emptied with other things, for nothing can remain empty, and, being without disordinate love for transitory things, it is filled with love of celestial things, and sweet Divine love, with which he arrives at the Fountain of the Water of Life, and passes through the Door of Christ crucified, and tastes the Water of Life, finding himself in Me, the Sea Pacific."[6]

"Oh, best beloved daughter, how glorious is that soul who has indeed been able to pass from the stormy ocean to Me, the Sea Pacific, and in that Sea, which is Myself, the Supreme and Eternal Deity, to fill the pitcher of her heart."[7]

[4] *Op. cit.*, p. 32.
[5] *Op. cit.*, pp. 74, 75, 77, 78.
[6] *Op. cit.*, pp. 138-139.
[7] *Op. cit.*, p. 192.

SELECTED BIBLIOGRAPHY

Editions

All the literary problems attaching to the life and doctrine of St. Catherine have by no means been resolved as yet. R. Fawtier's *Sainte Cathérine de Sienne: Essai de critique des sources,* 2 volumes (Paris, 1927-1930), first properly alerted scholars to the scope and nature of the problems, and since then, because of him, the problems have become somewhat lessened. Thus the edition of the *Dialogue* by E. Franceschini (Milan, 1942) is generally reliable; that of the *Prayers* by I. Taurisano (Rome, 1932), only slightly less so.

Translations

The English version of the *Dialogue* by Algar Thorold has gone through many editions. Of complementary interest is *Saint Catherine of Siena as Seen in Her Letters,* translated and edited by Vida D. Scudder (New York, 1905).

Studies

H. C. Scheeben discusses possible influences upon Catherine's doctrine in "Katharina von Siena und ihre 'Seelenführer,'" *Geist und Leben,* XXX (1957), 281-293, 369-379. Perhaps overly systematic in its treatment of so unsystematic an experience, *L'unione mistica in Santa Caterina da Siena* by Reginald Garrigou-Lagrange, O.P. (Florence, 1938), is yet a stimulus to thought.

XXI

BLESSED
JAN VAN RUYSBROEK

(1293—1381)

COMPARISONS have a way of being odious. Accordingly, the reader's indulgence must be here solicited because comparisons, rather more odious than usual, must here be made.

How unpleasant the procedure will be may be immediately divined from this: giants such as Origen and Augustine and Bernard before him, and giants such as John of the Cross and Paul of the Cross after him, are to be seen as of lesser stature than this Prior of an obscure religious community in fourteenth-century Flanders. Who would not be made uncomfortable by such a prospect?

Born just south of Brussels in the village of Ruysbroek, whence his name, Jan became a secular priest at the age of twenty-four and for over a quarter century served at the collegiate church in Brussels itself. During this time he was in touch with the local Beguines, semireligious communities of women much given to charitable works and untraditional doctrines. Perhaps affected by their doctrine of the contemplative life he retired in 1343 with some friends to the Forest of Soignes just outside Brussels. Eventually he became an Augustinian and officially the Prior of his group. Nothing of these exterior events suggests the kind of man he really was. That can be learned (and scholars learn more each day) only from his writings, the most completely theological ever composed by a mystic.

The least happy doctrine of the Beguines, that one can attain to the immediate vision of God while yet on earth, he made—with capital reservations—his own. To do so at any time would be a hazardous business. To have done so then, after the condemnation of Beguine doctrine by the Council of Vienne in 1312, was especially so. But, so towering was his theological stature and so simple and true was his own mystic experience, Ruysbroek carried it off.

Three elements are distinguishable in his mystical doctrine: exemplarism, introspection, and union.

His exemplarism is superficially similar to that of Eckhart. The life of the Trinity is one of perpetual egress and regress from the unity of Nature to the plurality of Persons and back again. In the "exemplars" (Eckhart's "ideal created existents") the Christian attains in some sort an eternal life that shares in this unending egress and regress of the Trinity simply because the Christian's soul is modeled after the Trinity. Here Ruysbroek shows himself the inheritor of concepts from both St. Augustine and William of St. Thierry. The three higher faculties of memory, understanding, and will proceed from the unity of the oneness of spirit. This oneness-threeness, naturally possessed, should be (and this was William's contribution) possessed supernaturally.

By introspection the Christian thus discovers in the depths of his soul the living image of God and consciously associates himself, there where grace is, with the life of the three Divine Persons.

The union, therefore, is a union in awareness: a union that is both "without means" (that is, without intermediaries) and "without difference" (that is, beyond all distinction or act of the Persons).

Ruysbroek, familiar with the aberrations of the Beguines, was acutely conscious of the possibilities of delusion. In *The Spiritual Espousals* he gave detailed and comprehensive norms for judging such experiences aright. Rather too extensive for adequate summary here, they come down to that rule, traditional in the Church from the time of Christ to St. Teresa and beyond, that they are to be known by their fruits. For Ruysbroek, they are fraudulent if they leave one proud and hard to get along with.

This man's head was in the clouds; his feet, always on the ground.

TEXTS [1]

THE LIFE OF CONTEMPLATION OF GOD

For the heavenly Father wishes that we should see, because He is a Father of light.[2] And therefore He speaks eternally, without mean and without ceasing, in the secret places of our spirit, one single unfathomable word and nothing more. And in this word He enunciates Himself and all things. And this word is nothing else than "See"; and this is the going-out and the birth of the Son of everlasting light, in Whom men recognize and see all blessedness.

If the spirit is now with God to contemplate God without means in this Divine light, there are three things which are necessary to man. The first is that he must be well ordered in all virtues from without, and that within he be unhindered, and that he be empty of all outward works, just as though he performed nothing. For if within he is preoccupied with any work of virtue, so he is distracted by images. As long as this lasts in him, he is unable to contemplate. Secondly, he must within depend upon God with compelling intention and love, just as a kindled and glowing fire that never again can be put out. And when he feels himself to be thus, then he is able to contemplate. Thirdly, he must have lost himself in a lack of manner, and in a darkness in which all contemplative men fare in delectation, and can never again find themselves in any way natural to the creature.

In the depths of this darkness, in which the loving spirit has died to itself, begins the revelation of God and the eternal life. For in this darkness there shines and there is born an incomprehensible light, which is the Son of God, in Whom we contemplate eternal life. And in this light we see. And this Divine light is given in the simple being of the spirit, where the spirit receives the clarity which is God Himself, above all gifts and above all works of the creature, in the empty idleness of the spirit in which it, through delectable love, has lost itself and has received the clarity of God without mean. And the spirit becomes immediately the very clarity which it receives.

Behold how this secret clarity in which man contemplates all that he has desired, in the manner of the emptiness of the

[1] From Blessed Jan van Ruysbroek, *The Spiritual Espousals*, edited and translated by Eric Colledge (London-New York, 1952-1953), pp. 181-190.
[2] *Cf.* James 1:17.

spirit, this clarity is so great that the loving contemplative sees and feels in his depths where he rests nothing except an incomprehensible light. And according to the manner of this single nakedness which embraces all things, he finds himself and feels himself to be that very light by which he sees, and nothing else.

And in this you have the first point of how one sees in the Divine light. Blessed are the eyes that see thus, for they possess the eternal life.

After we have thus come to see, we may joyfully contemplate the eternal coming of our Bridegroom, and this is the second matter, of which we will now speak.

What is then this coming of our Bridegroom which is eternal? That is the new birth and a new illumination without cease. For the depths from which the clarity shines forth, and which are the clarity itself, are living and fruitful. And therefore the revelation of the eternal light is ceaselessly renewed in the hidden places of the spirit. Behold, all works of the creature and all exercises of virtue may here pass away, for here God alone is His only work in the highest excellence of the spirit. And here there is nothing else than an eternal contemplation and beholding of the light, with the light and in the light. And the coming of the Bridegroom is so swift that He is always come and is always dwelling within us with all His riches; and ceaselessly and ever and again He is coming in His own Person with new clarity, just as if He never were come before. For to be come consists in an eternal now, without time, which is constantly received in new joy and new delight.

Behold how the gladness and the joy which this Bridegroom brings in His coming are unfathomable and immeasurable, for so is He Himself. And therefore the eyes of the spirit, with which it contemplates and gazes upon its Bridegroom, are opened so wide that they never may be closed again. For this beholding and contemplating of the spirit remains eternally in the secret revelation of God, and the understanding of the spirit is opened so wide against the coming of the Bridegroom that the spirit itself becomes the wideness which it comprehends.

And so with God is God comprehended and seen, wherein lies all our blessedness. This is the second point concerning how we ceaselessly receive in our spirit the everlasting coming of our Bridegroom.

Now the Spirit of God says within the secret out-flowing of our spirit: "Go out in an eternal contemplation and delectation, according to the manner of God."

All the riches which are natural in God we possess through

love in God, and God possesses them in us, through the immeasurable love which is the Holy Ghost. For in this love men savour everything for which they can yearn. And therefore through this love we die to ourselves and go forth in a loving flowing-out, in darkness, and lacking all manner. There the spirit is embraced in the Holy Trinity, eternally remaining in the superessential unity in rest and in delectation. And in this same unity, according to the manner of fruitfulness, the Father is in the Son and the Son in the Father, and all creatures are in Them both. And this is above any differentiation of Persons, for here, so far as reason is concerned, we understand the nature of Fatherhood and Sonhood in a living fruitfulness of the Divine natures.

Out of this there springs and begins an everlasting going-out and an everlasting work without beginning. For here is a beginning that has no beginning. For since the Almighty Father in the depths of His fruitfulness has perfectly comprehended Himself, the Son is the everlasting Word of the Father, proceeding forth as a Second Person in the Divinity. And through the everlasting birth, all creatures proceed forth everlastingly, before ever they have been created in time. So they have seen and acknowledged God in themselves, discreetly according to the *ratio vivens,* and with that difference which is His, not, however, a difference in every respect, for everything which is in God is God.

This everlasting going-out and this eternal life which we evermore have in God, and which we are without ourselves, this is a cause of our created being in time. And our created being depends upon the everlasting Being, and it is essentially one with that Being. And this everlasting being and life which we have and are in the eternal wisdom of God, that is like to God. For it remains eternally without differentiation in the Divine Being, and it flows out eternally, through the birth of the Son, with difference and with differentiation according to the *ratio vivens.* And through these two points our being and life are so like to God that they ceaselessly acknowledge and imagine Him in this likeness as He is in Being and in Person. For even though, as the reason is concerned, all is here discretion and difference, this likeness is still one with that same image of the Holy Trinity which is the wisdom of God, in which God contemplates Himself and all things in an eternal instant before which nothing came, after which nothing goes. With a single glance He contemplates Himself and all things; and this is the image and likeness of God, and our image and our likeness, for in this God makes the image of Himself and of all things. In this image like to God, all creatures have an everlasting life, outside themselves, as it were in their everlasting exemplar. And the Holy Trinity made us in this ever-lasting image and in this likeness.

And therefore God would have us go forth from ourselves in this Divine light, and supernaturally attain to this image, which is our own life, and possess it with Him, operatively and in delectation, in everlasting blessedness. For there indeed we discern that the bosom of the Father is our own deepness and source, wherein we begin our life and our being. And out of our own deepness, that is, out of the Father and out of all that lives in Him, there shines an eternal clarity, which is the birth of the Son. And in this clarity, that is, in the Son, the Father and all that lives in Him is made manifest to Himself. For all that He is and all that He has He gives to the Son, except only His attribute of Fatherhood, which He Himself retains. And therefore all that lives in the Father, concealed in unity, lives in the Son, flowing out and made manifest; and evermore the simple deepness of our everlasting image remains hidden in darkness and without manner. But the unmeasured clarity which shines forth from this makes manifest that concerning God which is hidden, and gives to it a manner. And all men who are exalted above their created nature into a life of contemplation are one with this Divine clarity, and they are the clarity itself. And they behold and feel and discover themselves, by means of this Divine light: they discover that they are this same single deepness, according to the manner of their uncreated nature, whence clarity shines forth without measure in a godlike manner, and yet remains evermore without manner, according as their being within is simple and single.

And therefore men who are inward and contemplative must go out, according to the manner of contemplation, beyond reason and beyond discretion; and beyond their created nature, with an everlasting beholding in this inborn light, and so they shall become transformed, and one with this same light by which they see, and which they are. And so contemplative men attain to that everlasting image in which they are made, and they contemplate God and all things without any discretion in a single act of beholding in Divine clarity. And this is the most excellent and the most profitable contemplation to which a man can attain in this life. For in this contemplation best of all does man remain free and master of himself, and he can increase in every meritorious form of living, each time that with love he turns inward, beyond all that men can understand. For he remains free and master of himself in inwardness and in virtue. And that beholding in the Divine light preserves him about all inwardness and above all virtue and above all merit, for it is the crown and the prize for which we strive, and which in this manner we now have and possess, for the life of contemplation is the light of heaven. But if we were set free from this our exile, then we should be more apt in our being to receive the clarity, and so should the glory of God better and more excellently shine forth upon us.

This is the manner above all manners in which man goes out in a Divine contemplation and in an everlasting beholding, and in which he is transformed and formed again in Divine clarity.

This going-out of the contemplative man is also loving. For through delectable love he passes beyond his created nature, and finds and savours the riches and the joy which are God Himself, and which cause the secret places of the spirit immediately to be transfused, when now he stands made like to the high excellence of God.

When the inward contemplative man has thus attained his everlasting image, and in this purity, by means of the Son, possesses the bosom of the Father, he is illumined with Divine truth. And each hour he receives afresh the everlasting birth, and he goes out, according to the manner of the light, in a Divine contemplation. And from this there springs the fourth point and the last, which is a loving meeting, in which above all else our highest blessedness consists.

You shall know that the heavenly Father, as He is a living depth, has gone operatively with all that lives in Him into His Son, as into the everlasting wisdom which is He; and this same wisdom, and all that lives in it, is operatively returned again into the Father, that is into the same depths whence it proceeds. And from this meeting perhaps springs the third Person, between the Father and the Son, that is the Holy Ghost, the love of Them both, Who is one with both of Them in the same nature. And the Holy Ghost embraces and transfuses, operatively and in delectation, the Father and the Son and all that lives in Them, with so great riches and joy that concerning this all creatures must evermore be silent. For the incomprehensible miracle that lies in this love everlastingly exceeds the comprehension of all creatures. But in the spirit, above himself and one with the Spirit of God, man understands and savours this wonder without wonderment, and tastes and sees without measure as God does, the riches which are God, in the unity of the living depths where man possesses Him according to the manner of His uncreated being.

Then this most blessed meeting in us according to God's manner is ceaselessly renewed operatively. For the Father gives Himself in the Son, and the Son in the Father in an everlasting delight, Each in the Other, and a loving embracing, the One of the Other. And this is renewed every hour in the bond of love. For just as the Father ceaselessly contemplates all things anew in the birth of His Son, so all things are loved anew by the Father and by the Son in the flowing-out of the Holy Ghost.

And this is the operative meeting of the Father and of the Son in which we are lovingly embraced through the Holy Ghost in eternal love.

Now this operative meeting and this loving embrace are in their depths delectable and without manner. For God's impenetrable lack of manner is so dark and so without manner that in itself it comprehends all the Divine manners, and the work and the attributes of the Persons in the rich embrace of Their essential unity; and in the abyss of God's namelessness it makes a Divine delectation. And in this there is a delectable passing-over and a flowing-away and a sinking-down into the essential nakedness, with all the Divine names and all manners and all living reason which has its image in the mirror of Divine truth: all these fall away into this simple nakedness, wanting manner and without reason. For in this unfathomable joy of simplicity, all things are embraced in a delectable blessedness, and the depths themselves remain uncomprehended, except it be in our essential unity with God. Before this all created personality must fail, and all that lives in God, for here there is nothing but an eternal resting in a delectable embrace of the flowing-out of love.

And this is in the being without manner which all inward spirits have chosen above all things. This is the dark silence in which all lovers are lost. But could we thus, as I have told, so prepare ourselves in virtues, we should then hasten to divest ourselves of this our mortal flesh, and we should launch ourselves on the waves of this blessedness, and no creature ever call us back again.

That we in delectation may possess this essential unity, and that we may clearly contemplate Unity in Trinity, grant to us that Love which denies no prayer addressed to its Divinity.

AMEN. AMEN.

SELECTED BIBLIOGRAPHY

Editions

The text of his writings, in the original Thiois, has been critically established by the Ruusbroec-Genootschap at Antwerp: *Werken*, 2nd edition, 4 volumes (Tielt [Belgium], 1944-1948).

Translations

The Seven Steps of the Ladder of Spiritual Love, translated by F. Sherwood Taylor (London, 1944); *The Spiritual Espousals,* translated by Eric Colledge (London-New York, 1952-1953). *The Kingdom of Lovers* and *The Spiritual Espousals* have been excellently translated into French by J. A. Bizet, *Ruysbroeck: Oeuvres choisies* (Paris, 1946).

Studies

Long familiarity with Neoplatonism, as well as with Ruysbroek, has allowed Paul Henry, S.J., to provide in the space of two articles a brilliant synthesis of Ruysbroek's mystical doctrine: "La mystique trinitaire du bienheureux Jean Ruysbroek," *Recherches de science religieuse,* XL (1952), 335-368; XLI (1953), 51-75. The definitive exposition, however, is that by Albert Ampe, S.J., *De Mystieke Leer van Ruusbroec over den Zieleopgang* (Tielt, 1957); readers more comfortable in French than in Flemish will be grateful for Father Ampe's own summary of his interpretation: "La théologie mystique de l'Ascension de l'âme selon le Bx. Jean de Ruusbroec," *Revue d' ascétique et de mystique,* XXXVI (1960), 188-201, 273-302.

XXII

THE "THEOLOGIA GERMANICA"

THE *Theologia Germanica*, composed in the latter part of the fourteenth century by an author whose identity is still unknown, has had an undeservedly stormy time of it in the history of religious ideas.

The popularity, particularly, of Luther's editions served it but ill, for it made it a weapon in the wild polemics of Reformation and Counter-Reformation. Most notably, what the *Theologia* described as an inner experience of the soul was made over into a blunt dogmatic statement: good works are worthless.

Actually, as recent studies have made clear, its doctrine is quite traditional, indeed much more traditional than what is to be found in the writings of Eckhart or Tauler or Suso, which, however, it so much resembles. Tauler, whose influence upon it was very real, influenced it only in those areas where he was himself at one with the earliest tradition of the Church Fathers.

The concern of the *Theologia Germanica* is the man within. His high destiny, it teaches, is conscious union with God. His way thereto is through three stages. The first is purgative, the removal of the dross of sense as well as the dross of sin. The second is illuminative, a fitting Divine bestowal upon one whose self-will has been wholly set aside. The third is unitive: the soul is alight with grace and aflame with love and therefore "deified or divine."

These last words should lift the eyebrows of those alone who are utterly innocent of any knowledge of the theology of the Greek Church Fathers. As the conventional misinterpretations of the *Theologia* amply attest, in the fourteenth century and after there were many such innocents abroad.

TEXTS [1]

THEOLOGIA GERMANICA

A man who should be possessed by the Spirit of God, so that
he should not know what he did or left undone, and thus
should have no power over himself, but the will and Spirit of
God should have the mastery over him, and work, and do, and
leave undone with him and by him, and what and as it would;
such a man were one of those of whom Saint Paul says: "For
as many as are guided and led by the Spirit of God, they are
the sons of God, and are not under the law," [2] and to whom
Christ said: "For it is not you that speak, but the Spirit of your
Father which speaks in you." [3] But I fear that for one man who
is truly possessed with the Spirit of God, there are a hundred
thousand or an innumerable multitude possessed with the
Devil. This is because men have more likeness to the Devil
than to God. For I-hood, selfhood, Mine, Me, and the like, all
belong to the Devil. . . . Behold one or two words can say all
that has been said by many words: "Be simply and wholly
sundered from thy Self." [4]

"I would fain be to the Eternal Good, what his own hand is
to a man." [5]

So long as a man loves parts and fragments, and above all
himself, and holds converse with them, and makes account of
them, he is deceived and grows so blind that he knows good no
more; for what is most convenient and pleasant and profitable
to himself and what is his, these he holds to be the Best, and
loves above all. Thus he never comes to the Truth. [6]

Now it is objected that there be many who vainly think and
say that they are already so wholly dead and are come so far
beyond the self, that they live in a state where they suffer nothing and are moved by nothing, just as if all men were living in
obedience, and there were no creatures. And thus they profess

---

[1] From *Theologia Germanica.* The translation of Susanna Winkworth,
completely revised to accord with the modern version of Joseph
Bernhart. Introduction and Notes by Joseph Bernhart translated by
Wil.ard R. Trask (New York-London, 1949-1950).
[2] Romans 8:14; 6:14.
[3] Matthew 10:20.
[4] Chapter XXII; *op. cit.,* p. 150.
[5] Chapter X; *op. cit.,* p. 129.
[6] Chapter XIX; *op. cit.,* p. 147.

to continue always in an even temper of mind, so that nothing comes amiss to them, howsoever things fall out, be it this or be it that. Nay, verily! the matter stands not so, but it is as we have said. It might well be thus, if all men were in obedience. But the one thing being not, so neither is the other.[7]

The One in which God and man are united, stands free of itself and of all things, and whatever is in it is there for God's sake and not for man's, or the creature's. For the essential existence of God is without this and that, and without selfhood and I-hood, and the like; but it is the nature and property of the creature to seek itself and its own things, and this and that, here and there, and in all that it does and leaves undone its desire is to its own advantage and benefit. Now where a creature or a man denies and forsakes himself and his own and his selfhood, there God enters in with His own, that is, with Himself.[8]

Saint Paul says: "When that which is perfect is come, then that which is imperfect, and that which is in part, are cast away." [9] Now mark: What is "that which is perfect," and what "that which is in part"? That which is perfect is an Existence which comprehends and includes all existences in Itself and in Its Essence; and without which and beside which, there is no true being; and in which all things have their life. For It is the Essence of all things and is in Itself unchangeable and immovable, yet It changes and moves all things else. But that which is in part, or the imperfect, is that which has its source in, or has sprung from, the Perfect; just as a brightness or a visible appearance flows out from the sun or a candle. And appears to be somewhat, this or that, and is called a creature. And of all these partial things, none is the Perfect; so also the Perfect is none of these partial things. The partial things can be apprehended, recognized, and expressed; but the Perfect cannot be apprehended, recognized, or expressed by any creature in the measure of its creaturehood. Therefore we call the Perfect "Nothing," for it is not of the nature of creatures, therefore the creature as creature cannot recognize nor apprehend it, name nor conceive it.

Now, "When that which is Perfect is come, then that which is in part is rejected." But when does it come? I say: When, as much as may be, it is known, felt, and tasted in the soul. For the lack lies altogether in us, and not in it. In like manner the sun lights the whole world, and is as near to one as to another

[7] Chapter XVII; op. cit., pp. 143-144.
[8] Chapter XXIV; op. cit., p. 154.
[9] Cf. 1 Corinthians 13:10.

yet a blind man sees it not; but the fault lies in the blind man, not in the sun. And as the sun may not hide its brightness, but must give light to the earth (wheresoever the sky is cleansed and purified); so also God, who is the highest Good, wills not to hide Himself from any, wheresoever He finds a devout soul that is thoroughly purified from all creatures. For in what measure we put off the creature, in the same measure are we able to receive the Creator; neither more nor less. For if mine eye is to see any thing, it must be purified, or become purified from all other things; for if heat and light are to enter, cold and darkness must needs depart; it cannot be otherwise.

But some might say: "Now since the Perfect cannot be recognized nor apprehended by any creature, but the soul is a creature, how can it be recognized in the soul?" *Answer:* That is why we say, "in the measure of its creaturehood." This is as much as to say, "every creature in its creature-nature and created state," for this is impossible to it by virtue of its I-hood and selfhood. For in whatsoever creature the Perfect shall be known, therein creature-nature, created state, I-hood, self-hood, and the like, must all be given up and done away. This is the meaning of that saying of Saint Paul: "When that which is perfect is come" (that is, when it is recognized), "then that which is in part" (that is, I-hood, and creature-nature, qualities, desire) "will all be rejected and counted for nought." So long as we think of these things at all and cleave to them with love, joy, pleasure, or yearning, so long the Perfect remains unknown to us.

But it might further be said: "You say that beside the Perfect there is no Essence; yet again you say that something flows out from it: now is not that which has flowed out from it, something beside it?" *Answer:* That is why we say: Beside it, or without it, there is no true Essence! That which has flowed out from it, is no true Essence and has no Essence except in the Perfect, but is an accident, a brightness, or a visible appearance, which is no Essence, and has no Essence except in the Fire whence the brightness flows out, as in the case of the sun or a candle.[10]

SELECTED BIBLIOGRAPHY

Editions

The edition, antedating Luther's, of 1457 was discovered by Franz Pfeiffer and re-edited by him (Stuttgart, 1851). It is still much in

[10] Chapter I; *op. cit.,* pp. 113-115.

use but is inferior to the re-edition of Willo Uhl, *Der Frankforter* (Bonn, 1912).

Translations

The English version by Susanna Winkworth (London, 1854) has always been widely popular. In the selections above it appears in a revised form.

Studies

That the doctrine of the *Theologia* is wholly traditional has been ably defended by J. Paquier, *L'orthodoxie de la théologie german-ique* (Paris, 1922), and J. A. Bizet, "La querelle de l'Anonyme de Francfort," *Etudes germaniques*, III (1948), 201-207. A quantity of more general information is provided by Prof. G. Baring in his discussion of which—the edition of 1497 or Luther's editions of 1516 and 1518—best represents the primitive text: "Neues von der 'Theologia Deutsch' und ihrer weltweiter Bedeutung," *Archiv für Reformationsgeschichte*, XLVIII (1957), 1-11. The recent discov-ery of a manuscript of the *Theologia* dating from the latter half of the fifteenth century has destroyed one myth. It proves that Luther neither abbreviated nor elaborated nor modified in any way the manuscript he edited. On this see K. Ruh, "Eine neue Handschrift des 'Frankfurters' Cod. 482 de Münchener Universitätsbibliothek," *Zeitschrift für deutsches Altertum und deutsche Literatur*, LXXXIX (1958/1959), 280-287.

XXIII

THE AUTHOR OF "THE CLOUD"

(c. 1345—1386)

It is not known who wrote the most famous treatise on the mystical life to come out of mediaeval England, *The Cloud of Unknowing;* the dates indicated above are the result of literary detective work on the types of extant manuscripts, on the authors he cites, and on the early authors who cite him. Because of its fame, he has come to be referred to simply as "The Author" of that one sole work. The practice, although traditional by now, is unfortunate. Greater than *The Cloud* by far is another of his works, *The Epistle of Privy Counsel.*

The Cloud is a forthright exposition of the mystical theology of the Pseudo-Dionysius with, however, the modification from knowledge to love that was effected by St. Maximus the Confessor and which the author apparently knew from the writings of one of the later Victorines, Thomas Gallus (d. 1240). Doctrinal and literary dependencies such as these are never congenial to the expression of personal experiences and so, not unexpectedly, there is little of the personally revealing in *The Cloud.* It is, if you will, mysticism by the book.

Not so *The Epistle.* Its purpose is to explain to one of his disciples some of the obscure passages in *The Cloud.* In it the author is very much his own man.

Whether *The Cloud* or *The Epistle* attest their author a mystic, I must leave to others to decide. That he was a good director of mystics, every page of each of these works bears witness.

Let the concluding words of *The Cloud* testify to his knowingness as a Christian: "Not what you are, not what you have been does God regard with His merciful eyes, but what you would be. . . ."

TEXTS [1]

THE CLOUD OF UNKNOWING

Lift up thine heart unto God with a meek stirring of love; and mean himself and none of his goods. And thereto look that thou loathe to think on aught but himself, so that nought work in thy mind nor in thy will but only himself. And do that in thee as to forget all the creatures that ever God made and the works of them, so that thy thought or thy desire be not directed or stretched to any of them, neither in general nor in special. But let them be, with a seemly recklessness, and take no heed of them.[2]

At the first time when thou dost it, thou findest but a darkness, and as it were a cloud of unknowing, thou knowest not what, saving that thou feelest in thy will a naked intent unto God. This darkness and this cloud, howsoever thou dost, is betwixt thee and thy God, and hindereth thee, so that thou mayest neither see him clearly by light of understanding in thy reason, nor feel him in sweetness of love in thine affection. And therefore shape thee to bide in this darkness as long as thou mayest, evermore crying after him whom thou lovest. For if ever thou shalt see him or feel him, as it may be here, it must always be in this cloud and in this darkness.[3]

All reasonable creatures, angel and man, have in them, each one by himself, one principal working power, the which is called a knowing power, and another principal working power, the which is called a loving power. Of the which two powers, to the first, the which is knowing power, God who is the maker of them is evermore incomprehensible; but to the second, the which is the loving power, he is, in every man diversely, all comprehensible to the full.[4]

[1] From *The Cloud of Unknowing, and Other Treatises,* edited and translated by Dom Justin McCann, O.S.B., 5th edition (Westminster-London, 1947).
[2] Chapter III; McCann, *op. cit.,* p. 5.
[3] Chapter III; *op. cit.,* p. 6.
[4] Chapter IV; *op. cit.,* p. 7.

And if ever thou shalt come to this cloud and dwell and work therein as I bid thee, thou must, as this cloud of unknowing is above thee, betwixt thee and thy God, right so put a cloud of forgetting beneath thee, betwixt thee and all the creatures that ever be made. Thou thinkest, peradventure, that thou art full far from God, because this cloud of unknowing is betwixt thee and thy God; but surely, if it be well conceived, thou art full further from him when thou hast no cloud of forgetting betwixt thee and all the creatures that ever be made. As oft as I say "all the creatures that ever be made," so oft do I mean, not only the creatures themselves, but also all the works and the conditions of the same creatures. I except not one creature, whether they be bodily creatures or ghostly; nor yet any condition or work of any creature, whether they be good or evil. But, to speak shortly, all should be hid under the cloud of forgetting in this case.

For although it be full profitable sometimes to think of certain conditions and deeds of some certain special creatures, nevertheless in this work it profiteth little or nought. Because mind or thinking of any creature that ever God made, or of any of their deeds either, is a manner of ghostly light; for the eye of thy soul is opened on it and close fixed thereupon, as the eye of a shooter is upon the prick that he shooteth to. And one thing I tell thee, that everything that thou thinkest upon is above thee for the time and betwixt thee and thy God. And insomuch thou art the further from God, that aught is in thy mind but only God.

Yea—and if it be courteous and seemly to say—in this work it profiteth little or nought to think of the kindness or the worthiness of God, nor on our Lady, nor on the saints or angels in heaven, nor yet on the joys of heaven: that is to say, with a special beholding to them, as though thou wouldst by that beholding feed and increase thy purpose. I trow that on nowise it should help in this case and in this work. For although it be good to think upon the kindness of God, and to love him and praise him for it: yet it is far better to think upon the naked being of him, and to love him and praise him for himself.[5]

And therefore travail fast awhile, and beat upon this high cloud of unknowing, and rest afterwards. Nevertheless a travail shall he have, whoso shall use him in this work; yea, surely! and that a full great travail, unless he have a more special grace, or else he have for long time used him therein. But I pray thee, wherein shall that travail be? Surely not in

[5] Chapter V; *op. cit.*, pp. 10-11.

that devout stirring of love that is continually wrought in his will, not by himself, but by the hand of Almighty God, who is evermore ready to work this work in every soul that is disposed thereto, and that doth what in him is, and hath done long time before, to enable him to this work.

But wherein then is this travail, I pray thee? Surely, this travail is all in treading down of the thought of all the creatures that ever God made, and in holding of them under the cloud of forgetting named before. In this is all the travail; for this is man's travail, with the help of grace. And the other above—that is to say, the stirring of love—that is the work of only God. And therefore do on thy work, and surely I promise thee he shall not fail in his.[6]

Look that nought work in thy mind nor in thy will but only God. And try to smite down all knowing and feeling of aught under God, and tread all down full far under the cloud of forgetting. And thou shalt understand that in this work thou shalt forget not only all other creatures than thyself, or their deeds or thine, but also thou shalt in this work forget both thyself and thy deeds for God, as well as all other creatures and their deeds. For it is the condition of a perfect lover, not only to love that thing that he loveth more than himself; but also in a manner to hate himself for that thing that he loveth.

Thus shalt thou do with thyself: thou shalt loathe and be weary with all that thing that worketh in thy mind and in thy will, unless it be only God. For otherwise surely, whatsoever it be, it is betwixt thee and thy God. And no wonder if thou loathe and hate to think on thyself, when thou shalt always feel sin a foul stinking lump, thou knowest never what, betwixt thee and thy God: the which lump is none other thing than thyself. For thou shalt think it oned and congealed with the substance of thy being: yea, as it were without separation.

And therefore break down all knowing and feeling of all manner of creatures; but most busily of thyself. For on the knowing and the feeling of thyself hangeth the knowing and the feeling of all other creatures; for in regard of it, all other creatures be lightly forgotten. For, if thou wilt busily set thee to the proof, thou shalt find, when thou hast forgotten all other creatures and all their works—yea! and also all thine own works—that there shall remain yet after, betwixt thee and thy God, a naked knowing and a feeling of thine own being: the which knowing and feeling must always be destroyed, ere the time be that thou mayest feel verily the perfection of this work.[7]

[6] Chapter XXVI; *op. cit.*, pp. 38-39.
[7] Chapter XLIII; *op. cit.*, pp. 55-56.

Without a full special grace full freely given by God, and also a full according ableness on thy part to receive this grace, this naked knowing and feeling of thy being may in nowise be destroyed. And this ableness is nought else but a strong and a deep ghostly sorrow.[8]

This sorrow and this desire must every soul have and feel in itself (either in this manner or in another), as God vouchsafeth to teach his ghostly disciples according to his good will and their according ableness in body and in soul, in degree and disposition, ere the time be that they may perfectly be oned unto God in perfect charity. . . .[9]

THE EPISTLE OF PRIVY COUNSEL

Look that nothing remain in thy working mind but a naked intent stretching unto God, not clothed in any special thought of God in himself, how he is in himself, or in any of his works, but only that he is as he is. Let him be so, I pray thee, and make him on no otherwise. Seek no further in him by subtlety of wit; let that belief be thy ground. This naked intent, freely fastened and grounded in very belief, shall be nought else to thy thought and to thy feeling but a naked thought and a blind feeling of thine own being; as if thou saidst thus unto God within thy meaning: "That that I am, good Lord, I offer unto thee, without any looking to any quality of thy being, but only that thou art as thou art, without any more."

Let that meek darkness be thy mirror and thy mind wholly. Think no further of thyself than I bid thee do of thy God, so that thou be one with him in spirit as thus, without any separating and scattering of mind. For he is thy being, and in him thou art what thou art, not only by cause and by being, but also he is in thee both thy cause and thy being. And therefore think of God in thy work as thou dost on thyself, and on thyself as thou dost on God: that he is as he is and thou art as thou art; so that thy thought be not scattered nor separated, but oned in him that is all; evermore saving this difference betwixt thee and him, that he is thy being and thou not his.[10]

Bear up thy sick self as thou art unto gracious God as he is, without any curious or special beholding to any of all the quali-

[8] Chapter XLIV; *op. cit.,* p. 56.
[9] *Op. cit.,* p. 57.
[10] *Op. cit.,* p. 96.

ties that belong to the being of thyself or of God, whether they be clean or wretched, gracious or natural, godly or manly. It mattereth not now to thee, but that thy blind beholding of thy naked being be gladly borne up in lustiness of love to be knitted and oned in grace and in spirit to the precious Being of God in himself, only as he is, without more.[11]

Well is this work likened to a sleep. For as in a sleep the use of the bodily wits is ceased, that the body may take his full rest in feeding and strengthening of the bodily nature: right so in this ghostly sleep the wanton questions of the wild ghostly wits and all imaginative reasons be fast bound and utterly voided, so that the silly soul may softly sleep and rest in the lovely beholding of God as he is, in full feeding and strengthening of the ghostly nature. And therefore bind in thy wits in offering up of this naked blind feeling of thine own being, and look ever (as oft I say) that it be naked and not clad with any quality of thy being. For if thou clothe it with any quality, as with the worthiness of thy being, or with any other privy condition that pertaineth to the being of man, forby the being of any other creature: then as fast thou givest meat to thy wits, by the which they have occasion and strength to draw thee to many things and to be scattered thou knowest not how. Beware of this deceit, I pray thee.[12]

SELECTED BIBLIOGRAPHY

Editions

All previous attempts to establish a critical text have been antiquated by Miss Phyllis Hodgson's *The Cloud of Unknowing* (London, 1944; reprinted with additions, 1958) which contains *The Epistle of Privy Counsel* as well.

Translations

For the general reader, Dom Justin McCann's modernization of his own critically established text is the best. For the more erudite, the French version of Dom M. Noetinger, *Le Nuage de l'inconnaissance* (Tours, 1925), has its own rewards.

[11] *Op. cit.,* pp. 98-99.
[12] *Op. cit.,* pp. 109-110.

Studies

Of capital importance is the series of articles by Conrad Pepler, O.P., in *The Life of the Spirit*, III (1948/1949), 8-15, 109-117, 169-176, 203-210, 304-311, 354-359. See as well Phyllis Hodgson, "Walter Hilton and *The Cloud of Unknowing*," *Modern Language Review*, L (1955), 395-406, for the question of authorship.

XXIV

WALTER HILTON

(d. 1396)

ALREADY in the writings of the author of *The Cloud* there is evidence that the atmosphere congenial to mysticism created by St. Edmund Rich over a century before had now become, in places, a lowering and threatening one. Hostility to mysticism was general. Pseudo-mystics, more extravagant than Rolle, were on the increase. Peace of mind for such as might be genuinely called to the mystical life was hard to come by. Fortunately, there were such sure guides as the author of *The Cloud*—and Walter Hilton.

Hilton, an Augustinian canon, was the author of many works in both Latin and English. *The Ladder of Perfection* was his masterpiece, combining within its ample compass traditional doctrine, personal experience, and a sympathy for the needs of others in just about equal quantities. The manner of the man is worthy of remark. He devoted no less than thirty-eight patient chapters to explaining how evil tendencies are best eradicated. And he did this for the lone anchoress he sought to help in his writing of *The Ladder*.

His doctrinal dependence on the Victorines is well known. His debt, little noticed, to William of St. Thierry is no less certain. His chief device for explaining the need and the nature of mystic experience is William's doctrine of man the image. Only one change, but quite significant, did he make: where his predecessor emphasized will, he found himself forced to emphasize knowledge. But intellectualism was not the result. Compare the "nothings" of the authentic Dionysians—whether the Victorines or the Rhineland mystics or Ruysbroek—with his figure of the image of sin, the sorrow and pain and blindness and darkness, the "nothing" which has to be borne because, he said, "inside this nothing Jesus is hidden in all His glory."

TEXTS [1]

THE LADDER OF PERFECTION

There are three degrees in the contemplative life. The first consists in a knowledge of God and of spiritual things, acquired by reason through the teachings of others and the study of Holy Scripture, a knowledge that lacks the spiritual affectiveness and inner savor which is a special gift of the Holy Spirit. Learned men and great scholars, after long studies and work in Holy Scripture, attain this degree to greater or less extent depending upon their native intelligence and their perseverance in their studies, simply using the general gift that God gives every man who has the use of reason. This knowledge is good and may be called a degree of contemplation inasmuch as it involves a seeing of truth and a knowing of spiritual things. And yet it is only similitude and shadow of contemplation because it lacks the spiritual savoring of God and the inner sweetness of love which no man can feel unless he loves much, for Our Lord's love is Our Lord's true well and to it no man comes who is stranger to Him. It is a kind of knowledge that is common to good men and bad alike because it can be had without the love of God. It is therefore not true contemplation; often enough heretics and hypocrites and carnal men have more of such knowledge than many true Christian men, and yet these men have not the love of God. . . . Of itself such knowledge is mere water, tasteless and cold. But if those who have it will offer it in humility to Our Lord and ask His favor, He will turn the water into wine as He did by His blessing in response to His Mother at the marriage feast. In other words, He will turn this tasteless knowledge into wisdom, the cold and naked reason into spiritual light and burning love by the gift of the Holy Spirit.[2]

The second degree of contemplation consists principally in affection without understanding of spiritual things. It is the degree often found in simple and uneducated people who give themselves wholly to devotion. It is felt in this way: a man

[1] I here follow the contemporary convention of simply modernizing slightly more the version by Evelyn Underhill. See Selected Bibliography.
[2] Book I, Chapter IV.

or a woman is meditating on God and by the grace of the Holy Spirit feels a warmth of love and a spiritual sweetness in remembering Christ's Passion or any of His deeds as man; or such a one feels a great confidence in God's goodness and mercy, His forgiveness of sins, and His great gifts of grace; or else there is felt a great affective dread and reverence for the secret judgments of God which remain unseen and for His righteousness; or, in prayer, one feels the thoughts of the heart ascend from all things earthly, all its powers uniting to stretch up to Our Lord in fervent desire and spiritual delight. At such a time, however, one has no clear intellectual perception of spiritual things or of the mysteries of Holy Scripture but only that at this time nothing is more pleasing than to pray or to think like this because of the savor and delight and consolation that it provides. One cannot explain really what it is, but one knows quite well that one feels it because out of it come many sweet tears, burning desires, and inexpressible griefs which scour and cleanse the heart of all the filth of sin and make it melt into the wondrous sweetness of Jesus Christ, obedient, responsive, and ready to do all the will of God to the extent that it seems to matter not what becomes of one so long as God's will is fulfilled. And there are many other such affections, more than I can describe. Such feelings cannot be had without great grace, and whoever has them, at that time, has the love of God. And this love cannot be lost or lessened, even though the fervor of it may pass away, except by mortal sin. There is comfort in that. . . .[3]

The third degree of contemplation is the highest that is attainable in this life. Both knowing and loving go to make it up. It consists in knowing God perfectly and in loving God perfectly, and that is when a man's soul is first cleansed of all sins and is formed anew, through the fullness of virtue, into the image of Jesus and then, at the visitation of grace, is withdrawn from all earthly and fleshly affections and from vain thoughts and musings on bodily matters and is, as it were, rapt out of his bodily senses; and then, by the grace of the Holy Spirit, he is enlightened so that he can see by his understanding the truth which is God and see spiritual things with a soft sweet burning love in him which is so perfect that by the ravishing of this love he is united for a time to God and is conformed to the likeness of the Trinity. The beginning of this contemplation can be felt in this life. Its consummation is reserved for the happiness of Heaven. Of this contemplation St. Paul speaks when he says that whoever cleaves to God is one spirit with Him,[4] meaning that, whenever a soul is joined to God in this

[3] Book I, Chapter V.
[4] I Corinthians 6:17.

rapture of love, then God and the soul are two no longer; they are one in spirit although not in nature. In this oneness a marriage is effected between God and the soul which shall never be dissolved.[5]

The second degree of contemplation might be called "love on fire with devotion"; the third, "love on fire with contemplation." The former is a lower degree and the latter is a higher. The former is the sweeter to bodily sense. The latter is sweeter to the spiritual sense because it is more inward, more spiritual. It is the more precious and the more wonderful for it is in truth a foretasting and an earnest of the joys of Heaven, perceived now dimly and in darkness, which will be completed and made wholly luminous in the bliss of Heaven. . . . It is the enlightening of the understanding joined to the joys of His love to which David refers in the Psalter: "To me night is as light in my joy."[6] That other degree of contemplation is milk for children; this is solid food for full-grown men of experienced judgment, able to distinguish good from evil, as St. Paul says, "Solid food is for the mature who are trained by practice to discern good from evil."[7] No one can exercise this gift fully unless he is first changed into the likeness of Jesus by the fullness of virtues. I do not think that any man living in this mortal flesh can have it constantly and completely, but only now and again when he is visited by grace. And, as I understand from the writings of holy men, such periods are very short, for a man will quickly subside into the sobriety of bodily feeling.

It is from love alone that this gift comes. As I understand him, St. Paul is relating his own experience when he says, "If we are beside ourselves, it is for God; if we are in our right mind, it is for you; because the love of Christ drives us on."[8] Whether we transcend bodily sense in contemplating God or remain soberly there, it is the love of Christ that drives us. St. Paul clearly describes this stage of contemplation and conformity to God: "All of us, face unveiled, looking upon the glory of the Lord are changed into His likeness from one degree of clarity to the next by the Lord who is Spirit."[9] In other words, he says of himself and of others made perfect: reformed first in virtue, our inward vision cleared, we behold as in a mirror the bliss of Heaven; we are changed and joined to His likeness, going from the clearness of faith to the clearness of knowledge, from the clearness of desire to the clearness of true love. All this is brought about in a soul, St. Paul says,

[5] Book I, Chapter VIII.
[6] *Cf.* Psalm 139:11.
[7] Hebrews 5:14.
[8] 2 Corinthians 5:13-14.
[9] 2 Corinthians 3:18.

by the Spirit of God. God it is who gives this degree of contemplation. He gives it where He will, to the learned or the simple, to men and women, to those busy with the governing of the Church and to solitaries. But it is a special gift. It is not common. And, although a man of active life may have this gift by a special grace, I believe that no man may have its full use unless he is a solitary and vowed to the contemplative life.[10]

SELECTED BIBLIOGRAPHY

Editions

A strictly critical text of *The Ladder* is only now in process of being established by a team of British scholars. For a discussion of the problems before them, see Miss Helen Gardner's "The Text of *The Scale of Perfection*," *Medium Aevum*, V (1936), 11-30.

Translations

The closest thing at the moment to a critical text is the slightly modernized version of Evelyn Underhill, which was based upon a limited selection of manuscripts: *The Scale of Perfection* (London, 1923).

Studies

Of especial value is Miss Gardner's "Walter Hilton and the Mystical Tradition in England," *Essays and Studies*, XXII (1937), 103-127.

[10] Book I, Chapter IX.

XXV

JULIAN OF NORWICH

(1343—p. 1416)

LANGUAGE, at best a vehicle of quite dubious reliability, seems
to collapse forthwith when it is a question—as it must be here
—of attempting to describe that most elusive of mystics, Dame
Julian of Norwich. For hers is a quality expressible, it would
seem, by words that possess nothing except their primitive and
simple meanings. And there are no words of that sort around
any more.

One would very much like, for instance, to call her
"homely." But the term would, I fear, conjure up today only
disquieting images of an ill-proportioned face, when all I
should have meant was a well-proportioned soul that was as
lightsome and orderly and ordinary as a farmhouse kitchen,
swept, shining, warmly redolent of familiar human living, with
something—eminently practical and savory—bubbling away
on the hob.

Again, she might be comprehensively described by the one
word, "buxom." Might, that is to say, were this not today
when the term would imply, rather ungraciously, that Julian
was fatter than is generally thought fashionable. Not her girth
—about which I know nothing and do not especially care—
but her Godward-ness would have been meant: utter pliability,
tractability, flexibility to His will in a way that was at once
lively and jolly and marked with a dignity and quiet kindliness.
All this, and more, so apposite to our purpose was compressed
within the primitive rich simplicity of the word "buxom." But
not any more.

And so it goes.

Such alarming inadequacies of our language to express the simple, and especially—as is really the problem here—to express the simple as luminously resident within transcendent mystery, have long stayed the pens of interpreters. What, timidly, people have done on a variety of occasions was to reproduce her own words, those fresh urgent little Melchizedeks of words that have no father or mother or distracting genealogy, pretty much as they are found in her *Revelations of Divine Love*. Latterly, however, there has been a striking change. Timidity overcome, scholars like Reynolds and Molinari and Walsh have courageously made the attempt to capture her quality in the tired and sophisticated embrace of modern English. It is a venturesomeness which, in however limited a way, I would emulate here; for one possible, incidental by-product of my doing so might well be the rejuvenation, though temporary, of our word "love."

The reality of love is the recurrent theme and the cohesive principle of all that Julian wrote as she put into words the accumulative meditation of years upon Christ's appearance to her from four to nine o'clock on the morning of the Third Sunday after Easter, May 8, 1373.

She tells us that when she was still a quite small child she had desired "three gifts of God's grace." The first gift was to be the thought of Christ's Passion; the second, bodily sickness "even unto death" when thirty years of age; the third was "to have of God's gift, three wounds . . . that is to say, the wound of true contrition, the wound of kind compassion, and the wound of earnest longing for God." And she says she asked the fulfillment of the first two desires "with a condition," that is, if such should be God's will; the last, however, she asked "mightily and without any condition." She confesses that she soon forgot the first two desires but that the third remained with her continuously.

Then came the illness, at the age of thirty and a half and apparently unto death. As she lay there, with bodily consciousness gone but her mental activity even more perfectly alerted, she remembered. "Then it came suddenly to my mind that I should desire the second wound, that of Our Lord's gift and of His grace I might be filled full, in body and in mind, with experience of His blessed Passion. . . . But in all this I desired never any bodily sight nor any manner of showing [vision] of God but only compassion—such as I believed a kindred soul might have with Our Lord Jesus."

But, with the compassion, she was accorded as well a "showing." It was of Christ's "precious crowning of thorns; and therein was contained and made manifest the Blessed Trinity with the Incarnation and the unity between God and man's soul." In that vision, she tells us, all others that followed were "grounded and oned."

It might be instructive sometime for someone to compare the visions and their consequences of both Julian and St. Teresa of Avila. With Teresa there was a like progression, based on awareness of the Passion, from an appreciation of voluntary suffering to a new humility and culminating in a prayer-life of exceptional solidity. Only when she began to engage in serious bodily mortification did her perspective clear and her prayer become strong. But one does not find in Teresa the expression of what "grounded" the progression. One finds it—that is her distinctive quality—in Julian. "Love is all its meaning." He that is Love is "the ground of our beseeching."

There best is love found where best love has been shown, in the Father's gift of His Son for the redeeming of men as spelt out in the Passion. There best is love known where best it is lived, in that return by compassion "such as I believed a kindred soul might have with Our Lord Jesus." There reality is best perceived where truth is best beheld, in the Godhead where, as St. Gregory anciently said, "Love enters in and knowledge cannot." There prayer is best made where union is best—is only—achieved, in love.

And the love throughout is, in intent at least for both Christian and Christ, wholly a giving and not a getting.

Such is the large, noble content of the word "love" for Julian.

TEXTS [1]

REVELATIONS OF DIVINE LOVE

Then I had an offer in my reason; it was said to me, as though by a friend: "Look up to heaven to his Father." Then through the faith that I felt I saw well that there was nothing between the cross and heaven that could have dis-eased me. Here then I must needs look up, or else answer. So I answered inwardly, with all the might of my soul, and said: "Nay, I cannot, for Thou art my heaven." This I said because I would not. For I would rather have been in that pain till doomsday than have come to heaven otherwise than by him. For I knew well that he who had bound me so sore, would unbind me when he would.[2]

[1] From *The Revelations of Divine Love of Julian of Norwich*, translated by James Walsh, S.J. (London-New York, 1961-1962).
[2] Chapter XIX; Walsh, *op. cit.*, p. 79.

As long as he was passible, he suffered for us. And now he is uprisen and no more passible, yet still he suffereth with us.[3]

I looked for the going forth of the soul with all my might, and thought to have seen his body wholly dead. But I saw him not so. For just at the time that it seemed to me his life could no longer last, and that the shewing of his end must needs be nigh, suddenly (I still beheld the cross) his blessed face changed. This change in him changed me, and I was as glad and merry as it is possible to be. Then our Lord brought to my mind these joyful words: "Where now is any trace of thy pain or of thy anguish?" And I was full of joy. I understood that in this life, as our Lord sees it, we are on his cross, dying with him in our pains and our passion. Then suddenly his countenance shall be changed upon us, and we shall be with him in heaven.[4]

For it is God's will that we have true liking, with him, of our salvation; and he willeth that we be mightily comforted and strengthened therein; and he willeth that our soul be thus happily occupied, with his grace. For we are his bliss, and in us he hath liking without end; and so shall we have in him, with his grace.[5]

After this our Lord shewed himself more glorified (if I saw aright) than I had seen him before. Wherein I was taught that our soul shall never have rest till it come into him, knowing that he is fullness of joy, homely, courteous and blissful: true life. Oftentimes our Lord said:

I it am, I it am; I it am that is highest; I it am that thou lovest; I it am that thou likest; I it am that thou servest; I it am that thou longest; I it am that thou desirest; I it am that thou meanest; I it am that is all; I it am that Holy Church preacheth and teacheth thee; I it am that shewed myself to thee here.

The number of his words passeth beyond my wits, and all my understanding, and all my powers; and they are the highest, as I see it. For therein is comprehended—I cannot tell what: except that the joy that I saw in the shewing of them passeth all that heart can think or soul could desire.[6]

[3] Chapter XX; *op. cit.*, p. 81.
[4] Chapter XXI; *op. cit.*, p. 82.
[5] Chapter XXIII; *op. cit.*, p. 85.
[6] Chapter XXVI; *op. cit.*, p. 90.

I saw that he is to us everything that is good and strengthening for our help. He is our clothing that, for love, wrappeth us up and windeth us about; embraceth us, all becloseth us and hangeth about us, for tender love; so that he can never leave us. And so, in this sight, I saw that he is to us everything that is good, as I understand it.

Also in this he shewed a little thing, the size of a hazelnut, which seemed to lie in the palm of my hand; and it was as round as any ball. I looked upon it with the eye of my understanding, and thought, "What may this be?" I was answered in a general way, thus: "It is all that is made." I wondered how long it could last; for it seemed as though it might suddenly fade away to nothing, it was so small. And I was answered in my understanding: "It lasts, and ever shall last; for God loveth it. And even so hath everything being—by the love of God."

In this little thing I saw three properties. The first is that God made it: the second, that God loveth it: the third, that God keepeth it. And what beheld I in this? Truly, the Maker, the Lover and the Keeper. And until I am substantially oned to him, I can never have full rest nor true bliss; that is to say, until I am so fastened to him that there is no created thing at all between my God and me. And this little thing that is made —it seemed as though it would fade away to nothing, it was so small. We need to have knowledge of this—that we should reckon as naught everything that is made, to love and have God who is unmade. For this is the reason why we are not all in ease of heart and of soul: that we seek here rest in this thing that is so little and where no rest is in; we know not our God that is almighty, all-wise and all-good. For he is very rest. It is his will to be known and it is his pleasure that we rest us in him. All that is beneath him sufficeth not to us. And this is the reason why no soul can be in rest until it is naughted of everything that is made. When the soul is willingly naughted, for love, so as to have him who is All, then is she able to receive ghostly rest.[7]

The highest prayer is to the goodness of God which cometh down to us, to the lowest part of our need. It quickeneth our soul, and maketh it to live; it maketh it to grow in grace and in virtue; it is nearest it in kind, and readiest to it in grace; it is, indeed, the very grace for which the soul seeketh and ever shall, until we know our God truly—he that hath us all beclosed in himself.[8]

[7] Chapter V; *op. cit.*, pp. 52-54.
[8] Chapter VI; *op. cit.*, p. 55.

He despiseth nothing of what he hath made. And he disdaineth not to serve us in the simplest offices that belong, in kind, to our body, for love of the soul that is made to his own likeness. For as the body is clad in clothes, and the flesh in skin, and the bones in flesh, and the heart in the breast; so are we, soul and body, clad and enclosed in the goodness of God. Yea, and more homely; for they all vanish, wasting away. But the goodness of God is ever whole and most near to us, without any comparison.[9]

Our kindly will is to have God, and the good will of God is to have us. Nor may we ever cease willing or loving, until we have him in fullness of joy. And then we may no more will. It is his will that we be occupied in knowing and loving until the time come that we be full filled in heaven; therefore was this lesson of love shewed, as ye shall see.[10]

After this, our Lord shewed me concerning prayer. In this shewing I saw two conditions for prayer—as our Lord understandeth it; one is rightfulness, the other is sure trust. For oftentimes our trust is not full; we are not sure that God heareth us, because (so we imagine) of our unworthiness, and the fact that we feel nothing at all—for we are as barren and as dry oftentimes after our prayers as we were before. Thus, in our feelings and in our folly is the cause of this weakness of ours; and this is my own experience.

All this our Lord brought to my mind at once, and shewed these words:

I am the ground of thy beseeching. First, it is my will that thou have it—and seeing that I make thee to desire it, and seeing that I make thee to beseech it and thou beseechest it, how could it then be that thou shouldst not have thy beseeching?

Thus in the first reason, with the three that follow, our Lord shewed a mighty comfort, as may be seen in these same words. In the first reason, where he saith "and thou beseechest it," he there sheweth the exceeding pleasure and endless reward that he willeth to give us for our beseeching. And the sixth reason (where he says "How could it then be?") was given as an impossibility. For nothing is more impossible than that we should seek mercy and grace, and not have it. For all the things that our good Lord himself maketh us to beseech, these he

[9] Chapter VI; *op. cit.*, p. 56.
[10] Chapter VI; *op. cit.*, p. 56.

hath ordained to us from without-beginning. Here then may we see that his proper goodness and not our beseeching is the cause of the goodness and the grace that he doeth to us; and that shewed he truly in all these sweet words where he saith "I am the ground." Our good Lord willeth that this be known amongst his lovers on earth; and the more we know it the more shall we beseech, if we understand it wisely—and that is our Lord's intention.

Beseeching is a true and grace-giving, lasting will of the soul which is oned and fastened to the will of our Lord, by the sweet and secret working of the Holy Ghost.[11]

Also to prayer belongeth thanksgiving. Thanksgiving is a true inward knowing, a turning of ourselves with great reverence and loving dread and with all our power to the working which our Lord stirreth us to: inwardly, with joy and thanksgiving. And sometimes the abundance of it breaketh out into speech, and we say, "Good Lord, be merciful, blessed may thou be." And at other times when the heart is dry, and we feel nothing, or when tempted by our enemy, we are driven by reason and by grace to cry out loud on our Lord, rehearsing his blessed passion and his great goodness. And so the power of our Lord's word pierceth the soul and quickeneth the heart, and bringeth it by his grace into true working, maketh it to pray most blissfully and have true joy in our Lord. This is a most lovely thanksgiving in his sight.[12]

Our Lord willeth us to have true understanding in what belongeth to our prayer, especially in three things. The first is to know by whom and how our prayer beginneth. By whom, he sheweth when he says "I am the ground": and how, by his goodness; for he saith, "First, it is my will." The second is to know in what manner and how we should use our time of prayer; this is, that our will be turned to the will of our Lord in joy. This is his meaning when he saith "I make thee to will it." The third is to know the fruit and end of our prayer; which is to be oned and like to our Lord in everything. To this meaning and to this end was all this lovely lesson shewed. He will help us, and he shall bring it about, as he says himself, blessed may he be!

For this is our Lord's will—that our prayer and our trust be alike, large. For if we do not trust as much as we pray, we fail in full worship to our Lord in our prayer; and also we hinder and hurt ourselves. The reason is that we do not know

[11] Chapter XLI; *op. cit.*, pp. 113-114.
[12] Chapter XLI; *op. cit.*, pp. 115-116.

truly that our Lord is the ground from whom our prayer springeth; nor do we know that it is given us by his grace and his love. If we knew this, it would make us trust to have of our Lord's gift all that we desire. For I am sure that no man asketh mercy and grace with sincerity, without mercy and grace being given to him first.[13]

Prayer is a right understanding of that fullness of joy that is to come, along with true longing and absolute trust that we shall savour and see the bliss that we are ordained to; which kindly maketh us to long. True understanding and love, with sweet grace-giving mindfulness in our Saviour, maketh us to trust; and thus it belongeth to our kind to have longing, and it belongeth to grace, to trust. In these two workings our Lord beholdeth us continually—for this is our duty, and his goodness cannot assign to us any lesser task than belongeth to our diligence to perform. And even when we do it, it shall seem to us as nothing. And true though this is, let us do what we can, and meekly ask for mercy and grace; and whatever is wanting in us, we shall find it in him. This is his meaning when he saith, "I am the ground of thy beseeching." In these blissful words and in the shewing I saw that all our wickedness and all our doubtful dreads may be fully overcome.

Prayer oneth the soul to God. For though the soul is ever like to God in kind, and like also in substance when restored by grace, it is often unlike to him in its condition, because of sin on man's part. But prayer is a witness that the soul willeth as God willeth, it strengtheneth a man's conscious working, and enableth him to receive grace. And hence he teacheth us to pray and mightily to trust that we shall have it. For he beholdeth us in love, and willeth to make us partakers of his good will and deed. Therefore he moveth us to pray for what it pleaseth him to do; and he willeth to reward us, and give us endless payment for the prayer and the good will that we have received of his gift. This was shewed in his words "and thou beseechest it." By these words God shewed such great pleasure and liking—as though he were beholden to us for every good deed that we do; and yet it is he that doeth it all. In as much, then, as we beseech him that we may do the thing that pleaseth him (it is as though he had said: "What couldst thou do to please me more than to beseech me mightily, wisely and willingly, that thou mayest do that which I will do to have done?"); it is thus that the soul by its prayer is in accord with God.

But when our courteous Lord, of his special grace, sheweth

himself to our soul, then we have what we desire; and we do not see, in that time, any thing more to pray for. All our intent and all our might is set wholly upon this beholding of him. And this is a high and ineffable prayer, as I see it. For all the reason why we pray is oned into the sight and the beholding of him to whom we pray, with marvellous enjoyment and reverent dread, and such great sweetness and delight in him that we can pray not at all, or only as he moveth us to do at the time. I know well that the more the soul seeth of God, the more she desireth him, by grace. But when we see him not so, then feel we need and cause to pray, because of our weakness and the unreadiness of ourselves to receive Jesus. For when a soul is tempested, troubled and left to herself because of her unrest, then it is time to pray, that she may make herself supple and docile, so as to receive God. (For by no manner of prayer can she make God supple to receive her: he is ever one and the same in his love.)

Thus I saw that whenever we see the need for prayer, then our Lord is with us, helping our desire. But when, of his special grace, we behold him plainly and see no further need of prayer, then we are with him; for he draweth us to him by love. I saw and felt that his marvellous and superabundant goodness filleth full all our powers; and saw also that his continual working in all manner of things is done so well, so wisely and so mightily that it surpasseth all our imagining —beyond all that we can explain or even conceive. Then we can do no more but behold him and enjoy: with a high and powerful desire to be entirely oned in him, to be received into his dwelling, to enjoy in his loving, to delight in his goodness. It is thus that we may, with his sweet grace in our own meek, continual prayer, come into him now, in this life, by many secret touchings and sweet ghostly sights and feelings, measured out to us according as our simpleness can support it. This is wrought, and shall be, by the grace of the Holy Ghost until we die in longing for love. Then shall we all come into our Lord—ourselves clearly knowing, God abundantly having —until we are all endlessly hid in God—him truly seeing and abundantly feeling, him ghostly hearing and delectably smelling, him all sweetly swallowing.[14]

Marvellous and stately is the place where the Lord dwelleth. And therefore he willeth that we readily turn us to his gracious touching, having more joy in his all-love than sorrow in our frequent fallings. For of anything that we may do, it is most worship to him that we live, in our penance, gladly and merrily

[14] Chapters XLII-XLIII; *op. cit.*, pp. 118-120.

for his love. For he beholdeth us so tenderly that he seeth all
our living here to be a penance. For the kind longing in us
for him is a lasting penance in us. Which penance he worketh
in us, and mercifully helpeth us to bear it. For his love maketh
him to long; his wisdom and his truth, with his righteousness,
maketh him to suffer us here; and in this manner he willeth
to see it in us. For this is our kindly penance, as to my sight.
This penance never goeth from us till what time that we be
full filled, and have him for our meed. And therefore he willeth that we set our hearts in our out-passing: that is to say,
from the pain that we feel into the bliss that we trust to have.[15]

I had, in a measure, touching, sight and feeling in three
properties of God. In which the strength and the effect of all
Revelation standeth. And they were seen in every shewing;
and most directly in the twelfth, where it is said often: "I it
am." The properties are these: life, love and light. In life is
marvellous homeliness: in love is gentle courtesy: and in light
is endless kindhood. These three properties were seen in one
goodness; into which goodness my reason would be oned—
cleaving to it with all its might. I beheld with reverent dread,
highly marvelling in the sight and in the feeling of the sweet
accord—that our reason is in God, understanding that it is the
highest gift that we have received: and it is grounded in Kind.
Our faith is a light, kindly coming from our endless Day
that is our Father God. In which light our Mother Christ[16]
and our good Lord the Holy Ghost lead us, in this passing
life. This light is measured discerningly, standing unto us, at
need, in the night. The light is the cause of our life: the night
is the cause of our pain and all our woe. For which woe we
deserve endless meed and thanks from God. For we, with
mercy and grace, willfully know and believe our light, going
therein wisely and mightily. And at the end of woe, suddenly
our eye shall be opened, and in clearness of sight our light
shall be full. Which light is God, our Maker, Father, and Holy
Ghost in Christ Jesus our Saviour. Thus I saw and understood
that our faith is our light in our night. Which light is God, our
endless Day.
This light is charity; and the measuring of this light is done
to us profitably by the wisdom of God. For neither is the light
so large that we can see clearly our blissful day, nor is it all
shut out from us. But it is a light such as we may live in

---

[15] Chapter LXXXI; *op. cit.,* p. 203.
[16] Mediaeval mystics had no hesitation in speaking of the maternal
aspects of Christ's love or in even addressing Him, accordingly, as
"Mother." See A. Cabassut, O.S.B., "Une dévotion médiévale peu con-
nue," *Revue d'ascétique et de mystique,* XXV (1949), 234-245.

profitably with labour—deserving the worshipful thanks of God. And this was seen in the sixth shewing, where he saith: "I thank thee for thy service and for thy labour. . . ."

And in this sight I marvelled highly. For notwithstanding our simpleness and our blindness here, our Lord endlessly beholdeth us, rejoicing in this working. And we can please him best of all by believing this truly, and rejoicing with him and in him. For as truly as we shall be in the bliss of God without end, him praising and thanking; so truly we have been in the foreknowledge of God, loved and known in his endless purpose from without-beginning. In which unbegun love he made us, and in the same love he keepeth us, and never suffereth us to be hurt in a way that our bliss might be lessened. And therefore, when judgment is given, and we are all brought up above, then shall we clearly see in God the secrets which now are hid from us. And then none of us shall be prompted to say of anything: "Lord, if it had been thus, it had been well"; but we shall all say with one voice: "Lord, blessed may thou be! For it is thus, and it is well. Now we see truly that all thing is done as was thine ordinance before anything was made." [17]

For charity's sake, let us pray all together with God's working, thanking, trusting, enjoying. For it is thus that our good Lord willeth us to pray, according to the understanding that I took in all his meaning, and in the sweet words that he said full merrily "I am the ground of thy beseeching." For I saw truly and understood in our Lord's meaning that he shewed it because he will have it known more than it is. In which knowing he will give us grace to love him and cleave to him. For he beheld his heavenly treasure with so great love on earth, that he willeth to give more light and solace in heavenly joy, in drawing our hearts from the sorrow and darkness which we are in.

And from the time that it was shewed, I desired oftentimes to know what was our Lord's meaning in it. And fifteen years after, and more, I was answered in ghostly understanding: "What, wouldst thou know thy Lord's meaning in this thing? Know it well. Love was his meaning. Who sheweth it thee? Love. Wherefore sheweth he it thee? For Love. Hold thee therein. Thou shalt know more in the same, but thou shalt never know other therein, without end."

Thus was I learned that love is our Lord's meaning. And I saw full surely in this, and in all, that before God made us, he loved us. Which love was never slaked, nor ever shall be. And

[17] Chapters LXXXIII-LXXXV; *op. cit.*, pp. 205-208.

in this love he hath done all his works. And in this love he hath made all things profitable to us. And in this love our life is everlasting. In our making we had beginning: but the love wherein he made us was in him from without-beginning. In which love we have our beginning. And all this shall we see in God without end.

Thanks be to God.[18]

SELECTED BIBLIOGRAPHY

Editions

Despite the popularity of Julian, we still have (1963) nothing better than popular modernizations of her work. A long-awaited critical edition of the original Middle English, by Sister Anna Maria Reynolds, C.P., and James Walsh, S.J., is promised in the "Early English Texts" series.

Translations

The Shorter Version of the *Revelations* has been translated into modern English by Sister Anna Maria Reynolds, *A Shewing of God's Love* (London, 1958). Father Walsh, having collated for the first time all three manuscripts of the Longer Version, has given us a modernization of unusual penetration and charm from which the selections above were made.

Studies

The definitive work is that of Paul Molinari, S.J., *Julian of Norwich: The Teaching of a 14th Century English Mystic* (New York-London, 1958). The literary and theological aspects of the *Revelations* have been most competently discussed by Sister Anna Maria Reynolds, "Some Literary Influences in the Revelations of Julian of Norwich," *Leeds Studies in English and Kindred Languages* (1952), pp. 18-28, and by Father Walsh in the Introduction to his modernization.

[18] Chapter LXXXVI; *op. cit.*, pp. 208-209.

XXVI

ST. CATHERINE OF GENOA

(1447—1510)

EVEN IF one should discount as pardonably exaggerated St. Catherine's condemnation of her early life, it would seem that she had a personal acquaintance with sin more extended and intimate than most of the saints. Entering a parentally arranged marriage at sixteen, she knew for years only unhappiness and suffering with her profligate husband and, by way of escape, sought out profligacies of her own. And, unlike most mystics, the completeness of mystical union would seem to have been hers from the first moment of her conversion on March 20, 1473. The two, the sinning and the sudden attaining to the heights, would appear to have been closely related.

Her conversion was effected by an abrupt awareness of the holiness of God that only gained in acuity from being set against her own unholiness. The awareness never left her, and her mystic experience to the end of her life was uniform. One might best describe it as a cauterizing sensation.

Her own subsequent analysis of it has contributed much not only to the historian's understanding of her own remarkable experience but, as well, to the theologian's understanding of the traditional doctrine of Purgatory. In both instances it is question of the soul being close to God, wrapped about with His love, all its defects exposed to His purity. A longing, a loving for God is, in such an intimate conjunction, a conflagration in which is lost, not without pain, one's impurity.

How the soul is thus cleansed of the impurity of sin was the burden of her *Treatise on Purgatory*. Her *Dialogue*, for all its archness, proffered the same, personally lived, explanation.

TEXTS[1]

THE DIALOGUE

This soul saw a certain ray of love come forth from the divine spring and turn towards man as though it would make him nothing. And she saw that when this ray was hindered, then, could God feel pain, His pain would be of the greatest there can be. All this ray had to do was to seek to pierce the soul, and if it failed only the soul was to blame. For to enter the soul the ray surrounds it on all sides, and yet a soul blinded by self-love perceives it not. . . . It was this ray of love which struck this Soul of which I speak. In one instant she saw and felt a fire of love which had come from that divine source and by which she was all but rapt from herself, without understanding, speech or feeling, busied only with this pure and simple love as God had shewn it her. This sight nevermore left her mind; evermore she saw this pure love turned on her.

It was also shewn her how unknowing she had been of this love and how many were her faults, and in her faults she saw herself and all she was apt to do against this pure love. Then she was sunk in such contempt for herself that she would have told her sins publicly through the town, and with an interior cry she uttered these words (for she could not do other): "O Lord, no more of the world for me! Not more sin!"[2]

Sometimes God lightened this hold His love had taken, letting the Spirit breathe and respond to the Soul and the Soul to the Body, and then the feelings of the Soul and the Body were fit to receive some comfort from created things and thus were given life.[3] But when God withdrew the Spirit to Himself all the rest followed, for then the Body was left as though dead, and was so strange to his natural way of being that when he came back to it he was utterly weak nor could be helped by created things.[4]

---

[1] From *Saint Catherine of Genoa, The Treatise on Purgatory and The Dialogue,* translated by Charlotte Balfour and Helen Douglas-Irvine, published by Sheed & Ward, Inc., New York; Sheed & Ward Limited, London, 1946.

[2] Part I, Chapter VIII; Balfour and Douglas-Irvine, *op. cit.,* pp. 56-57.

[3] Catherine, as many other mystics, distinguishes between "soul" and "spirit." "Soul," "Spirit," and "Body" are here capitalized because they are characters who have speaking roles in *The Dialogue.*

[4] Part II, Chapter II; *op. cit.,* pp. 87-88.

Then God shed on the creature another ray of love which filled her soul, and was so abundant that her body too was restored, and she felt only love and heart's joy so that she thought herself in Paradise. She was kept in this state until all love lower than God had been consumed in her and she was left with love for God alone and in Him was all recollected. God vouchsafed many graces to this creature, sending her very pleasant savours on which she and all her friends in God were fed, and words of love like burning arrows which pierced the hearts of those who heard her. Even her body was, through her mind, set on fire; it seemed as though her soul would leave her body to join what she loved. The time was one of great peace and contentment in which the creature fed only on life eternal.[5]

The Lord: If thou knewest how much I love thee, thou couldst never know anything more in this life, for it will kill thee; or if indeed thou still didst live, it would be by a miracle. And if thou sawest thy wretchedness clearly, knowing My goodness and the great and pure love with which I never cease to work for man, thou wouldst live in despair. For such is My love that it would destroy not only the body but the soul too, if that were possible. My love is infinite and I cannot but love what I have created; My love is pure, simple and clear; with this love only can I love.

To whomsoever understood the least spark of My love all other love would seem false, as in truth it is. The cause of My love is no other than that love itself. And since thou art not able to understand it, abide in peace nor seek what thou canst not find. This love of Mine is best known by an inward feeling. A man gets it when, by its working, it separates him from what in him is man, for man is his own hindrance. . . . My will is that thou meddle no more with My works, for always thou wouldst steal from them, making thine own what befits thee not. I will finish the work without suffering thee to know aught of it; I will part thee from thy Spirit who shall be drowned in My abyss.[6]

For God works in us according to His good pleasure, so subtly and secretly that the man in whom the work is done is unaware of it. For man must feel the martyrdom sent him by God, and otherwise would feel it less. For if he were aware of the work he would not cease to steal from God, even against his own will, because of the evil instinct and the bad habits hidden in the most secret part of his soul. But God knows that

[5] Part II, Chapter IV; *op. cit.*, pp. 92-93.
[6] Part II, Chapters V and XI; *op. cit.*, pp. 94 and 107.

unless He provide man cannot live in this extremity, and therefore provides for him secretly, in divers ways and at divers times, according to his need. At first God's providence is clearly shewn by signs, but little by little God lessens the number of these signs, as He sees man gain strength for the fight. And the stronger a man is in the beginning, the more may he look to suffer great martyrdom in the end. Verily, God provides for every man according to his need, but what He provides in secret is so great that it cannot be compared with what He provides openly, and until death He never ceases.[7]

The Lord: Other work I do unseen: with the finest golden thread, which is My hidden love, I come down to man, and to the thread a hook is fixed which catches his heart. He feels the wound but knows not who has caught and tied him; he cannot and would not move, for it is I, his object and his end, who draw the thread, but this he understands not. I, however, who hold the thread in My hand, still draw him to Me with a love so fine and piercing that he is overcome and conquered and rapt from himself. As a man on the gallows touches not the earth with his feet but hangs in mid air by the rope which kills him, so also this spirit hangs by the thread of this finest love which kills all man's hidden, lurking and unknown imperfections. And all that he loves thereafter he loves with the love of this thread which he feels binding his heart. So also are all his other works wrought by this love, and by grace they are made acceptable to Me. It is I who work of My pure love; man meddles not in it. I, having taken this man into My care and drawn him to Myself, work thus, and enrich him with My benefits, so increasing them that at the hour of his death he is drawn by the thread of love and drowned unawares in the divine abyss. And though man, in the state of which I have spoken, seems a thing dead, lost and abject, he has nevertheless found his life, hidden in Me, in whom are all the treasures and riches of eternal life. Nor can that be told or thought which I have prepared for My beloved soul.[8]

SELECTED BIBLIOGRAPHY

Editions

The definitive text has been established by Umile da Genova, O.F.M. Cap., *Teologia mistica di S. Caterina da Genova: Edizione critica dei manoscritti catariniani*, Volume II (Turin, 1962).

[7] Part II, Chapter XI; *op. cit.*, p. 108.
[8] Part III, Chapter I; *op. cit.*, pp. 111-112.

Translations

Besides the English version by Balfour and Douglas-Irvine from which the selections above were taken, there is an excellent French version by Pierre Debongnie, C.S.S.R., *La grande dame du pur amour* (Paris, 1960).

Studies

Still classic, Baron Friedrich von Hügel's *The Mystical Element of Religion,* 2nd edition (London, 1923), discusses perceptively and at length doctrine, authorship, and influence. Precisions have been suggested by Umile da Genova, "*L'Opus Catharinianum* et ses auteurs," *Revue d'ascétique et de mystique,* XVI (1935), 351-380.

XXVII

ST. IGNATIUS LOYOLA

(1491—1556)

SAINTS, for the most part, keep their secrets well. For every Augustine or Thérèse of Lisieux, whose words are windows through which anyone may gaze at will, there are dozens of others whose words are walls of a superlative opacity. Just such a one, splendidly secretive all these years behind walls of his own construction, is St. Ignatius Loyola.

Yet, as every schoolboy knows, there is really no staying the pens of biographers when their ink-pots are full and a market awaits. Ignorance, which perhaps should stay them, appears rather to awaken ingenuity instead.

It was a notably insomnious ingenuity that presided at the slow creation over the centuries of the Ignatius most people know: the "soldier-saint"; unlettered; slow and stiff of intellect; the exigent idealism of the impoverished nobility whence he sprang continually tilting with the windmill pragmatism of his peasant surroundings; Don Quixote de Loyola, ceaselessly nudged this way and that across the face of Europe by Providence until he founded the Company of Jesus, an ecclesiastical light-infantry of an Order military in its discipline and (innocuously) martial in its intent and ever at the ready to man each disputed barricade of the Church with the all-purpose weapon; the *Spiritual Exercises,* firmly in hand and the cry, *ad majorem Dei gloriam,* frenziedly in mouth. A pity that, except in the imaginations of hard-pressed biographers and of their readers, this Ignatius never existed. He sounds such fun.

St. Ignatius' secret today as through all those yesterdays remains his own. But today there are biographers who have not been content to remain outside his wall of words kicking their heels and cursing their fate and making, *faute de mieux*, ingenious guesses about what manner of man he might be. And of late, armed with the scholar's tools, they have effected small, venturesome breaches here and there in the wall so that today one can at least catch glimpses of the man within.[1] One does not, of course, see him whole. But what one does see makes it clear that St. Ignatius is quite other than ingenuity had led previous generations to believe.

Something of that "otherness" I would attempt to describe and discuss here, limiting myself to two of the most fascinating and hitherto unsuspected aspects of the man behind the now slowly crumbling wall: the theologian of the spiritual life and the mystic.

To begin with, he was the first because he was the second; his discoursing on God and on all things else in their relation to God, which is theology's function, was initially caused and consistently formed and deepened thereafter by his experience of God. In other words, his was a deliberate transfer from personal experience to doctrinal utterance—truly an alarmingly perilous business for anyone to engage in. The danger, of course, is that one tends to make men, made in the image of God, in one's own image. It was a danger he succeeded somehow in avoiding. How he did so may be disputed, but there is no gainsaying that he did. Thus, although they trust they bear a family resemblance to their father Ignatius, Jesuits do differ somewhat markedly; they always have; precisely to the extent that they remain his sons, they always will. Again, one need only recall how diversely hundreds of laity, priests, and nuns were formed to sanctity by him during the days when he was practically the spiritual director of all Europe. It would seem that he avoided the danger usually inherent in the method because his mystical experience and the theology based upon it went so very deep, moving in an area beneath individual differences and according solidity and meaning to them all. Such at least is the conviction which will pervade these introductory observations.

The mystical experience of St. Ignatius was of a piece from the very beginning. His own relating of the initial instance (told, as was his custom, in the third person) will serve to situate discussion:

> One day he went out of devotion to a church which stood a little over a mile from Manresa. . . . The road there

[1] I have in mind such worthy pioneers as James Brodrick, S.J., *Saint Ignatius Loyola* (London, 1956), and Hugo Rahner, S.J., *St. Ignatius Loyola: Letters to Women* (London, 1960).

runs along the river. Occupied with his devotions as he
went along, he sat down for awhile facing the river that
ran below. As he sat there, the eyes of his understanding
began to open. Without having any vision he understood
—knew—many matters both spiritual and pertaining to
the Faith and to the realm of letters and that with such
clearness that they seemed utterly new to him. There is
no possibility of setting out in detail everything he then
understood. The most that he can say is that he was given
so great an enlightening of his mind that, if one were to
put together all the helps he has received from God and
all the things he has ever learned, they would not be the
equal of what he received in that single illumination. He
was left with his understanding so enlightened that he
seemed to be another man with another mind than the
one that was his before.[2]

This signal experience by the River Cardoner would seem to
have taken place in the autumn of 1522.

Already the year had been one of exceptional graces. As he
lay in the diminutive Castle of Loyola, convalescing from
wounds sustained defending the fortress at Pamplona in July
of the previous year, he had asked that books of romance and
chivalry be brought him to help pass the time. None could be
found. So they brought him instead the four fat tomes of
Ludolph the Saxon's *Life of Christ* and a Castilian translation
of *The Golden Legend*. Now a veritable library on the life of
our Lord and a collection of saintly lives generously laced
throughout with the legendary would not, one would think,
be precisely this man's cup of tea. For this man, at thirty, was
in many ways still a boy of thirteen. The fairer of the opposite
sex still peopled his imagination unduly. Daydreams of large
feats of prowess in which he would signalize himself (particularly in feminine eyes) jostled for attention as much as
ever. But to the dreams of the boy undergoing court training
at Arévalo was now added a stain, dark and disturbing, relic
of the subsequent sordid exploits of the man; that would seem
to be the only difference. Yet boredom did its work uncommonly well. Ignatius, "much addicted to gambling and dissolute in his dealings with women, contentious and keen about
using his sword,"[3] found himself in spite of himself browsing
from time to time in the gentle books that had been provided

---

[2] I translate the Spanish of the *Autobiography* as contained in *Obras
Completas de San Ignacio de Loyola* (Madrid, 1952), pp. 49-50.
[3] The description of Ignatius at this time is provided by Juan Polanco,
his secretary and companion later in life. Quoted in Brodrick, *op. cit.*,
p. 45.

him. As weeks passed, a pattern of reading and reverie formed itself. And, increasingly, the reading would provide the matter of the reverie. But not always. The thought of one woman in particular, he tells us, "carried him away to such an extent that he would be wrapt up in it for two, three or four hours, without being conscious of the passage of time."[4] Yet he did find himself musing, however briefly, about St. Dominic or St. Francis and thinking that he should do such things as they. From this alternating of the sacred and the profane in his idly wandering thoughts there came, one significant day, a lesson: He enjoyed his profane thoughts, but when they passed he was left discontented and dry. He enjoyed his holy thoughts, but when they passed he continued to be filled with the joy and gaiety and lightsomeness of spirit they had induced. This rudimentary lesson in how to distinguish the workings of good and evil influences upon one would—nuanced and broadened and deepened—become, of course, a valued part of the *Spiritual Exercises* in later years. But its chief value, even if one has the eventual composing of the *Exercises* solely in mind, would seem to have been this: the frivolous extrovert, gross in his spiritual ignorance, who had never apparently been properly introduced to himself, learned the worth of introspection. It was a lesson he was never to forget. Operative in every line of the acute psychology of the *Exercises* is an informed awareness of the positive role of feelings in the life of the spirit. Now, in the months that followed, he applied his lesson to good purpose as he concluded to the authentic or counterfeit coinage of such things as successive visions of our Lady and Child, of a "very beautiful object shining with the likeness of many eyes," of the Trinity under the form of three keys of a musical instrument. He was ready, when it came, for the mystical experience upon the bank of the Cardoner.

In recalling the event thirty years later he was careful to record that it was not a vision. "Without having any vision he understood—knew—many matters. . . ." It was an instance of Ignatian mysticism in what might be called its pure state. All other instances of which we have record had a visionary accompaniment of one sort or another which can make the interpreter's task, difficult at best, more difficult still. For mystic experience is one thing. Visions are something else again. They must be always and everywhere distinguished one from the other. But where the one ends and the other begins it would often take a Daniel come to judgment to determine. Especially is this so with mystics who, as Ignatius, are also visionaries. Great, therefore, is the historical value of his account of this one vision-less occurrence for in every other re-

[4] Brodrick, *op. cit.,* p. 66.

spect it is identical with every other mystic experience he is reported to have had in the years that followed. A description of Ignatian mysticism "in its pure state," it is accordingly given priority of treatment here.

What it describes as having happened that day on the bank of the River Cardoner was a direct experience of the Godhead which flooded the recipient's intellect with knowledge.

It is to this "knowledge" that one should chiefly attend. It was not knowledge delimited and defined and accorded in concepts: his inability then or later to express it in so many words is sufficient indication that it was question of a direct *experience* in the order of knowing quite as that of the majority of other mystics is a direct experience in the order of loving. It was, further, knowledge that was had in an act of judgment, in an affirmation of the true which was accorded him, by Truth, in the very substance of his being.

The mind boggles, I know, at anything so difficult to grasp as what is being suggested here: the occurrence of a human affirmation was yet a "received," a "passive" act. Yet the contrarieties involved are basically no different from those theology encounters in its efforts to explain the divine operation which is operative in every act of every man, and they need not detain us here.

What must, however, be inquired into more closely is the level upon which this experience occurred, for to understand it is to understand both the role of the visionary in his other experiences and how those experiences could be so satisfactory a basis for his distinctive theology of the spiritual life.

The suggestion was made above that "an affirmation of the true . . . was accorded him . . . *in the very substance of his being.*" By "substance" I meant what Thomism conventionally means by the term: the abiding existential substrate of faculties, of habits, of acts in the human composite. One may call it, more descriptively, the *fundo del alma* with St. Teresa or the *Seelengrund* with Meister Eckhart; it matters little. Whatever expression is used, what one would indicate is that which is ontologically prior to, and normative of, *all* differentiations of the volitional or intellective order. Here, where (in Thomist theory) habitual grace is received, was apparently infused that knowing affirmation. Ignatius' direct experience of the Godhead always seems to have had its effect in these psychic deeps and nowhere else. A being of volition and intellection, he was transformed there where there is no intellection but only its generic matrix.

Because knowing is an existing, it is a truism that one knows as one is. Ignatius ever after knew differently because he was different ("he seemed to be another man"), and the basis of this new being and new knowing was the affirmation of truth which was accorded him then and thereafter.

If there is a magisterial cohesion and depth in his theology combined with a fragmentary and often disconcertingly superficial mode of expression—and there is—the reason lies in the mode of his mystic experience. He came himself to refer to it, more often than not, as being like the entry into his depths of a "white light." Think, then, of this infused act of affirmation as a lucent whiteness which contains within itself all colors of the spectrum, blended, their variety imperceptible, now only a luminous oneness. Of such all-containing light, received upon a level prior to all conceptualizing, there could not be in his theology anything more than scattered refractions. Yet each refraction, each reflected ray, is in harmony with every other because of the common hidden source. Hidden, unexpressed because inexpressible, the source gives coherence to what is disparately visible and, more important still, affords a dimension in depth to what appears only on surfaces.

There is always among the mystics an all but unbridgeable chasm between experience and expression. In Ignatius it was absolutely unbridgeable. Most other mystics have experienced God with the totality of their spiritual being; not only the substance of the soul but its faculties as well are suffused with His felt presence; they have in consequence been able to build a bridge of sorts from experience to expression because the basic organs of expression, the faculties, had themselves partaken of the experience. With Ignatius this was not so. Only the substance of his being was affected.

There would seem to have been two chief results from this relatively limited nature of his mystic experience: it was of almost unbroken duration throughout the last years of his life, and it was—paradoxically enough—theologically more informative than a less limited experience would have been.

It would seem to be the rare and exceptional mystic whose experience of God is practically constant. Marie of the Incarnation perhaps was such a one. St. Ignatius certainly was. The ability he had of "finding God in all things," which was the admiration of his later contemporaries, would seem to have been something much more than the practice he recommended to his Jesuit sons. That, however helpful and salutary, was largely based upon a theology of the *als ob:* one should accept things "as if" coming from the hands of God, one should attend the superior's will "as if" he were Christ, and so on. As is clear from the few pages of his spiritual diary that have come down to us (February 2, 1544, to February 27, 1545), he could *experience* God's presence almost at will. All that was required was an explicit advertence which in the days recorded in the diary he could not always effect but which in subsequent years, according to the testimony of his companions, he found not the slightest difficulty in doing. What he did at such times, it seems, was merely advert consciously and deliberately to what he was already experiencing, for to suggest that he or anyone else could have an authentic mystic experience at will is a particular nonsense I have no intention of indulging in here. And by this free advertence his awareness of what habitually he was experiencing came more sharply into focus—he "found" God.

A homely example may serve to clarify the central point here. Take a young man; he is wonderfully in love; his step has a new resiliency; his eye, a new brightness; all the world, which in accord with the adage loves him, is bright and gay. His happiness, so prolific in felicitous consequences whether ambulatory or oculatory or social, is habitual. He goes to sleep at night with a smile on his face; he awakes in the morning with it still there. Now and again (say, first thing in the morning) he asks himself, wonderingly, why he feels so happy. And, with his answer to himself and with the advertence it involves, his happiness comes more sharply into focus and he experiences it more fully—he "finds" it. Substitute "God" for "happiness" and one has not too inexact an idea of what Ignatius could do and why he could do it.

He could do much else besides. Unlike the majority of mystics, who when they have their experience of God are so invaded that they can experience nothing else, Ignatius was able to carry out the most absorbing and distracting occupations. He could do so because the experience was limited to the substance of his being. There was no ligature of the faculties. Intellect and will remained free to engage in any and all employments. Because they were left free in this experience of Himself, God could accord it to Ignatius uninterruptedly throughout whole years of his life. For it does not seem in the designs of Providence, this side of Paradise, that anyone for long should be only and totally absorbed in Him.

As theologian of the spiritual life, Ignatius again is a mystic with a difference. He provided no such enrichments of the Christian heritage as have Origen or Bernard or John of the Cross with their characteristically subtle analyses of the mystic encounter. It would perhaps be to engage in profitless speculation to wonder, at this late date, if ever he was tempted to try. All the indications are that he never was. He might have been had there been a progression and a variety in his experience. But there was none. Or had there been darkness in it or doubts about it. But, again, there was none. Most important, however, was the experience's leaving the faculties untouched, for it was only with the data provided upon that level that traditionally one began one's analysis. There were no such data. There was only that single, magnificent datum of his conscious juncture, deep in his being, with the operative Godhead. Within it he knew, he tells us, how God created, how the divine Persons proceeded, how Christ is present in the Eucharist, etc. Thence he learned, experientially, before ever he sat in the theology classrooms of Paris, the doctrine of the instrument.

Today, the beneficiaries of successive revivals in Thomism and in liturgical studies, theologians are only beginning to explore to our common profit the rich relevance of instrumental causality for an understanding of the Christian dispensation and the manner of God's acting within it. From the day by the Cardoner to his death decades later in Rome, St. Ignatius saw everything in terms of it. The hundreds of letters of spiritual counsel he wrote or had written for him, the Constitutions of his Order, the *Spiritual Exercises,* all are dominated by this one master intuition. To be apt and pliant instruments in the hands of God is the end of all being for all upon this earth—that is his constant theme and, theologically, it is impossible to think of one more basic or better. It is a doctrine that can be parodied, as it was in the *canard* that Jesuits taught the end justified the means. It can, if cut from its roots in the liturgy, end a stick much to the liking of activists with a particular apostolic drum to beat. It can easily be turned inside out and made an excuse for the lack of personal initiative. But, with a modicum of good sense and a mountainous patience in its application to oneself and to others, it introduces one infallibly if not to the luminous experience of Ignatius at least to the expression, equally luminous, of the will of Him whom Ignatius thus learned to serve.

Perhaps the paradox indulged in above will by now have been pardoned. The mysticism of St. Ignatius was theologically more informative than a less limited experience would have been because it conveyed an insight into reality which is valid for whatever time or place or condition, which undercuts all differences in schools of spirituality and diversities of possible apostolates and varieties of character or temperament while according an added firmness and meaning to them all.

One could hardly wish it to have been otherwise.

TEXTS [5]

SPIRITUAL DIARY

Going to Mass. Before it, not without tears; during, abundant and very calming. Very many insights into the most Holy Trinity which enlightened my mind to the degree that it seemed to me that I could never learn so much by hard study; reflecting later on what I comprehended by sense and sight I still had this impression—yes, even if I were to study all my life.

Immediately after Mass, brief prayer with these words: "Eternal Father, confirm me; Son, etc., confirm me." [6] A great flood of tears over my face and a growing determination to continue saying Masses in Their honor (and I agreed to, according to a number that I would decide upon later). Many deep sobs. Found great intimacy and certainty in an increased love of His Divine Majesty.

In general the insights during and before Mass had to do with the selection of the Mass prayers, when one addresses oneself to God, to the Father, or to the Son, etc.; on the operations of the Divine Persons and Their procession, sensing and seeing rather than understanding. All this corroborating what had been done, I was heartened about the future.

This same day, even while I was going about the city with much joy of soul, representation of the most Holy Trinity as I looked now at three people, now at three animals, now at three other things, and so on.

Wednesday. Before beginning prayer, a desire full of devotion to do so. After beginning, great devotion that was warm or luminous and sweet without any insights yet tending towards inner certainty. Did not terminate in any Divine Person.

Later I was confirmed regarding the past in recognizing the evil spirit of the past, that is to say, the one that would

[5] I translate from the Spanish text established by Arturo Codina, S.J., in the *Constitutiones Societatis Iesu,* Rome, IV, 1934, 86-158. The *Diary* consists solely of the pages devoted to the period February 2, 1544, to February 27, 1545, which alone St. Ignatius did not succeed in destroying before his death. The passages here translated cover only February 19-29, 1544.

[6] During these days he was engaged in writing the Constitutions of the Jesuits and was trying to determine what the poverty of his Order should consist in. He had himself tentatively come to a decision and sought by his Masses at this time confirmation that it was in accord with the will of God.

have me doubt and be impatient towards the most Holy Trinity, as I have already noted.[7]

With this recognition, felt within a fresh movement to tears, and also later, before and during Mass, very great devotion, peaceful and tranquil, tears, some insights.

Before and after, feeling or believing, the desire of going on left me, particularly afterwards, with this great tranquillity or satisfaction of soul. For it seemed to me that I should not continue the Masses of the most Holy Trinity unless this were in order to give thanks or to fulfill my promise, but not out of any necessity of confirming what had taken place.

Thursday. During prayer, the whole time, continuous and very great devotion, burning light and spiritual relishing, drawing partly to a certain elevation.

Later, as I was getting ready in my room, at the altar and in putting on the vestments, a few spiritual impulses and a tendency to tears. Mass over, remained in great spiritual repose.

At Mass, the whole time, tears in greater abundance than yesterday and, one or more times, speechless. Sensed then such spiritual insights that I seemed to understand that there was, so to speak, nothing more to know concerning the most Holy Trinity. The reason was this: when previously I wished to find devotion in the Trinity I did not want to search for it nor to find it by saying prayers to the Father and I did not prepare myself for it because it did not seem to me that consolation or illumination was to come from the most Holy Trinity. But, during this Mass, I knew, I sensed or saw—God only knows—that in speaking to the Father, in seeing that He was a Person of the most Holy Trinity, I was moved to love the Trinity entirely, the more so because the other Persons were in It essentially. I experienced the same thing during prayer to the Son, the same thing during prayer to the Holy Spirit, rejoicing in any one of the Persons and feeling consolations, attributing them to all three Persons and finding my happiness in their pertaining to all three of Them. It seemed so important to me to untie this knot[8] or this something or other that I never got through saying to myself, speaking of myself, "Who are you, then? Where do you come from? etc. What did you deserve? Or whence did it come? etc."

Friday. During the usual period of prayer, the whole time,

[7] On the previous Monday he recorded his impatience with God at his not being as yet manifestly confirmed in his decision.

[8] Scholars are divided about the nature of this "knot." Most say it was Ignatius' difficulty in reconciling the one Divine Nature with the three Divine Persons. It seems simpler to say that it was the stubborn business of confirmation in his decision which he still awaited while acutely aware of his unworthiness.

much help from grace that was hot and in part luminous and much devotion although for my part I sometimes felt an urge to escape into myself, yet the help from the grace did not lessen. Later, readying the altar, some tendency to tears, saying over and over again, "I am not worthy to invoke the name of the most Holy Trinity." This thought and this repeating moved me to great inner devotion and, while putting on the vestments, a greater openness of the soul to tears and sobs. Beginning Mass and going on to the Gospel, I celebrated with much devotion and with much help from burning grace that seemed to struggle with some thoughts as fire with water.

Saturday. In the usual period of prayer, nothing at the beginning; from midway to the end much devotion and satisfaction of soul with some indication of a luminous clarity.

While I prepared the altar, Jesus coming to mind, I was moved to follow Him. It seemed to me interiorly that, since He is the head of the Society, this is an argument for proceeding in complete poverty that is greater than all other human reasons although I thought that all these other reasons, which I had weighed in making my decision, pointed to the same conclusion. This thought moved me to devotion and tears and to such certainty that, even if I had not found tears during Mass or Masses, etc., I thought this feeling would be sufficient to keep me firm in time of temptation or trial.

Going out and putting on the vestments I continued to think such thoughts as these. They increased in number and seemed to be a confirmation although I received no consolation on that account. It seemed to me in some way to have been the work of the most Holy Trinity that Jesus showed Himself or made me sense His presence, reminding me of the day when the Father placed me with the Son.[9]

As I finished vesting, desirous so to impress within myself the name of Jesus that I would for the future be strengthened and, as it were, confirmed, a fresh attack of tears and sobs assailed me. Beginning the Mass, aided by great grace and devotion, with peaceful tears for a long time. Even when Mass was over, great devotion and tendency to tears continued until the moment of unvesting.

Throughout the Mass, experienced various feelings in confirmation of the matter mentioned. And, at the moment when I held the Blessed Sacrament in my hands, there came to me from within the word and the intense urging never to abandon Him for all of heaven or earth or etc. Felt fresh move-

[9] The reference here is to the vision he had in November, 1537, at La Storta outside Rome in which he saw the Father and the Son; and the Son, carrying His cross, was given Ignatius as companion by the Father. This was the vision which had definitely made clear to Ignatius the type of apostolate that would be his.

ments, devotion, and spiritual relish. I added: "for my part, for all that it depended on me." Made this restriction with regard to the companions who had signed.[10]

Later, during the day, each time that I recalled or that there simply came to me the memory of Jesus, a certain feeling or intellectual vision with continuous devotion and confirmation.

Sunday. During the usual period of prayer, from beginning to end, the help of a very intimate and sweet grace, full of warm gentle devotion. Preparing the altar and putting on the vestments I saw a representation of the name of Jesus in much love. Confirmation and great determination to follow Him, tears and sobs.

All during Mass, very great devotion and many tears, often loss of speech. The devotion and the feeling was totally directed towards Jesus, my being unable to direct it to the other Persons unless to the first Person as the Father of such a Son. And then spiritual reactions: "How He is Father and how He is Son!"

Mass over, at prayer the same feeling towards the Son. And then when I wanted confirmation by the most Holy Trinity I felt that it was given me by Jesus who showed Himself to me and gave me overwhelming inner strength and certainty of confirmation. Without fear of the future. Came to mind that I beg Jesus to obtain my pardon from the most Holy Trinity, great devotion, with tears and sobs, and hope of obtaining grace, finding myself much strengthened and confirmed about the future.

Later, near the fireplace, a new representation of Jesus with abundant devotion and a tendency to tears. Later, walking down the street, representation of Jesus, with strong movements and tears. After speaking to Carpi,[11] and also on my way back, felt great devotion. After dinner, especially after I went through the Vicar's door at Trani's,[12] sensed or saw Jesus, many inner motions and many tears. Begged and besought Jesus to obtain my pardon from the most Holy Trinity and continued to feel within me great confidence that He would obtain it. At these times, sensing or seeing Jesus, I felt so great a love within me that I thought nothing could happen in the future that would be able to separate me from Him or

[10] It had been decided by Ignatius and his first Jesuits in 1541 that the churches of the Society would have fixed revenues. Ignatius now was determined on absolute poverty even in regard to the churches but with the reservation that he would submit his decision to these companions "who had signed" the earlier rules relating to poverty.

[11] The Cardinal who was the official Protector of the Society.

[12] The Vicar was the Vicar of Rome, Filippo Archinto, and Trani was the Cardinal who was patron of a house that Ignatius had opened for new converts.

cause me to doubt the graces or the confirmation I had received.

Monday. First prayer with very great devotion which increased later, warmth and assistance of abundant grace. And yet, for my part, because I was disturbed I found myself distracted. Not asking or seeking confirmation, but desiring reconciliation with the three Divine Persons. Later, dressed for the celebration of Mass, not knowing to whom I should recommend myself or where I should begin, the thought came to me while Jesus was communicating Himself to me: "I want to go on" and thus it was that I began the confession *Confiteor Deo* as Jesus said in the Gospel for the day, "Confiteor tibi, etc."[13] Pursued therewith the confession with new devotion and not without a tendency to tears and began the Mass with much devotion, warmth, and tears, often losing the ability to vocalize. In the prayers to the Father, it seemed to me that Jesus presented them to Him or that He went along with them to the Father as I said them. Sense or seeing impossible to express.

Mass over, desire to reconcile myself with the most Holy Trinity. Begged that of Jesus not without tears and sobs, reassuring myself and not asking not even feeling any need of being confirmed nor even to celebrate Masses for this purpose but only to bring about my reconciliation.

Tuesday. The first prayer untroubled and undistracted and with much devotion. In the second half even more devotion although, especially in the first part, I experienced a certain weakness or indisposition of the body.

Once I was dressed,[14] and still in my room preparing for Mass, fresh devotion and inner urgings to tears upon recalling Jesus. Felt great confidence in Him. It seemed to me that He was in favor of interceding for me so long as I neither wanted nor sought out a new or firmer confirmation of the past. Remained tranquil and at peace on this point. I then began to beg and beseech Jesus to shape me to the will of the most Holy Trinity in the manner that seemed best to Him.

Later, while putting on the Mass vestments, this representation of the help and the love of Jesus grew. Began Mass not without great devotion, at peace and in repose. With a slight tendency to tears. It seemed to me that, with less tears, I was the more satisfied and content to let myself be guided

---

[13] The Mass that day was that of St. Matthias. Accordingly, the "Gospel for the day" read in the Mass was that of Matthew 11:25-30. The "confession" to which he refers is the public protestation of unworthiness voiced by the celebrating priest at the beginning of Mass.

[14] Somewhat unusual, but for him quite characteristic, the first period in the Saint's long hours of daily prayer was had in bed before ever he got up.

by the Divine Majesty to whom it pertains to give or withdraw His graces as and when it suits Him best. After this, near the fireplace, this contentment increased with a new inner urging and love of Jesus. I no longer had within me that former contradiction regarding the most Holy Trinity.[15] And so much devotion towards the Trinity continuing throughout the Mass.

Wednesday. In the usual prayer, sufficiently good and as usual, to the halfway point. Then, increasing greatly to the very end, with abundant devotion, peace and spiritual sweetness. Afterwards an unbroken devotion remained in me while I got dressed in my room and all the while commended myself to Jesus, not in order to obtain some further confirmation of whatever sort, but in order that He do me His best service in the presence of the most Holy Trinity etc. and that I be, in the most effective way, in His grace. Received then some light and strength.

Going into the chapel, during prayer, a sensing or, more precisely, a seeing beyond the capacities of nature of the most Holy Trinity and of Jesus who presented me, or placed me, or served as my intercessor before the most Holy Trinity in order that this intellectual vision be given me. And in this sensing and this seeing overcome with tears and love. But directed towards Jesus and the most Holy Trinity a feeling of respect closer to reverential love than to anything else.

Later, in the same fashion, a feeling that Jesus played the same role when I thought to pray to the Father. Impression and inward feeling that it was He that did everything in the presence of the Father and of the most Holy Trinity.[16]

Began Mass with an abundance of tears.[17] And, all during Mass, without interruption, abundance of devotion and tears. Likewise, suddenly, I clearly beheld the same vision of the most Holy Trinity that I had before; and throughout there grew in me a still greater love of His Divine Majesty. At times lost the power of speech.

[15] Again, Ignatian scholars disagree about this "former contradiction" as they do about the "knot" above. But it would seem to be question here, as his frequent begging for pardon attests, of his impatience with God at his not being more quickly confirmed.

[16] The reader may by now have come to marvel at this distinction that St. Ignatius seems to make between the second Person of the Trinity and the Trinity. The distinction is real and valid: it is question throughout of Jesus as man and therefore as mediator and intercessor. *See* 1 Timothy 2:5.

[17] And surely, by now, the reader must wonder about the nature and function of these frequent tears in a grown and psychically well-balanced man. A helpful analysis is provided by Jean Joseph Navatel, S.J., *La Dévotion sensible, les Larmes et les Exercices de Saint Ignace*, No. 64 in the "Bibliothèque des Exercices" (Enghien, 1920).

Mass over, during prayer and later by the fireplace, several times there was intense devotion towards Jesus. With special inner tendencies to tears, or more. While I write this my understanding is drawn to the vision of the most Holy Trinity; a vision, although not so clear as before, of the three Persons.

During Mass, while saying "Domine Jesu Christe, Filie Dei vivi, etc.,"[18] I seemed to understand that I had first seen Jesus, as I said,[19] white—that is to say, His humanity—and I sensed Him now in my soul in a different way—that is to say, not only the humanity but that He was completely my God, etc. Fresh flowing of tears and great devotion, etc.

Thursday. During the entire usual period of prayer, abundance of devotion. Great help from a warm, luminous, amorous grace. Going into the chapel, added devotion. Once I was on my knees, revelation or vision of Jesus at the feet of the most Holy Trinity, and then movements and tears. This vision was not of the same duration or the same clarity as that of Wednesday, although it seemed to me to be of the same sort. Later, during Mass, tears, great devotion, some helpful thoughts. And, after Mass, not without tears.

Friday. During the usual period of prayer, from the beginning to the very end, very great devotion and very luminous, cloaking my sins and preventing me from thinking of them. Outside, at the church, before Mass, a vision of the heavenly fatherland or of its Lord in the form of a seeing by intelligence of the three Persons, and, in the Father, the second and the third. During Mass, now and again, abundance of devotion without either insights or being moved to tears.

When Mass was over, the same vision of the fatherland or of its Lord, without distinction of Persons, but clearly as has happened to me many times, now more, now less. The whole day, special devotion.

SELECTED BIBLIOGRAPHY

Aside from the *Exercitia Spiritualia* (Madrid, 1919) and the *Diary* (Rome, 1934), among the writings of St. Ignatius the following are of utmost importance: the conclusion to the first redaction of the "Examen" (*Constitutiones Societatis Iesu,* Rome, II, 1936, 125), the fourth chapter of the definitive "Examen" (*op. cit.,* pp. 85-89, especially nn. 44-46, which treat of the spirit one should have would he respond properly to his vocation, while the

[18] The opening words of the second of three prayers said by the celebrating priest before his Communion in the Mass.

[19] Apparently he said so in an earlier part of the *Diary* which has not survived.

previous locus referred to treats of the interrelations of nature and grace); in the *Constitutiones* themselves, P. III, c. 1 (spiritual formation of novices), IV, 4 (maintenance of fervor among scholastics), VI (obligations of Jesuit life and the means given to fulfill them), VIII, 1 (union of minds and hearts), IX, 1-2 (qualities of the General, with which one should compare IV, 10 [nn. 4-5] on the qualities of Rectors), X (the means of conserving and increasing the Society of Jesus).

Among the writings by others than Ignatius but of close Ignatian inspiration one should consult the letter to the Scholastics at Coimbra (*Epistolae S. P. Ignatii*, Madrid, I, 1903, pp. 495-508— the work of Polanco or of Ferrao) and Polanco's famous "Letter on Obedience" (*op. cit.*, III, 1905, 669-681). Comparably informative is Jerome Nadal's *Scholia in Constitutiones et Declarationes S. P. Ignatii* (Prato, 1883), declared normative by the second General Congregation (1565) in its 42nd Decree.

Of the multitudinous interpretations of the "spirituality of St. Ignatius" the best are Erich Przywara, *Majestas Divina:* Ignatianische Frömmigkeit (Augsburg, 1925) [*ET* by Thomas Corbishley, *The Divine Majesty* (Cork, 1951), which unfortunately omits the important Epilogue of the original]; P. de Chastonay, *Die Satzungen des Jesuitenordens* (Einsiedeln, 1938), pp. 169-275 [*ET*, anonymously done, *Les Constitutions de l'Ordre des Jesuites*, (Paris, n.d.), pp. 154-248]; F. X. Lawlor, "The Doctrine of Grace in the *Spiritual Exercises*," *Theological Studies*, III (1942), 513-532; Jean Daniélou, "La vision ignatienne du monde et de l'homme," *Revue d'ascétique et de mystique*, XXVI (1950), 5-17 [*ET by T. R. Royce*, "The Ignatian Vision of the Universe and of Man," *Cross Currents*, IV (1954), 357-366]; Joseph de Guibert, *La Spiritualité de la Compagnie de Jésus* (Rome, 1953), pp. 97-140; and Miguel Nicolau, "Notas de la Espiritualidad jesuítica," *Manresa*, XXV (1953), 259-288.

XXVIII

ST. TERESA OF AVILA

(1515—1582)

THE TITLE of this book is *Varieties of Mystic Experience*.
This section of this book might, with strict justice, be entitled
"Varieties of Mystic Experience in Saint Teresa." For with the
others considered thus far it has been question of one distinctive and characteristic experience presented as a peak
towards which all else led. But with Teresa it is question of
several distinctive and characteristic experiences, now one and
now another being presented as the peak towards which all
else led.

Writing five years before her death, Teresa in *Interior Castle*
presented spiritual marriage as the peak and all other mystic
experiences she had as intermediate degrees. There is no difficulty in admitting that they were chronologically intermediate.
But were they logically so? The attempt seems to have been
made to present them as if they were. Yet there is also recurrently the assigning as the basic distinctive characteristics of
one experience what are later assigned as the basic distinctive
characteristics of another. They would seem, therefore, to have
been different experiences rather than progressive parts of the
same experience.

It is the besetting temptation of even the best of interpreters
to arrange data from the mystics in an ascending line. More
often than not, no real wrong is committed in giving in to the
temptation because, more often than not, so proceeded the
individual mystic's life. But, I fear, it would be very wrong
to accede to the temptation here and simply plot out the experi-

210

ences of Teresa as successive and exclusive stages of one experience.

She herself reports these varieties:

In her *Life* (1562–1565) she writes of four degrees of prayer, Meditation (Chapter 11), Prayer of Quiet (Chapter 14), Sleep of the Faculties (Chapter 16), and Union (Chapter 18). This last is a true union in which one is unable to do anything—unable to reason, unable to read—and which, brief, usually comes about after long mental prayer.

In *The Way of Perfection* (1565–1566), Prayer of Recollection (Chapter 28) is followed by Prayer of Quiet (Chapter 30), which she says is "a supernatural state" in which all the faculties are stilled and the will is held captive; it goes on for days. There follows Prayer of Union (Chapter 31).

In her *Fifth Relation* (1576), she writes of Prayer of Recollection followed by Quietude and then the Sleep of the Faculties, where the will alone is in union. Union, in which all the faculties are engaged, is followed by Rapture, and the culmination is the Wound of Love.

The selections given here are from *Interior Castle*. They describe the experience she had towards the close of her life, an experience not wholly like that of any other mystic nor even of a piece with her previous experiences.

TEXTS [1]

INTERIOR CASTLE

Prayer of Quiet

To understand it better, let us suppose that we are looking at two fountains, the basins of which can be filled with water. There are certain spiritual things which I can find no way of explaining more aptly than by this element of water; for, as I am very ignorant, and my wits give me no help, and I am so fond of this element, I have observed it more attentively than anything else. . . . These two large basins can be filled with water in different ways: the water in the one comes from a long distance, by means of numerous conduits and through human skill; but the other has been constructed at the very

[1] From *The Complete Works of St. Teresa*, Volume II, translated and edited by E. Allison Peers from the critical edition of P. Silverio de Santa Teresa, C.D., published by Sheed & Ward, Inc., New York; Sheed & Ward Limited, London, 1946.

source of the water and fills without making any noise. If the flow of water is abundant, as in the case we are speaking of, a great stream still runs from it after it has been filled; no skill is necessary here, and no conduits have to be made, for the water is flowing all the time. The difference between this and the carrying of the water by means of conduits is, I think, as follows. The latter corresponds to the spiritual sweetness which, as I say, is produced by meditation. It reaches us by way of the thoughts; we meditate upon created things and fatigue the understanding; and when at last, by means of our own efforts, it comes, the satisfaction which it brings to the soul fills the basin, but in doing so makes a noise, as I have said.

To the other fountain the water comes direct from its source, which is God, and, when it is His Majesty's will and He is pleased to grant us some supernatural favour, its coming is accompanied by the greatest peace and quietness and sweetness within ourselves—I cannot say where it arises or how. And that content and delight are not felt, as earthly delights are felt, in the heart—I mean not at the outset, for later the basin becomes completely filled, and then this water begins to overflow all the Mansions and faculties, until it reaches the body. It is for that reason that I said it has its source in God and ends in ourselves—for it is certain, and anyone will know this who has experienced it, that the whole of the outer man enjoys this consolation and sweetness.[2]

Apparently, as this heavenly water begins to flow from this source of which I am speaking—that is, from our very depths —it proceeds to spread within us and cause an interior dilation and produce ineffable blessings, so that the soul itself cannot understand all that it receives there. The fragrance it experiences, we might say, is as if in those interior depths there were a brazier on which were cast sweet perfumes; the light cannot be seen, nor the place where it dwells, but the fragrant smoke and the heat penetrate the entire soul, and very often, as I have said, the effects extend even to the body. Observe— and understand me here—that no heat is felt, nor is any fragrance perceived: it is a more delicate thing than that; I only put it in that way so that you may understand it. People who have not experienced it must realize that it does in very truth happen; its occurrence is capable of being perceived, and the soul becomes aware of it more clearly than these words of mine can express it. For it is not a thing that we can fancy, nor, however hard we strive, can we acquire it, and from that

[2] IV, ii; Peers, *op. cit.*, pp. 236-237.

very fact it is clear that it is a thing made, not of human metal, but of the purest gold of Divine wisdom. In this state the faculties are not, I think, in union, but they become absorbed and are amazed as they consider what is happening to them.

It may be that in writing of these interior things I am contradicting what I have myself said elsewhere. This is not surprising, for almost fifteen years have passed since then, and perhaps the Lord has now given me a clear realization of these matters than I had at first. Both then and now, of course, I may be mistaken in all this, but I cannot lie about it . . . I am speaking of it just as I understand it.

The will certainly seems to me to be united in some way with the will of God; but it is by the effects of this prayer and the actions which follow it that the genuineness of the experience must be tested.[3]

Prayer of Union

Do not think it is a state, like the last, in which we dream; I say "dream," because the soul seems to be, as it were, drowsy, so that it neither seems asleep nor feels awake. Here we are all asleep, and fast asleep, to the things of the world, and to ourselves (in fact, for the short time that the condition lasts, the soul is without consciousness and has no power to think, even though it may desire to do so). There is no need now for it to devise any method of suspending the thought. Even in loving, if it is able to love, it cannot understand how or what it is that it loves, nor what it would desire; in fact, it has completely died to the world so that it may live more fully in God. This is a delectable death, a snatching of the soul from all the activities which it can perform while it is in the body; a death full of delight, for, in order to come closer to God, the soul appears to have withdrawn so far from the body that I do not know if it has still life enough to be able to breathe. I have just been thinking about this and I believe it has not; or at least, if it still breathes, it does so without realizing it. The mind would like to occupy itself wholly in understanding something of what it feels, and, as it has not the strength to do this, it becomes so dumbfounded that, even if any consciousness remains to it, neither hands nor feet can move; as we commonly say of a person who has fallen into a swoon, it might be taken for dead.[4]

[3] IV, ii; *op. cit.*, pp. 237-238.
[4] V, i; *op. cit.*, p. 248.

Betrothal

Let us now begin to treat of the way in which the Spouse deals with [the soul], and see how, before it is wholly one with Him, He fills it with fervent desire, by means so delicate that the soul itself does not understand them, nor do I think I shall succeed in describing them in such a way as to be understood, except by those who have experienced it; for these are influences so delicate and subtle that they proceed from the very depth of the heart and I know no comparison that I can make which will fit the case.

All this is very different from what one can achieve in earthly matters, and even from the consolations which have been described. For often when a person is quite unprepared for such a thing, and is not even thinking of God, he is awakened by His Majesty, as though by a rushing comet or a thunderclap. Although no sound is heard, the soul is very well aware that it has been called by God, so much so that sometimes, especially at first, it begins to tremble and complain, though it feels nothing that causes it affliction. It is conscious of having been most delectably wounded, but cannot say how or by whom; but it is certain that this is a precious experience and it would be glad if it were never to be healed of that wound. It complains to its Spouse with words of love, and even cries aloud, being unable to help itself, for it realizes that He is present but will not manifest Himself in such a way as to allow it to enjoy Him, and this is a great grief, though a sweet and delectable one; even if it should desire not to suffer it, it would have no choice—but in any case it never would so desire. It is much more satisfying to a soul than is the delectable absorption, devoid of distress, which occurs in the Prayer of Quiet. . . .[5] Oh, what confusion the soul feels when it comes to itself again and what ardent desires it has to be used for God in any and every way in which He may be pleased to employ it! If such effects as have been described result from the former kinds of prayer, what can be said of a favour as great as this? Such a soul would gladly have a thousand lives so as to use them all for God, and it would like everything on earth to be tongue so that it might praise Him. It has tremendous desires to do penance; and whatever penance it does it counts as very little, for its love is so strong that it feels everything it does to be of very small account and realizes

[5] VI, ii; op. cit., pp. 275-276.

clearly that it was not such a great matter for the martyrs to suffer all their tortures, for with the aid of Our Lord such a thing becomes easy. And thus these souls make complaint to Our Lord when He offers them no means of suffering.[6]

Spiritual Marriage

In this Mansion everything is different. Our good God now desires to remove the scales from the eyes of the soul, so that it may see and understand something of the favour which He is granting it, although He is doing this in a strange manner. It is brought into this Mansion by means of an intellectual vision, in which, by a representation of the truth in a particular way, the Most Holy Trinity reveals Itself, in all three Persons. First of all the spirit becomes enkindled and is illumined, as it were, by a cloud of the greatest brightness. It sees these three Persons, individually, and yet, by a wonderful kind of knowledge which is given to it, the soul realizes that most certainly and truly all these three Persons are one Substance and one Power and one Knowledge and one God alone; so that what we hold by faith the soul may be said here to grasp by sight, although nothing is seen by the eyes, either of the body or of the soul, for it is no imaginary vision. Here all three Persons communicate Themselves to the soul and speak to the soul and explain to it those words which the Gospel attributes to the Lord—namely, that He and the Father and the Holy Spirit will come to dwell with the soul which loves Him and keeps His commandments. . . .

This Presence is not of course always realized so fully—I mean so clearly—as it is when it first comes, or on certain other occasions when God grants the soul this consolation; if it were, it would be impossible for the soul to think of anything else, or even to live among men. But although the light which accompanies it may not be so clear, the soul is always aware that it is experiencing this companionship. We might compare the soul to a person who is with others in a very bright room; and then suppose that the shutters are closed so that the people are all in darkness. The light by which they can be seen has been taken away, and, until it comes back, we shall be unable to see them, yet we are none the less aware that they are there.[7]

[6] VI, iv; *op. cit.*, pp. 291-292.
[7] VII, i; *op. cit.*, pp. 331-332.

SELECTED BIBLIOGRAPHY

Editions

Obras de Santa Teresa, edited and annotated by Silverio de Santa Teresa, O.C.D. (Burgos, 9 volumes, 1915-1924), is standard. Convenient manual editions of the Silverio text are available.

Translations

Good English versions of *The Life* and of *Interior Castle* have been provided by David Lewis, 5th edition (London, 1916), and the Benedictines of Stanbrook (London, 1912) respectively. The best version is that by E. Allison Peers, *The Complete Works of St. Teresa* (from which the selections above have been taken).

Studies

Alois Mager, O.S.B., *Mystik als seelische Wirklichkeit* (Salzburg, 1945), pp. 144-203, brings strong theological insight to his interpretation. Historical perspective is the chief recommending feature of Louis Oechslin, O.P., *L'Intuition mystique de sainte Thérèse* (Paris, 1946); psychological perspective, of Marcel Lépée, *Sainte Thérèse d'Avila: Le réalisme chrétien* (Paris, 1947).

XXIX

ST. JOHN OF THE CROSS

(1542—1591)

To INTERPRET aright the mystical experience of St. John of the Cross, this, it would seem, must chiefly be kept in mind: his ability to adjust his expression of it to literary conventions, whether those of the popular poetry of his day or those, then current, of the theology classroom. I have particularly in mind here his easy, almost eager, adapting of his exposition to the Dionysian schema. Just as he uses the verse forms of pastoral poetry to say obviously unpastoral things, so also he uses the thought patterns of the Pseudo-Dionysius to say—not so obviously—un-Dionysian things. Where our mysterious sixth-century Syrian provides an ontology of what mystical experience ought to be, St. John provides psychological description of what his own mystic experience actually was.

Three levels of that experience can best engage our attention here: the Dark Night, the Betrothal, and the Spiritual Marriage.

In the second book of *Dark Night*[1] he describes a dark contemplation which is "the inflowing of God into the soul."

For him, it will be recalled, there is "darkness" whenever the faculties of sense or of spirit are denied their own native act while the soul is yet being acted upon; and there is always an element of terror present.

In this "dark contemplation," then, the spiritual faculties are denied their native act: nothing is "seen" or known in the ordinary way, nothing is willed in the ordinary way; the fac-

[1] Chapter V.

217

ulties are assailed and overwhelmed by a presence they are unable to grasp. It is, he says, as though one were to look at the sun with the naked eye and the eye, because of its weakness, were to recoil blinded and in pain. Pain is paramount. This is the "horrible night" comparable only to Purgatory.

Is it mystic experience in the strict sense, the experiential awareness of the presence of God? I would suggest that it is. It is the pain-filled awareness of majesty and munificence entering into the wretched and the poor, of consummate holiness touching human vileness, of infinite strength "assailing" human weakness: "Beneath the power of this oppression and weight the soul feels itself so far from being favored that it thinks, and correctly so, that even that wherein it was wont to find some help has vanished with everything else."[2] It is an experience, it is worth noting, not of the Trinity but of the One God.

In the Betrothal the presence of God is experienced by the will alone, which, purified now, reacts without pain to the impress upon it of the Divine Will,[3] where there is pain in the other experience there is delight here in a state "wherein the Spouse grants the soul great favors and visits it most lovingly and frequently." The Purification continues, but it is joy-filled. Desire is its consequence: "The yearnings of the caverns of the soul are wont to be extreme and delicate." Who is the Spouse? The three Divine Persons. But the three Divine Persons as one "for They all work in one."[4] The interpreter naturally wonders here whether St. John is simply repeating a theological axiom (all acts extrinsic to the Trinity are common to all three Persons) or reporting an experience. It would seem that he is doing the second, because he will speak of the Word, for instance, or of the Holy Spirit and then promptly add that this is no more than a manner of speaking, "for They all work in one."

The Spiritual Marriage is a state which differs from that of the indwelling of the Trinity in the souls of all mankind only in that the indwelling is now experienced: "God dwells secretly in all souls and is hidden in their substance; for, were this not so, they would be unable to exist. But there is a difference between these two manners of dwelling and a great one. . . . He dwells not secretly with respect to the soul which is in this state of perfection, for it feels this intimate embrace within it."[5] It is comparable, he says, to the Beatific Vision in Heaven, the sole difference being its transiency: "[God] is there, habit-

---

[2] Chapter V, n. 7.
[3] *Living Flame*, First Redaction, Stanzas II-III.
[4] Stanza II, n. 1.
[5] *Living Flame*, Second Redaction, Stanza IV, n. 14.

ually, as it were, asleep in this embrace with the bride, in the substance of the soul; and of this the soul is quite conscious, and habitually has fruition of Him, for, if He were forever awake within it, communicating knowledge and love to it, it would be already living in glory."[6]

TEXTS [7]

SPIRITUAL MAXIMS

He that desires to be alone, without the support of a master and guide, will be like the tree that is alone in the field and has no owner. However much fruit it bears, passers-by will pluck it all, and it will not mature.[8]

The fly that clings to honey impedes its flight; and the soul that would cling to spiritual sweetness impedes its liberty and contemplation.[9]

At eventide they will examine thee in love.[10]

He that knows how to die to all things will have life in all things.[11]

ASCENT OF MOUNT CARMEL

Stanzas

Wherein the soul sings of the happy chance which it had in passing through the dark night of faith, in detachment and purgation of itself, to union with the Beloved.

On a dark night,   Kindled in love with yearnings—oh, happy chance!—

[6] Stanza IV, n. 15.
[7] From *The Complete Works of Saint John of the Cross,* translated and edited by E. Allison Peers, Volumes I-III, new edition, revised (Westminster-London, 1953).
[8] Peers, *op. cit.,* Vol. III, p. 219.
[9] *Op. cit.,* Vol. III, p. 221.
[10] *Op. cit.,* Vol. III, p. 225.
[11] *Op. cit.,* Vol. III, p. 235.

I went forth without being observed,   My house being now at rest.

In darkness and secure,   By the secret ladder, disguised—oh, happy chance!—
In darkness and in concealment,   My house being now at rest.

In the happy night,   In secret, when none saw me,
Nor I beheld aught,   Without light or guide, save that which burned in my heart.

This light guided me   More surely than the light of noon-day,
To the place where he (well I knew who!) was awaiting me—A place where none appeared.

Oh, night that guided me,   Oh, night more lovely than the dawn,
Oh, night that joined Beloved with lover,   Lover transformed in the Beloved!

Upon my flowery breast,   Kept wholly for himself alone,
There he stayed sleeping, and I caressed him,   And the fanning of the cedars made a breeze.

The breeze blew from the turret As I parted his locks;
With his gentle hand he wounded my neck And caused all my senses to be suspended.

I remained, lost in oblivion; My face I reclined on the Beloved.
All ceased and I abandoned myself,   Leaving my cares forgotten among the lilies.[12]

In order to arrive at having pleasure in everything,
Desire to have pleasure in nothing.
In order to arrive at possessing everything,
Desire to possess nothing.
In order to arrive at being everything,
Desire to be nothing.
In order to arrive at knowing everything,
Desire to know nothing.
In order to arrive at that wherein thou hast no pleasure,
Thou must go by a way wherein thou hast no pleasure.

[12] *Op. cit.,* Vol. I, p. 10.

In order to arrive at that which thou knowest not,
Thou must go by a way that thou knowest not.
  In order to arrive at that which thou possessest not,
Thou must go by a way that thou possessest not.
  In order to arrive at that which thou are not.
Thou must go through that which thou are not.

  When thy mind dwells upon anything,
Thou art ceasing to cast thyself upon the All.
  For, in order to pass from the all to the All,
Thou hast to deny thyself wholly in all.
  And, when thou comest to possess it wholly,
Thou must possess it without desiring anything.
  For, if thou wilt have anything in having all,
Thou hast not thy treasure purely in God.[13]

  In order to conquer all the desires and to deny itself the pleasures which it has in everything, and for which its love and
affection are wont to enkindle the will that it may enjoy them,
[the soul has] to experience another and a greater enkindling
by another and a better love, which is that of its Spouse; to the
end that, having its pleasure set upon Him and deriving from
Him its strength, it should have courage and constancy to deny
itself all other things with ease.[14]

  We may say that there are three reasons for which this
journey made by the soul to union with God is called night.
The first has to do with the point from which the soul goes
forth, for it has gradually to deprive itself of desire for all
the worldly things which it possessed, by denying them to itself; the which denial and deprivation are, as it were, night to
all the senses of man. The second reason has to do with the
mean, or the road along which the soul must travel to this
union—that is, faith, which is likewise as dark as night to the
understanding. The third has to do with the point to which it
travels—namely, God, Who, equally, is dark night to the soul
in this life. These three nights must pass through the soul—or,
rather, the soul must pass through them—in order that it may
come to Divine union with God. . . . These three parts of the
night are all one night; but, after the manner of night, it has
three parts. For the first part, which is that of sense, is comparable to the beginning of night, the point at which things
begin to fade from sight. And the second part, which is faith,
is comparable to midnight, which is total darkness. And the

---

[13] Book I, Chapter XIII; *op. cit.,* Vol. I, pp. 59-60.
[14] Book I, Chapter XIV; *op. cit.,* Vol. I, p. 61.

third part is like the close of night, which is God, the which part is now near to the light of day.[15]

DARK NIGHT OF THE SOUL

This dark night is an inflowing of God into the soul, which purges it from its ignorances and imperfections, habitual, natural and spiritual, and which is called by contemplatives infused contemplation, or mystical theology. Herein God secretly teaches the soul and instructs it in perfection of love, without its doing anything, or understanding of what manner is this infused contemplation. Inasmuch as it is the loving wisdom of God, God produces striking effects in the soul, for, by purging and illumining it, He prepares it for the union of love with God. Wherefore the same loving wisdom that purges the blessed spirits and enlightens them is that which here purges the soul and illumines it.

But the question arises: Why is the Divine light (which, as we say, illumines and purges the soul from its ignorances) here called by the soul a dark night? To this the answer is that for two reasons this Divine wisdom is not only night and darkness for the soul, but is likewise affliction and torment. The first is because of the height of Divine Wisdom, which transcends the talent of the soul, and in this way is darkness to it; the second, because of its vileness and impurity, in which respect it is painful and afflictive to it, and is also dark.

In order to prove the first point, we must here assume a certain doctrine of the philosopher, which says that, the clearer and more manifest are Divine things in themselves, the darker and more hidden are they to the soul naturally; just as, the clearer is the light, the more it blinds and darkens the pupil of the owl, and, the more directly we look at the sun, the greater is the darkness which it causes in our visual faculty, overcoming and overwhelming it through its own weakness. In the same way, when this Divine light of contemplation assails the soul which is not yet wholly enlightened, it causes spiritual darkness in it; for not only does it overcome it, but likewise it overwhelms it and darkens the act of its natural intelligence. For this reason Saint Dionysius and other mystical theologians call this infused contemplation a ray of darkness—that is to say, for the soul that is not enlightened and purged—for the natural strength of the intellect is transcended and overwhelmed by its great supernatural light. Wherefore David

[15] Book I, Chapter II; op. cit., Vol. I, pp. 19-21.

likewise said: That near to God and round about Him are darkness and cloud; not that this is so in fact, but that it is so to our weak understanding, which is blinded and darkened by so vast a light, to which it cannot attain. For this cause the same David then explained himself, saying: "Through the great splendour of His presence passed clouds"—that is, between God and our understanding. And it is for this cause that, when God sends it out from Himself to the soul that is not yet transformed, this illumining ray of His secret wisdom causes thick darkness in the understanding.

And it is clear that this dark contemplation is in these its beginnings painful likewise to the soul; for, as this Divine infused contemplation has many excellences that are extremely good, and the soul that receives them, not being purged, has many miseries that are likewise extremely bad, hence it follows that, as two contraries cannot coexist in one subject—the soul —it must of necessity have pain and suffering.[16]

We observe that a ray of sunlight which enters through the window is the less clearly visible according as it is the purer and freer from specks, and the more of such specks and motes there are in the air, the brighter is the light to the eye. The reason is that it is not the light itself that is seen; the light is but the means whereby the other things that it strikes are seen, and then it is also seen itself, through its reflection in them; were it not for this, neither it nor they would have been seen. . . . Now this is precisely what this Divine ray of contemplation does in the soul. Assailing it with its Divine light, it transcends the natural power of the soul, and herein it darkens it and deprives it of all natural affections and apprehensions which it apprehended aforetime by means of natural light; and thus it leaves it not only dark, but likewise empty, according to its faculties and desires, both spiritual and natural. And, by thus leaving it empty and in darkness, it purges and illumines it with Divine spiritual light, although the soul thinks not that it has this light, but believes itself to be in darkness, even as we have said of the ray of light, which, although it be in the midst of the room, yet, if it be pure and meet nothing on its path, is not visible. With regard, however, to this spiritual light by which the soul is assailed, when it has something to strike— that is, when something spiritual presents itself to be understood, however small a speck it be and whether of perfection or imperfection, or whether it be a judgment of the falsehood or the truth of a thing—it then sees and understands much more clearly than before it was in these dark places.[17]

[16] Book II, Chapter V; *op. cit.*, Vol. I, pp. 381-382.
[17] Book II, Chapter VIII; *op. cit.*, Vol. I, p. 395.

VERSES UPON AN ECSTASY OF
HIGH CONTEMPLATION

I enter'd in—I knew not where—
And, there remaining, knew no more,
Transcending far all human lore.

I knew not where I enter'd in.
'Twas giv'n me there myself to see
And wondrous things I learn'd within,
Yet knew I not where I could be.
I'll say not what was told to me:
Remaining there, I knew no more,
Transcending far all human lore.

That was the love, all else above,
Of perfect peace, devotion deep.
In the profound retreat of love
The path direct I learn'd to keep.
Such secret knowledge did I reap
That, stammering, I could speak no more,
Transcending far all human lore.

Herein so deeply was I vers'd,
Throughly absorb'd and borne so high,
So far my senses were immers'd
That destitute of sense was I.
My soul was dower'd from on high
With power of thought that thought no more,
Transcending far all human lore.

He that in truth attains to this
Is lost to self upon the earth.
All that, before, he knew as his
Appears to him of little worth.
His knowledge comes anew to birth,
Yet, resting there, he knows no more,
Transcending far all human lore.

The nearer I approach'd the cloud,
The less I understood its light,
That, howso darksome was its shroud,
Illumin'd all the gloomy night.

Wherefore a soul that knows that sight
Can never compass knowledge more,
For this transcends all human lore.

This wondrous knowledge knowing naught
Is of a power so sov'reign high
That wise men's reasoning and thought
Defeat it not, howe'er they try.
Ne'er can their intellect come nigh
This power of thought that thinks no more,
Transcending far all human lore.

Built on so excellent a plan
This summit of true knowledge is
That neither wit nor power of man
Can ever reach such heights of bliss.
He that can climb as high as this
Through knowledge that can know no more
Shall aye transcend all human lore.

Would ye unto this summit climb?
Then know wherein its nature lies.
'Tis an experience all-sublime,
God's Self reveal'd before our eyes.
His clemency the means supplies
Whereby man understands no more,
Yet far transcends all human lore.[18]

SELECTED BIBLIOGRAPHY

Editions

Obras de San Juan de la Cruz, 5 volumes, edited and annotated by Silverio de Santa Teresa, O.C.D. (Burgos, 1929-1931), is usually—but not always—to be given the preference over *Obras del místico doctor San Juan de la Cruz,* 3 volumes, critically edited with introduction and notes by Gerardo de San Juan, O.C.D. (Toledo, 1912-1914).

Translations

The Complete Works of St. John of the Cross, translated by David Lewis (London, 1864), is frequently reprinted with inci-

[18] *Op. cit.,* Vol. II, pp. 425-426.

dental revisions and corrections. The best version is that of the late Professor Peers; it is used in this book.

Studies

Much of latter-day interpretation of St. John derives directly from the stimulus provided by Jean Baruzi, *Saint Jean de la Croix et le problème de l'expérience mystique* (Paris, 1924); whatever one's disagreements with certain of his basic positions, Baruzi's book is still indispensable. Even more learned, much more temperate, much less inspiring is *San Juan de la Cruz: su obra científica y su obra literaria,* 2 volumes, by Crisógono de Jesús, O.C.D. (Madrid, 1929).

XXX

MARIE
OF THE INCARNATION

(1599—1672)

A WIFE, then a mother, then a widow, then a cloistered nun, then a missionary among the Indians of New France, the gentle girl from Tours in Old France ended by contributing much the most magnificent pages in the history of mysticism. That the pages are poorly composed one can forgive because of what they contain. One treads one's way with uncommon patience through the tangle of her metaphors and the incongruities of her syntax, aware that, clearheaded and literate, she could do no other in her rare moments of privacy in the busy mission house at Québec.

The *Relation of 1654* is her spiritual autobiography, written in response to the repeated requests of her son who, by now, was one of Paris' most famous Benedictines, Dom Claude Martin. Having her son's specialized interests in mind, she divided her account according to the thirteen states of prayer she passed through. It might be instructive to summarize them here.

The First was marked by the loss of affection for temporal things; positively, it was liturgical prayer in its simplest form. The Second was an uninterrupted praying to Christ during a time singularly free of peace and quiet when, a young widow, she was doing the work of three men. Mortification (a word that means "a dying"), both within and without, characterized the Third State. The Fourth State was one of increased passivity, in that she felt more acted upon by God than acting herself; in this State, Christ, still the object of her prayer, became especially the word, and the Bible became her most congenial reading; God accorded her "the grace of His holy presence," which was a feeling that had nothing of the spatial or localized about it: "My imagination was not engaged but everything occurred in the understanding and the will, spiritually with great pureness."

The Fifth State was "religious" in the sense that, not a nun, Marie seemed to herself to be one within the private portable convent of her body. The three Persons of the Holy Trinity manifested Themselves to her in the Sixth State; it was a state which knew its own special anguish because the Trinitarian Godhead showed Itself as "an abyss of love to the bottom of which she could not go, yet she wanted to be 'abyssed' in this abyss."

With the Seventh came Spiritual Marriage, union with the second Person and an increased awareness of the other two Persons.

Two points might profitably be mentioned here in passing. The easy convention adopted by most who write about the mystics—that Spiritual Marriage is the term of the mystical ascent—stands in need of revision; Marie, at this point, had still far to go. The belief, often expressed, that mystics who have been married never have recourse to marriage symbolism she also proves to be groundless.

The Trinitarian aspect was even more to the fore in the Eighth State and suffering, again, was most marked. The Ninth lasted from 1633 to 1639 when, now an Ursuline nun, her experience was centered with the will of God. After the event, it is easy for us to say that she was thus being prepared for an apostolic and missionary role and, saying that, we would speak true. But there seems to have been rather more to it than this. According to the distinction in which theologians have long taken much pleasure, it was more than the "signified will" of God (what He wanted her to do); it was the "essential will" of God (which is identical with His essence). This interpretation seems justified by what followed in the Tenth State: here even the awakened desire for a life of missionary activity was submerged in the will of God, and consciousness of her own will, as distinct, was lost.

The Eleventh was a state of further suffering. Some interpreters, astonished that the Spiritual Marriage was only a stage and not the term of Marie's mystical ascent, attempt quite reasonably to stay their wonderment by reflecting that hers, unlike St. Teresa's, was an apostolic and missionary vocation. The reflection does not deserve to be so consoling. There would appear to be precious little difference between the activities of Teresa in Spain and Marie in Canada. The difference is to be thought in nothing that exterior, but rather—and perhaps with a Pauline *O altitudo!*—in that God continues to be wonderful in His saints.

The Twelfth lasted eight years, 1639 to 1647, and was of a sort almost without parallel in any other mystic we know of. Temptations of a most brutal and sordid kind constantly shouldered their way into her mind and imagination. I call them "temptations" because Marie herself does so, but the term is somewhat less than exact: they had all the qualities of temptations except that of being tempting. Throughout these eight long years they were never attractive. They were always revolting. Permanent residents in the soul, they inspired constant horror. "During this Purgatory," she writes, "the Incarnate Word is never lost from sight. But he who appeared only as love and who formerly overwhelmed the soul with His caresses is now the one who crucifies it and, in all its parts, separates it from the spirit."[1] The separation is effected by the separateness of the effects experienced. While all is turbulence and pain and horror in the soul, in the spirit is peace and quiet and happiness.

The Thirteenth State would seem to have lasted to the end of her life, a period of some twenty-five years. She described it, as she did the previous twelve, in her *Relation of 1654,* and the further explanations she sent her son in subsequent years manifest no change. It was a state she comprehensively described as "poverty." Much as other mystics use the philosophic term "annihilation" to indicate the experience of the reality of the Godhead before which they are as nothing, Marie used the Gospel term "poverty" to indicate her experience of the opulence of the Godhead—to her, poor, had been given the Kingdom.[2] Richness received is the master idea in her description of this state of poverty. Soul is no longer separated from spirit. Peace is no longer the property of one lone part of her being but pervades it wholly.

The nun on the Rock of Québec, confined to a small perilous space hacked out of the forest, instructing her small In-

---

[1] However unusual the experience, Marie's distinction between soul and spirit in describing it is usual among many of the mystics—Origen, William of St. Thierry, Mechtilde of Magdeburg, Ruysbroek, Catherine of Genoa—who felt forced to differentiate between the multiplicity of spiritual operations and potentialities (the "soul") and the oneness in which they are rooted (the "spirit"). It is upon the "spirit" that God's action is directly experienced in the culminating stages for such mystics. The distinction, of course, is that between *psuché* and *pneuma* in the Pauline writings (*cf.* Hebrews 4:12).

[2] *Cf.* Matthew 5:3.

dians, managing her primitive convent, was the girl from Tours now magnificently grown. One may wonder at the long torturous stages of that growth, but one can only acclaim the result —her whom Bossuet called the "Teresa of the New World."

TEXTS [3]

Once when I was at prayer—this was about two years after my conversion [4]—I was greatly recollected within. Then was it shown me how God is like a great ocean and that, as the ocean cannot stand anything unclean but casts it from itself, so also this great ocean of purity which is God will have nothing that is unclean, casting from Himself all that is dead and dirty.[5]

Wherever I was, whatever job I might be doing, I was unable to be other than absorbed by, buried in this Being that surpasses comprehension. Nor could I look upon creatures in any other way. The result was that I used to see God in everything and everything in God. This limitless Majesty was in my sight like a great and vast ocean which, overflowing its bounds, covered and inundated and surrounded me completely.[6]

RELATION OF 1654 [7]

It may well be that I express myself obscurely. Yet I myself understand myself well enough. It is just that I find it impossible to describe so much as a thousandth part of the imprints and workings which my Divine Spouse has effected in my soul. . . . I simply content myself with giving the substance of what the Spirit who leads me allows me to say. Nevertheless, I am now going to provide a small discourse in the following chapter so as in some fashion to make myself understood

---

[3] I translate throughout from the critical text established by Dom Albert Jamet, O.S.B., *Marie de l'Incarnation: Ecrits spirituels et historiques,* 4 volumes (Paris-Québec, 1929-1939).
[4] This "conversion" was the signal grace of March 24, 1620, when Marie made "the firm resolve . . . to think no more of the world nor of the hopes it proffered in order to be wholly God's." *Life* cited in Jamet, I, 153, note "a."
[5] *Relation of 1633;* Jamet, Vol. I, p. 154.
[6] Letter to her director in *Life;* Jamet, Vol. I, p. 354.
[7] Jamet, Vol. II, pp. 451-466.

concerning the stripping of the soul, the victim state, and true spiritual poverty.

God having created the rational soul free and having endowed it with faculties to work out its salvation with His grace and the other helps and aids that He has confided to His Church, founded by the Precious Blood of Jesus Christ, the soul becomes aware of its dignity through the operations of grace which effectively lay bare to it both the destiny to which it is called and that of which it is capable if only it is faithful. It would force itself to be responsive with an unremitting straining towards its sovereign and unique Good. If this tension is pure, the Divine Goodness, which alone knows this His creature and scrutinizes the most intimate areas of its spirit, floods the soul with light and fire and passionate love and gives it finally the key with which to enter into His knowledge and love and gives it possession of His riches.

Seeing itself so overwhelmed, the soul wants to walk about in these rich and fertile pastures, in these gardens, in these rooms which have been laid open to it. There the faculties take their delight tasting a wisdom that is impossible to describe. The divine delights and banqueting and repose that are accorded it there, the holy intoxications that assail it there, make it sing a nuptial song. . . . All this comes about without its doing anything. Rather is it invaded with a spiritual abundance whose sense and meaning is to liberate love. Then are there rejoicings and tears which make the soul a paradise. There is the enjoying of God in an intimacy impossible to describe. All this flows over into the senses; the entire sense part of the soul is penetrated by it. . . . This sense part is disgusted wholly by creatures because it has been purified, as though with fire, by the sweetness of spiritual goods. Yet it would return to creatures quickly enough if, by a strength it cannot see, it were not bound under "the laws of the Spirit which the carnal man understands not." [8] This strength sets it, as it were, in the ranks of the dead although it is not dead altogether. But it is wounded to the point of being able to do nothing to prevent the higher part of the soul from peacefully enjoying the good things that it alone possesses. In this death (I call it "death" in a spiritual sense) there are many degrees because there are many sources and resources, innumerable stores of ruses and tricks in fallen nature which at every instant would make us monkeys. But, to change the image, the Spirit of God steps in and clears His royal table of all these leftovers of food that were never meant for the soul. At this point the true distinction between the higher and lower parts of the soul becomes known.

[8] 1 Corinthians 2:14.

But this is not all. We are at only the first step of the entrance into the victim state and the possession of poverty of spirit.

Nature, being thus annihilated first by penance and then by privation of all that kept it in existence and made it pliable to whatever the Spirit willed,[9] is humbled indescribably. All this while the higher part is truly content to see itself free of what hindered it most. Now, truly pure, it can rejoice in its sovereign and unique Good. Now understanding and will have lights and loves in that manner—indeed, beyond that manner —I spoke of above.

But the Spirit of God wishes all for Himself. Seeing the understanding (however purified it may have become, forever mingled with something of its own and with something of its own doing) present in His actions—an extreme impurity in this spiritual state—at a stroke He, the master, calls a halt. The soul is, as it were, held in suspense and made utterly incapable of the ordinary actions of this state which, indeed, it did not consider to be actions because in their simplicity they were all but imperceptible.

The will, having been rapt into God and known His embrace, has need no longer of the understanding to provide it with fuel for its flames; on the contrary, because of its large abounding fecundity, it would do it hurt. The will is now a queen who takes her delight in her Divine Spouse, in intimacies of which it were better for the Seraphim to speak in their language of fire than a creature that possesses only a tongue of flesh incapable of expressing such lofty things as these.

Years pass in this way. But the Spirit of God, who is the unfailing source of all purity, wishes to triumph further upon the will. And although it is He that effects these Divine motions and He that has it singing its unbroken nuptial song, nonetheless the will still adds something of its own. This He cannot permit. He wishes, as though jealous, to be absolute master. . . . Hence that loving activity (which, so delicate, is sweeter in the embracing of the Divine Spouse than sweetness itself and, like an endless chain, binds her about and centers her within His sovereign and singular goodness) ceases and [the will] is placed on the level of memory and understanding. . . . See then the poor victim. See whither the Spirit of God, infinitely desiring the purity of souls espoused to the Son of God, leads souls in order to give them to Him for His delight. This bed is a narrow one.

After this Divine action, so crucifying for faculties so noble,

[9] The meaning here would seem to be that gone, now, are the familiar and habitual desires, ideals, thoughts which, directed upon God, made the soul "pliable" to grace and "kept it going," as we would say today.

what happens? Is one to think that the faculties can thus stay fixed and rigid and, as it were, ranged among the dead?

It is incredible how painful the retrenchment is. Especially painful is it during the solemn ceremonies of the Church when the very mysteries of our redemption are presented. Formerly they had been a delicious food. Now, where all had been light-some and pleasant as the Spirit dispensed the holy mysteries, the faculties can no longer abide. Sometimes a person who is led along this way becomes frightened, being unable to understand how it can be the right way since one is no longer able to abide what, in the Church, is holiest and most glorious. Such a one does violence to himself, wishing to drag the understanding out of the lethargy into which he thinks it has fallen. The attempt, however, is futile, ignorant, and a mark of imperfection. After many repeated violent efforts one learns by experience that there is nothing to be gained in this because the faculties of the soul have, supernaturally, lost their ability. And yet, this native tendency of the soul to use faculties as noble as these is really done to death only when the Spirit of God puts it to death. He is inexorable in this matter. As I have said, the dwelling must be freed of all noise for this Spouse who delights in peace and quiet.

The will is now no longer active in love. The soul, united in its center, remains actively in love in the embraces of the Spouse. . . . This is to be remarked: to the degree that the spirit suffers interiorly in being cleansed of all impurity, God allows many crosses exteriorly to the end that all be fulfilled according to the words of St. Paul, "He conformed them to the image of His Son. . . ."[10] I repeat it! It is necessary to go through great trials, interior and exterior, which would terrify the soul that foresaw them. They would even make one give up everything in order not to proceed further in such an experience did not a hidden strength sustain one. For it seems that the waters of tribulation through which one has passed . . . have extinguished the fire which perfected so gently that higher part of the soul when the faculties had been deprived of their exercise and when, alone, the soul enjoyed God in purity of spirit. Indeed, the poor soul does not know where or what it is. A cloud has formed about it that shuts out the view and, it seems, cuts it off from the portion it had in its sovereign and unique Good, the adorable Word Incarnate.

And He finally, in pity for the soul, dissipates the cloud. . . . Now, in its possession of the goods of the adorable Word Incarnate and of Himself, it is more fecund than ever. . . .

It was necessary that I provide this small dissertation on my personal experiences in order, in some fashion, to make under-

[10] Romans 8:29.

standable what I wanted to say about spiritual and substantive poverty of spirit and the victim state.

The state which I now experience, compared with what I have previously described, is a completely extraordinary clearness about the ways of the adorable Spirit of the Word Incarnate. I know, experientially in great pureness and certainty, that here is Love Himself intimately joined to me and joining my spirit to His and that "all that He has said has spirit and life" in me.[11] Particularly does my soul experience being in this intimate union with Him.

It is the same with the eternal Father and the Holy Spirit. By this impress is known the truth and certainty of what this adorable Lord and Master said to His Apostles in His final discourse with them and in His prayer to God His Father[12] in the first instance responding to Philip who asked to see the Father: "Philip, who sees Me, sees the Father. Why do you say, Show us the Father? Do you not believe that I am in the Father and that the Father is in Me? etc."[13]

This mode of union is most lofty and most pure. And, although I speak of "the holy Word Incarnate," it is not because I have an image of Him but because, in a spiritual pureness and simplicity, the soul has the experience that the Father and the Word Incarnate are one with the adorable Spirit, although there is no confusion of Persons. And this soul is aware of the Divine operations of the adorable Word Incarnate by the Spirit. With these motions, impressions, and operations the same Spirit has me speak now to the eternal Father, now to the Son, now to Himself. Without reflecting on it, I find myself saying to the Father: "O Father, in the name of Your beloved Son, I say to You this." And to the Son: "My Beloved, my dearest Spouse, I ask that Your will be fulfilled in me" and such other things as the Spirit suggests to me. And I have the experience that it is the Holy Spirit that links me to Father and to Son. I find myself frequently saying to Him: "Divine Spirit, guide me in the ways of my Divine Spouse." I am continuously engaged in this divine exchange in a fashion and a manner so delicate, so simple, and so intense that there is no way of expressing it. It is not an act. It is not a sigh. It is an air so gentle in the center of the soul where God has His dwelling that, as I have already said, I cannot find words to express it. My converse with the adorable Majesty contains only what the Spirit makes me say. It is by Him that I speak because in this language of the spirit in such exchanges as these wherein His Divine Majesty wills to dignify my lowliness

[11] *Cf.* John 6:63.
[12] *See* John 14-17.
[13] John 14:8.

I am entirely incapable of doing anything except through His very delicate urging. And, since it is so delicate, how could my tongue express what my spirit is unable to distinguish because so simple and pure and ever more and more and more simple.

The entire time of my spiritual exercises, which I have just completed, was passed in this way.[14]

Today what were imprinted upon my mind were these words of Our Lord, "I am the vine and My Father is the vine-dresser; every branch which does not bear fruit in Me He will cut off and He will prune what bears fruit so that it will bear more fruit."[15] To me this passage signified the reasons for the various states of purgation which I described above. And it indicated the importance of being united to our Divine Vine, the adorable Word Incarnate, so as to live only by His vitality, which is His Divine Spirit, that high point of the spiritual life and that consummation of the Saints of living no longer except in Him, as St. Paul says.[16]

There is still another disposition, in which I find myself, that seems derivative from that I spoke of in the preceding section. It descends upon me most often when I am alone in my room, having just come from some community exercise—especially from Holy Communion—more than at any other time. I receive an impression in my soul. I do not conceive it as coming from without; I speak of it this way only in order to express myself. It is a reality so lofty, so ravishing, so transcendent, so simple, and so beyond the scope of what falls within the meaning of human discourse that I am unable to express it otherwise than to say that I am in God, possessed by God, and that God would soon overwhelm me by His loving gentleness and strength were I not sustained by another impression which follows it and does not pass but tempers His greatness as something not to be sustained in this life. Were there not this tempering by this second impression, which is always related to the adorable Word Incarnate, my Divine Spouse, I could not continue to exist, my soul having life only in Him in this substantive state of my love day and night and at every minute.

The effects of this state are always annihilation and true root knowledge that one is nothing, is powerlessness itself. There results, too, a lowly opinion of oneself and of all one does which one directly perceives to be mingled with imperfec-

---

[14] The reference is to the spiritual exercises in the technical sense, that is, the *Spiritual Exercises* of St. Ignatius Loyola. She has just finished her annual period of prayer and retirement patterned on the book of Ignatius.

[15] John 15:1-2.

[16] *Cf.* Galatians 2:20.

tion; of this the mind is certain, and this keeps the soul in deep humility however elevated it might be capable of being. And there is fear as well, but without any uneasiness that one might be deluded in the ways of the spirit and accept what is false for what is true. This fear serves to awaken self-denial and a spirit of compunction. Equally, this fear awakens peace—a peace which comes from the acceptance of trials, sufferings, and the cross; however they come, one receives them from God's hand as the chastisement of a good Father who corrects, with love, His child, who right after the chastisement flings himself into His lap.

This state effects as well a great patience under crosses and an entire bent and inclination towards peace and amiability with everyone; a mild inner sentiment of good will towards those by whom one has been offended, with whom one seeks out contacts so as, without any show, to treat them as friends either in what one says or in what one does or in the face one wears or in anything else capable of winning the heart and making them see that one has nothing against them; and, finally, this state effects a total aversion for indignation, no least feeling being kept of the insults and injuries that one receives from one's neighbor. What faults and imperfections one commits are from forgetfulness and distraction; yet they grow ever less because nature has lost its vigor on account of the working within it of God.

Among the effects of this state are the acceptance of suffering in love and union with the adorable Word Incarnate, for one flows lovingly into Him; a great love of one's vocation and of the state to which God calls one and the disposition to do everything, to undertake everything out of love so as to remain faithful; an ever greater love for the life and practice of God's Church in which only purity and sanctity is seen; a total intent to let oneself be led, to submit one's judgment to those who hold the place of God.

SELECTED BIBLIOGRAPHY

Editions

The best text, although never completed, is that of Albert Jamet, O.S.B., *Marie de l'Incarnation: Ecrits spirituels et historiques*, 4 volumes (Paris-Québec, 1929-1939). Paul Renaudin has provided a singularly helpful selection from her writings in his *Marie de l'Incarnation, Ursuline* (Paris, 1942).

Studies

Henri Bremond is his usually acute self in his analysis of the person and doctrine of Marie: *Histoire littéraire du sentiment religieux en France,* Volume VI (Paris, 1933), pp. 1-176. But the laurel goes to Paul Renaudin, whose *Marie de l'Incarnation, Ursuline de Tours et de Québec: Essai de psychologie religieuse* (Paris, 1935) is a masterpiece of its kind. The tangle of Marie's vocabulary has been sorted out, not without success, by Mother Aloysius Gonzaga, O.S.U., *The Mystical Vocabulary of Venerable Mère de l'Incarnation and Its Problems* (Washington, 1956).

XXXI

QUIETISM

IT IS THE convention these days to give the name "Quietism" to any system of spirituality which does not put great store in human activity. It has proved itself a handy convention particularly when one does not approve of the system under discussion. But, whatever its pragmatic and polemical utility, this way of using words serves to make even vaguer and more confused a matter of moment which is in itself already too vague and confusing. I refer to that movement of the seventeenth century to which the names of Molinos and Madame Guyon and Fénelon are, in everyone's mind, attached. Of it, then, the attempt will be made to speak exclusively here.

Confusion on several scores awaits the interpreter who would properly assess Quietism. Its proponents used a vocabulary—"annihilation," "detachment," "abandonment," "deification," etc.—which had a long and noble history in orthodox spirituality before ever they put it to their particular purposes. Again, the areas of spiritual doctrine which they emphasized had always, in the most vital periods of the Church, been emphasized. Further, the number and probity of their followers were both so great that it seems a piece of callous and quite un-Christian effrontery for the latter-day historian to pass unfavorable judgment on their doctrine. Of these three sources of confusion, the last surely is the most potent: it unnerves one's writing arm and makes one uncomfortably distrustful of one's eyesight as one reads the relevant documents. The procedure here, therefore, will be simply to reinsert the vocabulary they used and the doctrinal areas they stressed within that historical context in which, whether rightly or wrongly, they were so well and widely received.

MOLINOS

Miguel de Molinos (1628-1696) was a Spanish priest and Doctor of Theology who was sent to Rome in 1663 by his superiors to provide data for the possible canonization of a priest of his province who had died, as the expression is, "in the odor of sanctity." That business dispatched, or perhaps simply shelved, Molinos stayed on in Rome as the most influential spiritual director the city had known in generations. Good people of every sort, from cart-haulers to Cardinals, put themselves under his guidance. In 1675 he published his *Spiritual Guide,* a small handbook of the contemplative life which was an immediate sensation. There were those who attacked its doctrine and had their efforts put on the *Index Librorum Prohibitorum.* There were others, more numerous, who defended it, and they received ecclesiastical advancement. Then, in 1685, when his influence with the people was at its peak and his favor in ecclesiastical circles was most marked and his friend, Innocent XI, was Pope, Molinos was arrested by the papal police, tried, and sentenced to life imprisonment for heresy.

The occasion of this sudden reversal of opinion would appear to have been the revelation of his personal immorality which in turn revealed what had hitherto remained hidden (perhaps even from himself): the antinomian implications of his doctrine. In the "Summation" of his trial he is to be found defending his own and his followers' sexual aberrations as sinless, purifying acts which, effected by the devil and passively permitted by the truly interior Christian, providentially deepen such a one's quiet repose in God.

The following, from the sixty-eight propositions that were condemned and which Innocent XI tells us Molinos admitted were his own, will sound familiar in vocabulary and stress to any reader not wholly ignorant of orthodox Christian spirituality:[1]

1. The faculties [of the soul] must be annihilated: this is "the interior life."
4. Natural activity is the enemy of grace and an impediment to the workings of God and genuine per-

[1] Original Latin text in Denzinger-Schönmetzer, *Enchiridion Symbolorum* (Freiburg, 1963), pp. 471-476.

fection because God wishes to work "in us without us."

5. Doing nothing the soul annihilates itself and returns to its source and origin, the essence of God, in which it remains transformed and deified. God remains in Himself because then there are no longer two things united but one sole thing. In this way God lives and reigns in us and the soul annihilates itself in the very source of its operations.

6. "The internal life" is that life in which neither light nor love nor resignation is known. It is not necessary to know God. In this way all goes well.

10. If one scandalizes others with one's faults, there is no need to give it a thought so long as one does not wish to give scandal. To be unable to give thought to one's own faults is a grace from God.

24. Whatever may be the thoughts that come to one in time of prayer—even if they are impure or against God or the Saints or the Faith and the Sacraments—so long as they are not deliberately fostered nor deliberately expelled but borne with indifference and resignation they do not impede the prayer of faith. Indeed they make it more perfect because then the soul remains more resigned to the Divine will.

57. By "acquired contemplation" one arrives at the state where one no longer sins either mortally or venially.

I have put in quotation marks some of the examples of traditional spiritual vocabulary most frequently favored by Molinos. There was an especial irony in his use of the phrase "God wishes to work 'in us without us,'" for this is the *in nobis sine nobis* of the most subtle and accurate and traditional expression of the Christian doctrine of grace, and it is precisely in the doctrine of grace that all Quietists have shown themselves egregiously inept. "Quietists," they emphasized personal activity to the extreme: to attain to quiet one must long be active in suppressing the possibilities of action. From this action results what, really, only the grace of God can confer: tranquillity, relative immunity to the allurements of sin, the experienced awareness of Him. At this point there comes to the fore the expression which was by then traditional in the Carmelite school of spirituality, "acquired contemplation." By it Molinos meant what the Carmelites called "infused contemplation," in which, for them, one is wholly passive. You would think that the passive aspect of this contemplation would recommend its acceptance by doctrinaire Quietists. But doctrinaire Quietists (this is one of the pretty anomalies of history) are always too enamored of action for that. Molinos' interpretation of "the interior life" provides corroborative proof. It becomes coterminous with a constricted area of the soul in which one can, because it is so limited, act. Thus an expression traditionally meaning no more than the priority that should be given to matters of the spirit becomes the label for an exclusive area of activity.

Exclusiveness, too, marks the emphasis placed on aspects of Christian spirituality that have always been stressed. Others before Molinos had advised annihilation, conformity to the Divine will, a quieting of the faculties, etc. But he advised *only* that. This doctrinal exclusivism is the hallmark of Quietism.

MADAME GUYON

Jeanne Marie Bouvier de la Mothe Guyon (1648-1717) after the death of her husband in 1676 turned, with a whim of iron, to mysticism. She made her own the doctrine of Molinos; and then, from 1681 to 1686, she tried to make it everyone else's doctrine, too, throughout the length and breadth of France. In the company of an unfortunate friar, François La Combe, she traveled everywhere, propagandizing as she went, until they were both arrested in 1687 on charges of immorality and heresy. The poor La Combe, surely the most vigorously directed of all spiritual directors, remained in prison for twelve years, but his protégée gained her freedom through the kindly offices of Madame de Maintenon, who desired to make a mystic of the King.

The chronicler becomes exhausted in trying to keep up with the activities of this champion of quiet. Now under Court patronage there was nothing that could subdue her explosive energy. She had already written her *Brief Method of Prayer,* the celebrated *Moyen Court,* which was destined for the general public. Her *Spiritual Torrents* she wrote even earlier but, destined only for her initiates, it circulated only in manuscript. Eventually her writings, in their definitive edition, were to fill thirty-nine fat volumes, and these were the days that saw most of them come into being. Only Madame de Maintenon, who made this period possible, could bring it to an end. She did. The King had not become a mystic after all, so this useless woman whose influence was as widespread as her own she conveniently disposed of by accusing her before Bossuet, the prodigious Bishop of Meaux. Therewith the focus of seventeenth-century Quietism shifted from Madame Guyon to Fénelon, who, undismayed by the thunders of Bossuet, came to her defense. He found himself obliged to defend such passages as these from her writings:[2]

To be willing to be nothing in the sight of God, to live in a total abandonment, in utter self-despair, to give themselves to Him when they are the most discouraged, to leave themselves in His hands and not to consider themselves when they are on the very edge of the abyss: this it is that is so rare and this it is that constitutes perfect abandonment. . . . If we tell them [who practice perfect abandonment] to go to confession, they do so for they are very submissive. But they say with their mouths what they are made to say, like a small child to whom one would say, "You must confess that." He confesses it without knowing what he says, without knowing whether it is true or not. . . . These souls can scarcely ever make their confession. . . . Before this the soul had been stripped of gifts and graces and the ability to do good. It had lost all good works such as external austerities, regard for the poor, readiness to help others, but it had not lost the theological virtues. Now, however, these too must be lost so far as their practice is concerned. . . . If a perfect soul tried to humble itself, it would be astonished as though it were guilty of unfaithfulness. It would even find it impossible because the state of annihilation through which it has gone has placed it below all humiliation; for in order to be humbled, we must be something. Nothingness cannot be brought lower. Its present state has situated it above all humility and all virtue by its transformation into God. . . . Nothing can harm souls that are perfectly abandoned since there is no longer anything hurtful for them because of their union with God who, in associating with sinners, contracts no defilement because of His essential purity. . . . The soul that thus no longer is can no longer sin. . . . You must put aside your defects when they are pointed out to you without departing from your firmly established immobility—even by a disavowal. What I say is bold, but this is your state. God never shows you a past fault so as to lead you to remedy it. He acts in the same way as a skillful gardener who shows his child the weeds without letting him pull them up; He wishes to do this Himself. . . . This soul would have nothing to ask [of God], nothing to desire, unless He Himself should give the impulse. It does not despise or reject Divine consolations. But graces of this kind are no longer appropriate

[2] I translate a conflation of texts from H. Delacroix, *Les grands mystiques chrétiens* (Paris, 1938), pp. 108-307.

to a soul as annihilated as it is and so established in its center and which, having lost all will in God's will, can no longer will anything.

In Madame Guyon, then, are to be found further exemplary instances of that exclusivism mentioned earlier. She was widely read in all the great mystical authors, but all they said—now speaking psychologically, now theologically, now metaphorically or symbolically—she interpreted theologically. Thus she could say that the perfectly abandoned soul does not sin in encouraging others to sin because such a soul is dead and therefore incapable of sinning, prettily confounding one's being psychologically mortified with what is true only of the resident on a mortician's slab. She had read in her authors of the necessity of grace and read into it the necessity of its being sensibly perceived: unless there is the felt push of grace, one remains inactive.

FÉNELON

François de Salignac de Lamothe-Fénelon (1651-1715) ascribed publicly to the "Articles d'Issy" in which, without being named, Madame Guyon was condemned in 1695 by Bossuet. (Madame Guyon publicly ascribed to them as well.) But the "Articles" were not models of doctrinal clarity. Both Bossuet and Fénelon, accordingly, set themselves the task of making their tenor clearer. Forty days before Bossuet's effort, *Instruction sur les états d'oraison,* appeared, Fénelon had managed to get his own into print. Its title expressed its intent. *Explication des maximes des saints sur la vie intérieure,* it sought to explain the sayings of the saints that were to be found in the writings of Madame Guyon and in her condemnation by the examiners of Issy in a way that would put her in a somewhat better light. It put Fénelon himself in a very bad light: the King exiled him to Cambrai (where he should have been, being Bishop of Cambrai, anyhow), and Rome condemned twenty-three of the doctrinal propositions it contained.

As Madame Guyon's doctrine was a modification of that of Molinos, Fénelon's was a modification of that of Madame Guyon. There is, accordingly, from the crudity of Molinos to the delicacy of Fénelon a clear and not altogether unhappy progression. Only when one replaces the statements of Fénelon within their historical context does their heterodoxy become at all apparent.

Fénelon had been much struck in reading contemporary lives of the saints by the frequency with which some, as St. Francis of Sales, had been tempted to despair. He thought to find the explanation of this seeming constant in holy lives in the Quietist acceptance of God's will. There were the "temptations" because in the final stage of passive purification the soul can become invincibly persuaded that it has been justly damned by God, and passively accept the damnation. The giving up of the desire to be saved is inevitable in one who loves God purely, which is to say, "passively."

Logically, then, if the pure love of God rids the perfect soul of the desire to be saved, indifference to the practice of virtue is equally inevitable and admirable.

To the objection that this refined and courtly Quietism seemed to be lacking in the sayings of the saints, Fénelon had a prompt reply. It was there, he said, by implication, and only initiates in a secret traditional doctrine, deriving from Clement of Alexandria in the early third century, were in a position to recognize it.

Fénelon accepted his condemnation by Rome and had the brief containing it read in all the churches of his diocese. His acceptance showed him still faithful in his fashion to Madame Guyon: although engineered by Bossuet and carried out by Rome, the condemnation was a passive purification upon arriving in Fénelon's quiet soul. He also said, human still, that everybody had misunderstood him.

SELECTED BIBLIOGRAPHY

Editions

MOLINOS: *Guía espiritual,* 3rd edition, edited by G. Amendola (Madrid, 1955). The charges against him, a set of 283 "Theses Damnandae," are to be found in *Analecta Iuris Pontifici, X* (1868/9), 570-594.

GUYON: *Oeuvres,* 39 volumes, edited by P. Poiret (Cologne, 1713-1732). An edition of the letters, more complete than that provided by Poiret, was edited by Philippe Dutoit-Mambrini at Paris in 1767.

FÉNELON: *Oeuvres,* 35 volumes (Versailles, 1820-1830); there is as yet no completely reliable edition of Fénelon's writings. Mlle. J. L. Goré has had the happy inspiration of providing three especially relevant but rare documents as Appendices to her *La notion d'indifférence chez Fénelon et ses sources* (Paris, 1956).

Translations

MOLINOS: An incomplete version in English of the *Spiritual Guide,* edited in 1906 by Kathleen Lyttleton, is frequently reprinted.

GUYON: *A Short Method of Prayer and Spiritual Torrents,* translated by A. W. Marston (London, 1875).

Studies

GENERAL: H. Heppe's *Geschichte der quietistischen Mystik in der katholischen Kirche* (Berlin, 1875) is still of value. For the ambience favorable to Molinos, see M. Petrocchi, *Il quietismo italiano del seicento* (Rome, 1948). Louis Cognet describes the French scene in his *Crépuscule des mystiques* (Tournai, 1958).

MOLINOS: For discussion and relevant documentation, see Paul Dudon, S.J., *Le quiétiste espagnole Michel Molinos* (Paris, 1921). The classic treatment is that of M. Menéndez Pelayo, *Historia de los heterodoxos españoles,* Volume IV (Madrid, 1947), pp. 253-274, to be complemented by J. Ellacuria Beascoechea, *Reaccíon española contra las ideas de Miguel de Molinos* (Bilbao, 1956).

GUYON: The most extended study is still that of Henri Delacroix, *Les grands mystiques chrétiens* (Paris, 1938), pp. 118-307. Ronald Knox is his usual perceptive and persuasive self in *Enthusiasm* (New York, 1950), pp. 319-352.

FÉNELON: The title of Henri Bremond's masterly *Apologie pour Fénelon* (Paris, 1910) could serve for the majority of books about Fénelon these days. A rather more temperate example is F. Varillon, S.J., *Fénelon et le pur amour* (Paris, 1957). How Fénelon and his chief adversary both managed to cite the mystics to their purpose is engagingly discussed by Henri Sanson, S.J., in his *Saint Jean de la Croix entre Bossuet et Fénelon* (Paris, 1953).

Appendix

ORIENTAL MYSTICISM

THE MYSTICISM of China and India largely antedates the period covered in this book but it would be foolishly pedantic, on that account, to omit all reference to it. Hence this appendix.

Just how old the classical mystical writings of China are, no one really knows. They were already a traditional heritage by the third century before Christ when the chief of them were gathered together under the title *Tao Tê Ching* (literally, *The Book of the Way and Its Virtue*), and ascribed without foundation to one Lao Tzu.

"Tao" means "road" or "path." For the Chinese mystics it signified not only the way the whole world operates but also the undifferentiated Reality from which the universe evolved.

Thus, The Way is the cause of all:

> The Way begot one,
>   And the one, two;
> Then the two begot three,
>   And three, all else.
>
> All things bear the shade on their backs
>   And the sun in their arms;
> By the blending of breath
>   From the sun and the shade,
> Equilibrium comes to the world.[1]

It is, as well, the sustainer of all:

> When The Way brings forth,
>   Its power fosters all:

[1] From *The Way of Life: Tao Tê Ching* by Lao Tzu, translated by R. B. Blakney (New York, 1955), p. 95.

> They grow, are reared,
>> And fed and housed until
> They come to ripe maturity.[2]

It is both origin and term:

> The Way is a void,
>> Used but never filled:
> An abyss it is,
>> Like an ancestor
> From which all things come.
>> A deep pool it is,
> Never to run dry!
>> Whose offspring it may be
> I do not know:
>> It is like a preface to God.[3]

Or again:

> Like the gods of the shrine in the home,
>> So The Way and its mystery waits
> In the world of material things:
>> The good man's treasure,
> The bad man's refuge.
>> Fair wordage is ever for sale;
> Fair manners are worn like a cloak;
>> But why should there be such a waste
> Of the badness in men?
>> How used the ancients to honor The Way?
> Didn't they say that the seeker may find it,
>> And that sinners who find are forgiven?
> So did they lift up The Way and its Virtue
>> Above everything else in the world.[4]

The Way is both transcendent and immanent: as the ultimate and nameless Reality, it is beyond the confines of the universe; as emanation, it is everywhere present to it. Under neither aspect is The Way a personal God.

The way to The Way is through personal purgation:

> The secret waits for the insight
>> Of eyes unclouded by longing;
> Those who are bound by desire
>> See only the outward container.[5]

---

[2] Blakney, *op. cit.*, p. 104.
[3] *Op. cit.*, p. 56.
[4] *Op. cit.*, p. 115.
[5] *Op. cit.*, p. 53.

Purgation is achieved through self-knowledge for

> It is wisdom to know others;
> It is enlightenment to know one's self.[6]

And again:

> The world may be known
> Without leaving the house;
> The Way may be seen
> Apart from the windows.
> The further you go,
> The less you will know.
> Accordingly, the wise man
> Knows without going,
> Sees without seeing,
> Does without doing.[7]

Small bright pebbles, polished smooth by long usage, are these poems. The reader will have no difficulty in recognizing the similarity of their doctrine to the later themes of Plotinus. But Plotinus would never succeed in speaking as sensibly—and as prettily—of the "void" as this:

> Thirty spokes will converge
> In the hub of a wheel;
> But the use of the cart
> Will depend on the part
> Of the hub that is void.

> With a wall all around
> A clay bowl is molded;
> But the use of the bowl
> Will depend on the part
> Of the bowl that is void.

> Cut out windows and doors
> In the house as you build;
> But the use of the house
> Will depend on the space
> In the walls that is void.

> So advantage is had
> From whatever is there;

[6] Op. cit., p. 86.
[7] Op. cit., p. 100.

But usefulness rises
From whatever is not.[8]

At much the same time that *Tao Tê Ching* was compiled, a similar task was performed in India on the doctrines of the traditional native mysticism; the *Bhagavad-Gita* (literally, *The Song of the Blessed One*) was the result. Emphasis throughout is on the method of attaining—of oneself—to mystical union.

The resemblances to Plotinus in the following selection (if one but abstract from the non-Plotinian homeliness of image) are most striking.

Arjuna:

Krishna,[9] how can one identify a man who is firmly established and absorbed in Brahman?[10] In what manner does an illumined soul speak? How does he sit? How does he walk?

Sri Krishna:

He knows bliss in the Atman[11]
And wants nothing else.
Cravings torment the heart:
He renounces cravings.
I call him illumined.
Not shaken by adversity,
Not hankering after happiness:
Free from fear, free from anger,
Free from the things of desire.
I call him a seer, and illumined.
The bonds of his flesh are broken.
He is lucky, and does not rejoice:
He is unlucky, and does not weep.
I call him illumined.

[8] *Op. cit.,* p. 63.

[9] One of the most widely worshipped deities of Hinduism, the greatest of the incarnations of Vishnu and variously represented in legend as warrior, cowherd, prankster, lover, slayer of dragons, he becomes in the *Bhagavad-Gita* God Himself.

[10] Signifying prayer in the *Rig-Veda*, Brahman came to represent the power behind the spell cast by prayer and finally, in the *Upanishads*, ultimate reality.

[11] Literally "breath," Atman came to signify "the self" and, in the *Upanishads*, the universal self so that the final reality was simply called "Brahman-Atman."

The tortoise can draw in his legs:
The seer can draw in his senses.
I call him illumined.

Thinking about sense-objects
Will attach you to sense-objects;
Grow attached, and you become addicted;
Thwart your addiction, it turns to anger;
Be angry, and you confuse your mind;
Confuse your mind, you forget the lesson of experience;
Forget experience, you lose discrimination;
Lose discrimination, and you miss life's only purpose.

The wind turns a ship
From its course upon the waters:
The wandering winds of the senses
Cast man's mind adrift
And turn his better judgment from its course.
When a man can still the senses
I call him illumined.
The recollected mind is awake
In the knowledge of the Atman
Which is dark night to the ignorant:
The ignorant are awake in their sense-life
Which they think is daylight:
To the seer it is darkness.

Water flows continually into the ocean
But the ocean is never disturbed:
Desire flows into the mind of the seer
But he is never disturbed.[12]

The resemblances to Hesychasm in the next extract are
perhaps even more marked:

The yogi[13] should retire into a solitary place, and live
alone. He must exercise control over his mind and body.
He must free himself from the hopes and possessions of
this world. He should meditate on the Atman unceasingly.
The place where he sits should be firm, neither too high

[12] From *The Song of God: Bhagavad-Gita*, translated by Swami
Prabhavananda and Christopher Isherwood (New York, 1954), pp.
41-43.
[13] The ascetic who seeks mystical union.

nor too low, and situated in a clean spot. . . . As he sits
there, he is to hold the senses and imagination in check,
and keep the mind concentrated upon its object. If he
practises meditation in this manner, his heart will become
pure. His posture is motionless, with the body, head and
neck held erect, and the vision indrawn, as if gazing at
the tip of the nose. . . . If a yogi has perfect control over
his mind, and struggles continually in this way to unite
himself with Brahman, he will come at last to the crowning peace of Nirvana, the peace that is in me. . . . When
can a man be said to have achieved union with Brahman?
When his mind is under perfect control and freed from
all desires, so that he becomes absorbed in the Atman,
and nothing else. "The light of a lamp does not flicker in
a windless place. . . ."[14]

And again:

Shutting off sense
From what is outward,
Fixing the gaze
At the root of the eyebrows,
Checking the breath-stream
In and outgoing
Within the nostrils,
Holding the senses,
Holding the intellect,
Holding the mind fast,
He who seeks freedom
Thrusts fear aside,
Thrusts aside anger
And puts off desire:
Truly that man
Is made free for ever.

When thus he knows me
The end, the author
Of every offering
And all austerity,
Lord of the worlds
And the friend of all men:
O son of Kunti
Shall he not enter
The peace of my presence? [15]

[14] Prabhavananda and Isherwood, *op. cit.*, pp. 65-66.
[15] *Op. cit.*, pp. 61-62.

The examination of the resemblances that exist between such instances of early Eastern mysticism and the mysticism, Christian and non-Christian, of the West does not fall within the purposes of the present book. Readers, however, whose curiosity has been aroused will have it, if not allayed, at least comforted in consulting the following studies:

Rudolf Otto, *Mysticism East and West* (New York, 1957); Louis Gardet, *Expériences mystiques en terres non chrétiennes* (Paris, 1953); and R. C. Zaehner, *Mysticism Sacred and Profane* (New York-London, 1961).

Other MENTOR-OMEGA Books

THE CONFESSIONS OF ST. AUGUSTINE
The classic autobiography of the man who journeyed from sin to sainthood. Newly translated by Rex Warner.
(#MT490—75¢)

THE ESSENTIAL ERASMUS
The first single volume in English to show the full range of thought of one of the great Catholic minds of the Renaissance. Selected and newly translated with introduction and commentary by John P. Dolan.   (#MT571—75¢)

THE ESSENTIAL NEWMAN   Vincent Ferrer Blehl, ed.
The central writings of the master of English prose who infused new vigor into the nineteenth-century Catholic Church. Selected and edited by an eminent Newman scholar.   (#MT488—75¢)

ELEMENTS OF CHRISTIAN PHILOSOPHY
by Etienne Gilson
The noted French philosopher illuminates the key ideas of the theology of St. Thomas Aquinas. (#MT489—75¢)

AMERICAN CATHOLIC DILEMMA by Thomas F. O'Dea
A well-known sociologist discusses the contributions of his fellow Catholics to American intellectual life.
(#MP404—60¢)

TWO CENTURIES OF ECUMENISM: The Search for Unity
by George H. Tavard
A study of successive efforts at Christian reunion from the Oxford Movement of the last century to the Ecumenical Council of the Church called by the late Pope John XXIII.   (#MT465—75¢)

A PREFACE TO METAPHYSICS   by Jacques Maritain
An introduction to the science of metaphysics in seven brilliant lectures by the distinguished French Neo-Thomist.   (#MP403—60¢)

MARIA MONTESSORI: Her Life and Work
by E. M. Standing
A friend and colleague of the great educator writes her biography and evaluates her contributions to modern education. With eight pages of photographs.
(#MQ425—95¢)

DISPUTED QUESTIONS *by Thomas Merton*
A provocatively written analysis of the dilemma of the
individual person in a highly organized society.
(#MT622—75¢)

THE LITTLE FLOWERS OF ST. FRANCIS OF ASSISI
Written by his followers, the lyric and inspiring account of the gentle medieval saint who surrendered
wealth and embraced all creation with tenderness. New
translation by Serge Hughes. (#MT593—75¢)

THE DEAD SEA SCROLLS AND PRIMITIVE CHRISTIANITY
by Jean Danielou
A Jesuit Professor at the Catholic Institute of Paris
demonstrates the relationship between the facts revealed in the ancient scrolls and the traditional view
of Christian faith. (#MP405—60¢)

THE CHRIST OF FAITH *by Karl Adam*
A scholarly discussion of the doctrine of the Catholic
Church as revealed in the life, works, personality, and
message of Jesus Christ. By an eminent German theologian and priest. (#MQ430—95¢)

THE LOVE OF LEARNING AND THE DESIRE FOR GOD
by Jean Leclercq, O.S.B.
A study of the manuscripts of the medieval monasteries
reveals their role in preserving the culture of the past.
By distinguished scholar and Benedictine monk.
(#MT432—75¢)

OF THE IMITATION OF CHRIST *by Thomas à Kempis*
The great 15th century classic of devotional literature
in a widely acclaimed modern translation of Abbot
Justin McCann. (#MT467—75¢)

CATHOLICISM *by Henri de Lubac*
One of the world's leading theologians discusses the
social traditions and ideals inherent in the teachings of
the Church, and their relevancy to modern problems.
(#MT573—75¢)

The Mentor Philosophers

THE AGE OF BELIEF: The Medieval Philosophers
selected and edited *by Anne Fremantle*
The wisdom of a spiritually harmonious age, the 5th to the 15th century, embodied in selections from the basic writings of its important philosophers.
(#MT463—75¢)

THE AGE OF ADVENTURE: The Renaissance Philosophers
selected and edited *by Giorgio de Santillana*
The basic writings of Da Vinci, Machiavelli, Erasmus, Montaigne, Copernicus, Kepler, Galileo, and other great philosophical innovators. (#MT437—75¢)

THE AGE OF REASON: The 17th Century Philosophers
selected and edited *by Stuart Hampshire*
Selections from the basic writings of Descartes, Leibnitz, Spinoza, and other great philosophers of the century of genius. (#MT367—75¢)

THE AGE OF ENLIGHTENMENT: The 18th Century Philosophers selected and edited *by Isaiah Berlin*
Basic writings of Berkeley, Locke, Hume and other brilliant philosophers of the rational and humanistic age. (#MT473—75¢)

THE AGE OF IDEOLOGY: The 19th Century Philosophers
selected and edited *by Henry D. Aiken*
The basic writings of Kant, Fichte, Hegel, Schopenhauer, Mill, Spencer, Nietzsche, Marx and other great 19th century thinkers. (#MT421—75¢)

THE AGE OF ANALYSIS: 20th Century Philosophers
selected and edited *by Morton White*
The philosophy of our day, in all its complexity and diversity, embodied in the writings of leading 20th Century philosophers. (#MT353—75¢)

THE BEST READING AT REASONABLE PRICES

mentor ➤ MENTOR ➤ paperbacks

MENTOR BOOKS *The earliest of "quality paperbacks," this distinguished publishing program presents sound, scholarly works in history, international affairs, the arts, archaeology, anthropology, psychology, philosophy, science, religion, and many other fields. Among the authors are Margaret Mead, Rachel Carson, Charles Darwin, Whitehead, Jung, Veblen, William James, and many other authorities of the past and present.*

MENTOR CLASSICS *The timeless works of Homer, Aeschylus, Plato, Vergil, Dante, Goethe, and other great writers, in superb English translations by eminent scholars, poets, and writers.*

MENTOR-OMEGA BOOKS *A new series presenting major works of Catholic scholarship, religious classics in translation as well as contemporary Catholic books of lasting value. Among the authors are Jacques Maritain, Christopher Dawson, Karl Adam, Etienne Gilson.*

Long-Range Publishing Programs

Unique, long-range editorial programs include *The Mentor Religious Classics*, presenting basic scriptures of Christianity, Judaism, Mohammedanism, Buddhism, and other world religions; *The Mentor Philosophers*, consisting of six volumes from the Middle Ages to the 20th Century; *Mentor; Ancient Civilizations*, offering archaeological discoveries of past centuries in six or more volumes; and many other multi-volume series published in conjunction with UNESCO (including the new *Mentor Unesco* Art books), university presses, and outstanding hardcover publishers.